Social Policy in Australia

Understanding for Action

Edited by Alison McClelland and Paul Smyth

OXFORD
UNIVERSITY PRESS

OXFORD
UNIVERSITY PRESS

253 Normanby Road, South Melbourne, Victoria 3205, Australia

Oxford University Press is a department of the University of Oxford. It furthers the University's objective of excellence in research, scholarship, and education by publishing worldwide in

Oxford New York

Auckland Cape Town Dar es Salaam Hong Kong Karachi
Kuala Lumpur Madrid Melbourne Mexico City Nairobi
New Delhi Shanghai Taipei Toronto

With offices in

Argentina Austria Brazil Chile Czech Republic France Greece
Guatemala Hungary Italy Japan Poland Portugal Singapore
South Korea Switzerland Thailand Turkey Ukraine Vietnam

OXFORD is a trade mark of Oxford University Press in the UK
and in certain other countries

National Library of Australia

Cataloguing-in-Publication data:

McClelland, Alison.
    Social Policy in Australia.
    Bibliography.
    Includes index.
    For tertiary students.
    ISBN 9 78019555 2812.

    ISBN 0 19 555281 4.

    1. Australia—Social policy . I. Smyth, Paul, 1947– . II.
    Title
361.610994

Typeset by Adrian Saunders
Printed in Hong Kong by Sheck Wah Tong Printing Press Ltd

CONTENTS

Tables   v

Figures   vii

Preface   viii

Acknowledgments   xi

Contributors   xii

Abbreviations   xiv

Part One
INTRODUCTION TO SOCIAL POLICY   1

1   **WHAT IS SOCIAL POLICY?**   5
    Alison McClelland

2   **VALUES, CONCEPTS, AND SOCIAL POLICY DESIGN**   21
    Alison McClelland

3   **A FRAMEWORK FOR UNDERSTANDING AND ACTION**   39
    Alison McClelland

4   **THE INSTITUTIONAL CONTEXT FOR DECISIONS AND ACTION**   70
    Alison McClelland

Part Two
THE HISTORICAL, INTERNATIONAL, AND CHANGING CONTEXT FOR ACTION

93

5 **THE HISTORICAL CONTEXT FOR ACTION**   **95**
   Paul Smyth

6 **AUSTRALIAN SOCIAL POLICY IN AN INTERNATIONAL CONTEXT**   **112**
   Paul Smyth

7 **CHANGES AND CHALLENGES**   **128**
   Paul Smyth

Part Three
AREAS OF SOCIAL POLICY ACTION

143

8 **EMPLOYMENT POLICY: UNEMPLOYMENT AND
   LABOUR MARKET INSECURITY**   **147**
   Stephen Bell and John Quiggin

9 **AUSTRALIAN SOCIAL SECURITY POLICY:
   DOING MORE WITH LESS?**   **161**
   Stephen Ziguras

10 **HOUSING POLICY IN AUSTRALIA:
   BIG PROBLEMS BUT OFF THE AGENDA**   **178**
   Tony Dalton

11 **HEALTH POLICY IN AUSTRALIA:
   MIND THE GROWING GAPS**   **195**
   Jenny M. Lewis

12 **EDUCATION POLICY: MARKETS AND SOCIETY**   **209**
   Jane Kenway

13 **COMMUNITY SERVICES:
   CHALLENGES FOR THE TWENTY-FIRST CENTURY**   **224**
   Deborah Brennan

14 **TAXATION: PAYING FOR POLICY**   **238**
   Alison McClelland

Bibliography   255
Index   276

TABLES

1.1	Definitions of policy and social policy	15
1.2	Definitions of welfare states	19
2.1	Concepts, welfare, and design principles	27
2.2	Examples of different forms of welfare in Australia	37
3.1	The scope of policy practice and situations requiring policy practice	40
3.2	A simplified framework for analysis	49
3.3	Different understandings of the problems of the tax system in the mid 1990s	56
3.4	Examples of two different consultation processes	60
3.5	Common implementation problems	66
4.1	Non-government groups: social policy role and influence	72
4.2	Examples of social policies with joint Commonwealth/state responsibility	85
6.1	Indicators of economic and social difference across selected OECD countries in the late 1990s/early 2000s	114
9.1	Main social security changes 1901–2005	162
9.2	Main social security payments (at April 2005)	168

11.1 Selected items of recurrent health expenditure
      by source of funds for 2000–01   197

11.2 Timeline of key health insurance events and
      changing views of health in Australia   199

11.3 Health expenditure as a percentage of GDP and
      life expectancy for selected countries   204

13.1 Persons employed in community service occupations:
      selected characteristics, 2001   229

13.2 Commonwealth-funded children's services and type of
      ownership, 2001   231

14.1 Glossary of tax/social security terms   241

14.2 Structure of taxation in Australia 2002–03   244

FIGURES

8.1	Unemployment in Australia 1960–2004	149
8.2	Persons in and not in the labour force	151
10.1	Housing tenure of households and total occupied dwellings 1911–2001	181
10.2	Metropolitan Melbourne: number of annual sales	191
10.3	House price increase in Australia (real price index)	191
12.1	The market process in education	215
14.1	General government revenue as a proportion of GDP 2002	242

PREFACE

Social policy influences the lives of individual Australians and the nature of our society. Social policy is both a goal and an instrument whereby particular societies determine how social needs are to be met and social rights recognised. In this book, we aim to give students, practitioners, and researchers of social policy an understanding of why this is so and how it operates. The book is intended to help readers appreciate how the social policy context affects individual lives, organisations, communities, and societies. It also introduces the reader to social policy as a discipline and an area of practice as it presents information and knowledge about how to analyse the impacts of social policy and how to develop and advocate for better social policy. As such, the book generally aims to provide information for understanding and action. It is intended to be helpful for people with a general interest in appreciating the social policy context of their lives and work, and for those who may be practitioners of social policy at different levels and in different ways, inside and outside of government. To assist the reader, more general and theoretical information is complemented with case studies and examples from practice.

The first part of the book introduces readers to the idea of social policy, its scope and terrain, how it can be analysed and influenced, and the institutional context for decisions and actions in Australia. Chapter 1 covers the importance of social policy, its contested nature, purpose, and forms, the broad scope of social policy and its relationship to other policy areas, including economic, environmental, and public policy, as well as with the welfare state. Ideas and values are critical influences on policy, and important concepts such as need, rights, equity, and efficiency are discussed in some detail in Chapter 2 following a presentation of the different ideologies and frameworks that are influential in how these concepts are understood and utilised in policy analysis and development. A framework for understanding and action, including key stages in the policy process, is introduced in Chapter 3. Chapter 4 covers the institutional framework for decision-making and the roles and relationships of the key players and institutions.

Chapters 5, 6, and 7, in the second part of the book, deal with the historical development of Australia's social policy and welfare state, place Australia's social policy in a comparative context, and conclude with a chapter about its changing nature, including emerging issues and critical debates. We cannot appreciate the nature of our unique social policy arrangements, nor can we identify the choices that we are free to make, without understanding our history. Chapter 5 therefore covers some of the critical choices and developments over Australia's early and later years, concluding that it is important to understand how, in both the early and post-Second World War years, social protection was combined with social investment in a way that allowed an integrated approach to economic and social policy. However past struggles around 'gender, immigration and reconciliation with the indigenous owners of the land', remain as critical challenges for equality and recognition. Other countries have made some similar and some different choices, and Chapter 6 analyses the different understandings of the critical factors affecting these choices, the development of welfare states, and how these have been translated into different welfare 'regimes'. The chapter goes beyond the traditional focus on European welfare states and extends our gaze to the social policy arrangements that are developing in Asia, as well as challenging the distinction thus far between studies of social development and comparative social policy. Chapter 7 identifies our future choices and challenges in the context of globalisation, the social policy stance and impacts of the Howard government, the changing nature of disadvantage, and the changing discourse around ideas such as social exclusion. This chapter reinforces the importance of returning to a focus on social investment for social and economic policy.

The third part of the book contains an analysis of the individual areas of social policy; the key policy areas that contribute to the welfare of different groups. We cover employment and wages, income support, housing, health, education, community services, and financing and taxation. Policies in these areas are central to the level and distribution of material well-being in Australia and impact, either directly or indirectly, on people's relationships and capacity to participate. Paid work is the most important source of income for most Australians and its distribution is a critical influence on inequality and poverty in Australia, and on well-being in a range of areas including health, personal relationships, and housing. But for those unable to obtain sufficient, well-paid work, or for whom full-time work is inappropriate due to age, disability, or caring responsibilities, the payments by government through Australia's income support arrangements provide an alternative to poverty or to dependency on the good-will and charity of others. Next to employment, the cost, quality, and accessibility of housing is the most important determinant of living standards, while participation in education and the availability of health care can contribute to future living standards (through their development of human capital) as well as impacting on current well-being (both material and quality of life). Community services can provide social support, relieve suffering, and develop capacity in a range of ways, while policies related to financing and taxation directly affect the distribution of income. They also have an important indirect effect as they can determine whether certain social policies are adopted.

This is a comprehensive book that introduces readers to the meaning of social policy and how it operates in Australia, as well as providing some guidance for social policy practice. It combines a general understanding of the meaning of social policy and the relevant Australian institutional arrangements with specific information about the particular areas relevant to social policy. It covers the past, the present, and emerging issues and debates. It places Australian social policy arrangements in an international context. This is because we understand ourselves more fully by comparing ourselves with others and because Australian social policy is influenced by debates and events in other countries. The book also contains a framework for understanding and intervening in the policy process in Australia. While this framework provides an aid to understanding social policy as an exercise in rational analysis and understanding, it is accompanied by an understanding of social policy as politics and power.

Social policy has been neglected in recent decades in Australia and has taken second place to economic policy. Social policy needs to be given much greater prominence in decision-making about how our society operates and we hope that this book will make a contribution to the improvement of social policy in Australia by providing readers with the enthusiasm and knowledge to be competent and effective policy actors.

Alison McClelland and Paul Smyth

ACKNOWLEDGEMENTS

We are very grateful to Stephen Bell, Deborah Brennan, Tony Dalton, Jane Kenway, Jenny Lewis, John Quiggin and Stephen Ziguras for their chapters on the different areas of social policy. Thanks also to Sally Collins for her substantial work in developing the individual chapters into a consistent and acceptable manuscript and to Margaret Green and Deborah Patterson for their additional assistance. We have benefited enormously from the assistance of the Oxford University Press at all phases of the development of our manuscript. We especially acknowledge the ever courteous and thoughtful Debra James, as well as Caitlin Matthews and Tim Campbell. We also mention the inspiration and learning derived from working with our colleagues and students in our respective universities. Our emphasis on researching for action no doubt also reflects the enormous influence on both our work of having directed research and policy at the Brotherhood of St Laurence in Fitzroy, Melbourne. Thanks to our colleagues there.

Alison McClelland and Paul Smyth

CONTRIBUTORS

Stephen Bell Associate Professor Stephen Bell is Head of the School of Political Science and International Studies at the University of Queensland. His main teaching and research interests are in governance and political economy, including the politics of economic policy. He is the editor or author of seven books and published widely in national and international journals.

Deborah Brennan Associate Professor Deborah Brennan is head of Government and International Relations at the University of Sydney. She is the author of *The Politics of Australian Child Care: Philanthropy, Feminism and Beyond* and has published extensively on Australian and international social policy (especially family and children's services) and gender and politics.

Tony Dalton Associate Professor Tony Dalton is Dean of Research for the Design and Social Context Portfolio at RMIT University and responsible for Urban and Social Policy in the RMIT University Australian Housing and Urban Research Institute (AHURI)/National Centre for Social and Economic Modelling (NATSEM) Research Centre. His long-term research and publications in the area of housing studies are closely connected to his participation in non-government sector policy and advocacy work.

Jane Kenway Professor Jane Kenway is Associate Dean/Research in the Education Faculty at Monash University. Her research expertise is in educational policy sociology with reference to schools and education systems in the context of wider social and cultural change. A particular focus of her research is on educational reform and issues of justice.

Jenny Lewis   Dr Jenny Lewis is Senior Research Fellow in the Department of Political Science at the University of Melbourne. She has taught health politics, health and public policy, published widely on health policy in academic journals, and worked for the Victorian government, including as a consultant. Jenny held a VicHealth/Department of Human Services Research Fellowship 2001–05.

Alison McClelland   Associate Professor Alison McClelland is Head of School, Social Work and Social Policy, at La Trobe University. Previously she was Director of Social Action and Research, Brotherhood of St Laurence and Deputy President of ACOSS. She has been a member of a number of government advisory committees and policy reviews over the past 25 years.

John Quiggin   Professor John Quiggin is a Federation Fellow in Economics and Political Science at the University of Queensland. Professor Quiggin is prominent both as a research economist and as a commentator on Australian economic policy.

Paul Smyth   Professor Paul Smyth is Professor of Social Policy at the Centre for Public Policy, University of Melbourne and General Manager of Social Action and Research at the Brotherhood of St Laurence in Fitzroy, Melbourne. Paul's career has married research and action and this is his eighth book on Australian social policy.

Stephen Ziguras   Dr Stephen Ziguras is a Principal Policy Analyst in the Department of Human Services and a Research Fellow at the Centre for Public Policy, University of Melbourne. He has worked in the areas of social security policy, welfare reform, employment, and labour market programs as well as in other areas of social policy.

ABBREVIATIONS

AASW Australian Association of Social Workers

AAT Administrative Appeals Tribunal

ABS Australian Bureau of Statistics

ACCI Australian Confederation of Commerce and Industry

ACOSS Australian Council of Social Service

ACROD Australian Council for Rehabilitation of Disabled

ACTU Australian Council of Trade Unions

AHURI Australian Housing and Urban Research Institute

AIG Australian Industries Group

AIHW Australian Institute of Health and Welfare

ALP Australian Labor Party

ANTS A New Tax System

ATC Australian Technical College

AWT Australians Working Together

AYPC Australian Youth Policy Action Coalition

BCA Business Council of Australia

BSL Brotherhood of St Laurence

CGT Capital Gains Tax

CIS Centre for Independent Studies

COAG Council of Australian Governments

CPI Consumer Price Index

CSHA Commonwealth State Housing Agreement

CWO Community Welfare Organisation

DEST Department of Education, Science and Training

DEWR   Department of Employment and Workplace Relations

DSP   Disability Support Pension

EMTR   Effective Marginal Tax Rate

EPAC   Economic Planning Advisory Council

EU   European Union

FaCS   Department of Family and Community Services

FIS   Family Income Supplement

FTB   Family Tax Benefit

GATS   General Agreement on Trade and Services

GATT   General Agreement on Tariffs and Trade

GDP   Gross Domestic Product

GMI   Guaranteed Minimum Income

GST   Goods and Services Tax

HACC   Home and Community Care Program

HECS   Higher Education Contribution Scheme

ILO   International Labour Organisation

IMF   International Monetary Fund

IPA   Institute of Public Affairs

JET   Jobs, Education and Training

NACA   National Aged Care Alliance

NAFTA   North American Free Trade Agreement

NGO   Non-Government Organisation

NIC   Newly Industrialised Country

NTEU   National Tertiary Education Industry Union

OECD   Organisation for Economic Cooperation and Development

PAYE   Pay As You Earn

PBS   Pharmaceutical Benefits Scheme

PPBS   Program Planning Budgeting Systems

SGC   Superannuation Guarantee Charge

TAFE   Technical and Further Education

TLM   Transitional Labour Market

VCOSS   Victorian Council of Social Service

WHO   World Health Organisation

WST   Wholesale Sales Tax

WTO   World Trade Organization

YA   Youth Allowance

Part One

INTRODUCTION TO SOCIAL POLICY

This first part of the book introduces readers to the idea of social policy, its scope and terrain, how it can be analysed and influenced, and the institutional context for decisions and actions in Australia. Chapter 1 covers the importance of social policy, its contested nature, purpose, and forms, the broad scope of social policy, and its relationship to other policy areas, including economic, environmental, and public policy, as well as with the welfare state. It shows how social policy has changed the nature of Australian life and the choices available to individual Australians. Social policy is the expression of intent or purpose. This expression may be in the form of a very detailed policy statement, a series of related statements, a very general statement of values or an informal agreement. Social policy is also reflected in the institutional arrangements that assist people's welfare and in the impact of those arrangements on people's lives. It is also an area of study involving knowledge and analysis that helps us understand the aims, context, and impact of social policy on people's lives. We can also understand social policy as a process; how we develop policies and persuade the relevant decision-makers to adopt them.

Ideas and values are critical influences on policy and important concepts such as need, rights, equity, and efficiency are discussed in some detail in Chapter 2. However, these concepts are not straightforward, and how they are understood and the priority given to them varies according to different assumptions about how people behave and societies develop, as well as different values about what constitutes 'the good' individual or society. These differences are reflected in different ideologies and philosophical traditions, which are also covered in Chapter 2. The final section of the chapter deals with some of the enduring design principles of social policy and the choices between them. Should we provide services to all (universal provision) or should we target assistance to the most needy? How should we provide welfare—through employers (such as superannuation), though the tax system (through rebates and concessions), or through direct services and payments? Such decisions are important as they influence who is able to benefit most from our social policy decisions.

And what is a helpful way to make such decisions and how can we analyse a policy decision to understand why it was made and how it will affect people's lives and the nature of our society? These questions are central for people wishing to make a contribution to the development of better policies—who wish to be effective policy practitioners. Chapter 3 responds to these questions by providing two frameworks: a framework for policy analysis and a framework for action, after considering different views about how policy change occurs. In the final chapter, we cover the institutional framework for decision-making. The institutional context affects how change occurs, including the power relationships between different key actors and institutions in the policy process, and what is achievable at any point of time. The chapter is in two sections. The first considers the roles and relationships of the different non-government groups and institutions relevant to social policy in Australia. The second then examines the government-related institutional arrangements in more detail.

1
WHAT IS SOCIAL POLICY?
Alison McClelland

Social policy aims to improve people's welfare, and is especially concerned with the welfare of those who are vulnerable. This book is about social policy in Australia—its purpose and meaning, how it operates now, how it has operated in the past, and the social policy challenges for the future. We show how social policy has affected the lives and choices of Australians over time. We also cover how social policy is made so readers can better understand the policy process and be more informed and skilled policy activists in their attempts to transform society.

In this first chapter the idea and scope of social policy is explored; why it is important, what it means, where it is made, and how it relates to other policy areas and to the welfare state.

THE IMPORTANCE OF SOCIAL POLICY

Social policy change has dramatically affected the lives and choices of Australians over time. Social policy matters. There are many examples of past policy activism in social policy related areas. In the area of health they include the introduction of the Pharmaceutical Benefits Scheme in the late 1940s and 1950s, and Medibank and Medicare in the 1970s and the 1980s. These changes increased access to medicines and health care, and also changed the way the costs of health care are distributed in Australia. For families, women and children, some relevant changes are:

- the introduction of Child Endowment in 1941, Family Allowance in 1976, and payments for single parents in 1973 and 1977
- the introduction of family planning in the 1960s
- the expansion of child care in the 1980s.

These changes have influenced the choices that women can make to have children and to combine work and family. They have also assisted families with the costs of raising children in different ways. In the areas of housing, examples include assistance with home ownership, the development of public housing in the 1940s and 1950s, and the introduction of assistance to low-income private renters in the 1980s. Another example is the introduction of anti-discrimination legislation in the 1980s at both Commonwealth and state levels, which enlarged the rights of minority groups, such as people with disabilities. Finally, the welfare to work policies of the 1980s and 1990s, including the more recent introduction of Work for the Dole, have changed expectations of the responsibilities of welfare recipients and the community in the provision of income support and labour-market assistance to people without work.

In the chapters about individual policy areas in Part Three of this book, some of these examples are covered in more detail. One such example, discussed in Chapter 11, concerns changes to health care through the introduction of a national public health insurance scheme, initially Medibank (introduced in 1975) and now Medicare (introduced in 1983). Medibank and Medicare represented a significant shift in health care policy. They provided for universal access to basic health care, replacing a system where coverage for health care costs was predominately through private health insurance, with a residual safety net for very low-income Australians. Medicare has significantly reduced the cost of basic health care for a large number of Australians, especially those Australians who were not previously covered through private health insurance or the residual safely net. The cost of health care also became more equitably distributed. The introduction of the Medicare levy meant that the financing of health care was related more to a person's capacity to pay, rather than their need for medical or hospital care. Families were no longer necessarily faced with large health care bills or the need to prove to public hospitals, through the means test, that they were poor, in order to receive free hospital care. These changes have made a big difference to the disposable incomes of many families in Australia, as well as ensuring a more equitable access to health care (McClelland & Scotton 1998). However, the goals, elements, and benefits of Medicare have been disputed and the policy has changed over time. Medibank, the initial version of what is now Medicare, introduced by the Whitlam Labor government in 1975, was very contested and was effectively abolished by the Fraser Coalition government in the latter part of the 1970s. The Hawke Labor government then introduced Medicare in 1983, but changes by the Howard government since 1996, through the introduction of the Private Health Insurance Rebate and then Medicare Plus (see later chapter on health policy), alongside developing financing pressures, have watered down the universal and public nature of Medicare.

The changes to Medicare and the different views about the desirability of the changes point to the contested nature of social policy. People have different views about what is good social policy and these views vary according to differences in values about what is desirable and in assumptions about what will work. Social policy therefore involves debates about values, and, in the case of Medicare, the continuing debates about the values of public and private financing and provision are central. Social policy also includes debates about the assumptions of the way individuals and societies behave. In the case of Medicare, there are ongoing debates about how people respond to free health care (for example, if bulk-billing leads to unnecessary visits) and about the behaviour of doctors. Policies are therefore rarely completely settled, but are frequently contested and revisited. Social policy changes are not always viewed as beneficial.

Much policy activism is therefore about improving poor policy, but again, what is regarded as poor policy will differ according to people's values and beliefs, and according to changing ideas about what works. Changes to policies about family and child welfare illustrate the influence of different beliefs and values, and changing knowledge about what works. There are continuing debates about parental versus children's rights and different views about how to protect children's interests, especially whether *at risk* children should stay with their natural parents or be placed in some form of substitute care. Changing values and ideas are further reflected in changes to income support policy. In recent years, there has been a move away from the view that income support is a right of citizenship. Income support is now more conditional on fulfilling certain obligations such as Work for the Dole. This change in orientation has been strongly criticised. However, others see these changes to income support as an improvement, as enlarging people's capacity to take responsibility for themselves (Mead 2000). Chapter 2 provides more detail about how differences in values and assumptions can influence the design of social policy in particular countries—for example, the use of income and assets tests in Australia's income support system. As a result of these differences in values and assumptions, social policy for many can have a dark side and is not necessarily about the improvement of personal welfare (Hill 2003), but may also be aimed at social control (for example, control of parenting behaviour or the actions of welfare recipients) in order protect the community's interest.

Policy activism can also arise as a response to changing needs or social conditions. One current example is the need for different services as a result of population ageing. Another is the pressure for policies to help parents find a better balance between work and family, as a result of the entry of more mothers into the paid work force and changing views about the parenting responsibilities of fathers. A range of current issues that involve policy activism include:

- the cost and access to aged care services and the balance between residential and community-based care
- balancing work and family
- the effectiveness and orientation of child protection services
- responses to sexual violence and abuse
- the welfare of Indigenous people
- the access and cost of utilities (water, gas, electricity) in the face of competition policy and scarcity of resources
- the treatment of asylum seekers in Australia
- early childhood intervention.

THE FORMS AND MEANINGS OF SOCIAL POLICY

Social policy has at least three different meanings. The first is social policy as an *output*—that is, a policy or set of policies, the arrangements and organisation to achieve the policy, and the impact of the policy. Second is social policy as a *discipline* or field of study (Alcock 1998) and third is social policy as a *process* for action to improve societal welfare.

Social policy as output

If we understand social policy as output, we see social policy as some kind of product, which, according to Baldock et al. (2003) may have different forms. It can be:

- *Social policy as intentions and objectives* (p. 8), meaning social policy as clarifying and debating what we want to achieve. This can be in the form of policy statements or informal agreements. Various examples are provided below.
- *Social policy as administrative and financial arrangements* (p. 12), meaning the way we organise our services and institutions to achieve these intentions and

objectives—for example, the organisation of our health and housing systems and of our welfare state overall. This is covered in more detail in chapters about individual policy areas and about the changing nature of Australia's welfare state.

■ *Social policy as outcomes* (p. 18), meaning the impacts of social policies, such as the extent of poverty, how different groups are treated, or the overall quality of life of the population. Parts Two and Three of the book also contain information about the outcomes of individual policy areas.

Social policies can vary in detail and formality. They can be formal statements with substantial detail about purpose and proposed action, a set of related formal statements, statements of general intention or purpose, and statements where values are articulated or informal agreements of intent that are not necessarily made explicit.

Social policy as formal statements with substantial detail

Working Nation is an example of social policy as a formal statement with substantial detail. Prime Minister Keating released it in 1994 after a significant policy review about the problem of unemployment, particularly long-term unemployment. This followed the large hike in unemployment and long-term unemployment after the very severe recession of the early 1990s in Australia. After he won the 'unwinnable' election in 1993, the Prime Minister promised to take particular action to improve the position of unemployed people. *Working Nation* (Keating 1994) contained a range of detailed proposals related to reducing unemployment and long-term unemployment. They covered:

■ industrial relations changes such as the introduction of a training wage that allowed employers to pay a lower wage to previously unemployed people when training was provided

■ labour-market programs such as the introduction of case management, the expansion of job subsidies to employers to take on long-term unemployed people, and the introduction of 'New Work Opportunities' (a form of job creation program)

■ the introduction of a Job Compact with the promise of a job or training for long-term unemployed people over eighteen months

■ some actions to promote regional development

■ changes to the operation of income support, including the introduction of reciprocal obligation and the easing of income tests applying to the receipt of unemployment payments when part-time work was obtained (see Edwards 2001; Keating 1994; Watson 2002).

Reciprocal obligation referred to the obligation of the community to provide opportunities for long-term unemployed people to obtain work alongside the obligation of the unemployed person to take up the opportunities, or otherwise to face some penalty.

Australians Working Together (AWT) (Vanstone & Abbott 2001) is another example of a more recent formal statement, somewhat related to the focus of *Working Nation*, but more concerned about the problem of welfare dependency than unemployment. AWT is a policy statement from the Howard Coalition government. It was developed by the Minister for Employment and Workplace Relations (Tony Abbott) and the Minister for Family and Community Services (Amanda Vanstone), following the recommendations of a review of welfare by a Reference Group on Welfare Reform in 2000. AWT is a statement of actions mainly designed to move people off welfare into work. It includes changes to the type and level of employment-related assistance available to unemployed people, people with a disability, parents, and other groups such as Indigenous people. It was introduced in the 2001–02 Commonwealth Budget and, as such, also contained details of the number of people to be assisted and the amount of funding to be allocated. Budget statements are frequently vehicles for the release of policy statements.

Both *Working Nation* and AWT represent certain emerging features of policy statements in Australia. First, they are often policy packages—a range of related measures to be introduced over a period of time, frequently, but not always, over a 4-year period. Second, they often involve action by a number of different ministers and departments, based on the understanding that complex problems require whole-of-government responses. Third, they can involve different areas of policy, such as employment policy and income-support policy changes in the case of *Working Nation* and AWT.

Policy as a set of policy statements

Policy is frequently represented as a set of policy statements rather than being encapsulated in one statement alone. This particularly applies to broad policy areas such as aged-care policy, employment policy, and so on. It can also apply to a policy issue where there is a series of related changes taking place in a number of different areas. For example, the policy issue of work and family is affected by a number of policy statements including statements from the Industrial Relations Commission about the leave entitlements and working conditions that apply to parents in paid work, the introduction of the Maternity Payment in the 2004–05 Federal Budget Statement that dealt with the income support available to parents who had a baby, and statements related to the expectations of work by parents who receive welfare payments. Superannuation policy is also reflected in a number of different detailed statements about the taxes applying to superannuation, the obligations for employers to pay superannuation, government support for low-income Australians who make additional contributions to superannuation, and the conditions under which contributions to superannuation can be made and benefits received.

Policy as more general statements of intent and values

Policies can also be more general statements of intent or of broad values. These are often political party documents, adopted at party conferences, or key Ministerial and Prime Ministerial statements. A good example of a very important general policy statement by a Prime Minister in Australia is the landmark Redfern address.by Paul Keating in 1992. In this statement, Keating identified the need for white Australians to recognise and respond positively to the dispossession of Indigenous people's land and way of life (Watson 2002). Another very different and more recent example is the Federal Treasurer Peter Costello's Intergenerational report, released as a general statement that articulated the long-term consequences of the ageing of Australia's population and general options for response (Costello 2002).

Social policy as informal agreements

Finally, social policy is not always articulated in a formal statement but it may be a more informal agreement to do things in a certain way. The informality may be deliberate, in order to circumvent the requirements of the formal policy. For example, it is sometimes said that during the 1980s recession, when jobs were not available, many workers in the old CES (Commonwealth Employment Service) had an informal policy not to implement the strict requirements of the work test that applied to unemployed people's eligibility for unemployment benefits. At other times the informal agreement may occur because the formal policy is poorly articulated and not communicated well to those who have to implement it, or because it is so general that it can be interpreted in a number of different ways.

Social policy as a discipline or area of study

The second way of understanding social policy is as a discipline, or area of study. By this we mean the activities involved in understanding the factors that influence particular social policies and in understanding the impact of such policies on people's lives and the nature of society. The study of social policy is ultimately concerned with understanding how the organisation of society affects well-being. The development of social policy as a discipline derives from the belief that we can change society in a planned and purposeful manner and improve people's welfare using knowledge and research. It has progressively developed with the development of the responsibility of the governments for the pursuit of social well-being.

Australian social policy has been strongly influenced by the development of social policy as a discipline in the UK, drawing on the Fabian tradition of commitment to social reform based on an intellectual understanding of society's needs and operation. This in turn drew on a tradition of research into social conditions in the nineteenth century UK by researchers such as Rowntree and Booth (Alcock 1998). However, Richard Titmuss is the person probably most responsible for the development of social policy as a discipline in the UK. Titmuss was important in articulating an ethical case for welfare and social policy (see Chapter 2) and developing a framework for analysing how different institutional arrangements affect well-being.

In Australia, research into social conditions was understandably later in its development. It is exemplified in the work of Professor Ronald Henderson, who came to Australia in the 1960s from the UK and undertook the first (and only) major inquiry into poverty in Australia. Proceeding it was the work of individuals and organisations, such as Oswald Barnett who developed a study group to understand the conditions of slums in inner urban Melbourne and to develop proposals for change, leading to the establishment of the Housing Commission in Victoria and the expansion of public housing.

Erskine (1998) identifies a number of features of the study of social policy. As the study of social policy is about an analysis of how policies impact on the welfare of individuals and groups, this means first having views about what constitutes welfare and, second, having the means to assess the impacts of policies on people's welfare. Third, it involves an understanding of how policies are 'institutionally organised and implemented' (for example, how the income support system operates) (Erskine 1998, p. 15). Fourth, it also means understanding 'the components of welfare', which may go beyond the examination of existing government policies to understanding how new social issues, needs, and arrangements can impact on people's well-being. For example, the changing labour-force participation of women means that we need to significantly re-examine our policies to meet the emerging issue of work and family. Finally, Erskine says it is wrong to think of social policy as one discipline. He sees it as a multidisciplinary area of study that 'draws on the methods and theories used in sociology, statistics, management science, history, law, economics, political science, philosophy, geography and social psychology to help explore well-being' (Erskine 1998, p. 15).

In this book, we cover how social policy operates as an area or field of study in Australia, including:

- the different theoretical frameworks about how policies are made
- how to analyse the impact of policies
- the role of Australian institutions in the development and implementation of policy
- how current policy is affected by the past and by actions and ideas in other countries
- the impact of change on social policy.

The book is designed to enable readers to develop knowledge of the analysis and appraisal of social policy in Australia.

Social policy as a process

Social policy can also be understood as a process—the activities people, groups, and institutions undertake in order to introduce new policies or to change existing policies. Much of what we mean by social policy as a process has been covered in the discussion above of social policy as an area of study or discipline. But in framing social policy as a process in this book, we emphasise the normative aspect of the policy process in the sense that we wish to enable readers to develop an understanding of how to be an effective policy actor or practitioner—the useful activities that are more likely to be effective in creating change. So our understanding of social policy as a process goes beyond the analysis of social policy and an analysis of the process of policy making, to a focus on the knowledge that can inform what may be regarded as useful actions in the policy process. By useful actions we mean actions that are more likely to lead to good policy change. And by good policy change we mean policy that improves societal well-being, while also acknowledging that what is regarded as good policy is open to debate and contest. In short, the book is also informed by the view that a good policy process is more likely to lead to good policy than a poor policy process (see Bridgman & Davis 2004 and Edwards 2001 for elaboration of the importance of the policy process).

This emphasis on the social policy process and the development of social policy practitioners also comes from the idea that good policy is more likely to occur if more people from different organisations and roles are equipped to contribute to policy development. Therefore, we need to help workers who have day-to-day information about what is happening on the ground to be able to intervene in the policy process, just as we need to assist those in designated policy position in government departments to be effective in their roles. We also need to help those affected by policies to be able to intervene effectively in the policy process. Chapter 3 therefore contains information about how to be a policy practitioner or policy actor at different levels.

DEFINITIONS OF SOCIAL POLICY— THE MAIN FEATURES AND SCOPE

Definitions and features

There are a number of different definitions of policy and social policy. Some are presented in Table 1.1 to illustrate the key features of social policy.

First, as already discussed, social policy has different meanings including particular policies, areas of study, or processes for action.

Second, social policy is more planned than random—it involves some kind of purposeful, intentional activity and often 'authoritative choice' (Bridgman & Davis 2004, p. 4). For example, the decision to introduce reform of family law and no-fault divorce in the early 1970s was not accidental. It arose from purposeful action to change laws seen to be out of step with changing values and the changed reality of marriage and separation.

Third, social policy is concerned about the welfare (or well-being) of individuals and groups in society. This book takes a broad definition of the meaning of welfare as explained further below.

Fourth, social policy is concerned with social relationships—the relationships between individuals, individuals and society, and different groups in society. This is important because individual and social well-being is very dependent on the quality of relationships.

Fifth, social policy is concerned with both overall welfare and also about how welfare or well-being is distributed among different groups according to important facets of life such as health, education, income, and employment.

Table 1.1 Definitions of policy and social policy

Policy can be taken to mean principles that govern action towards given ends.	Titmuss 1974 cited in Dalton et al. 1996
Policy can be seen as: ■ a label for a field of activity ■ an expression of general purpose or desired state of affairs ■ specific proposals ■ decisions of government arising from crucial moments of choice ■ formal authorisation—a specific act or statute ■ a program—a particular package of legislation, organisation, and resources ■ output—what government actually delivers, as opposed to what is has promised or has authorised through legislation ■ the produce of a particular activity ■ theory—if we do X then Y will follow ■ a process unfolding over a long period of time.	Bridgman & Davis 2004, p. 5, adopted from Hogwood & Gunn 1990.
[Public] Policy is the continuing work done by groups of policy actors who use available public institutions to articulate and express the things they value.	Considine 1994, p. 4
The study of social policy is concerned with those aspects of public policies, market operations, personal consumption, and interpersonal relationships that contribute to, or detract from, the well-being or welfare of individuals or groups. Social policy explores the social, political, ideological, and institutional context within which welfare is produced, distributed, and consumed. It seeks to provide an account of the processes that contribute to or detract from welfare and it does this within a normative framework that involves debating moral and political issues about the nature of the desired outcome.	Erskine 1998, p. 19
Social policy contains both products and outcome-particular policies, as well as processes of critical reflection, action, and contest between people. Social policy is concerned with social goals, purpose, and values.	Dalton et al. 1996, p. 4
Social policy is 'actions aimed at promoting social well-being'.	Alcock in Hill 2003, p. 1

Sixth, social policy is concerned with the articulation of objectives and principles, and critically involves debates about values as well as action to achieve them. Different values and beliefs will mean there are different understandings about what constitutes welfare and also about how welfare is best promoted. The examples of the continuing and changing debates about Medicare and child protection earlier in this chapter illustrate the role of debates about values such as individual freedom, personal or social responsibility, and commitment to equality, in the development and analysis of social policy.

Seventh, the process of social policy involves rational analysis but also political contest about different values and the position of different groups. The analysis of social policy therefore requires an understanding of the power relationships within society and is informed by different theories about power and how it is exercised.

Finally, while social policy is concerned with debates about values and ideologies, it also draws on empirical knowledge to inform the analysis of social problems and the assessment of solutions. Social policies are based on assumptions about what might work (Bridgman & Davis 2004). Social policy also uses analytic frameworks to understand how this knowledge can be used in a systematic and rigorous manner.

The scope of social policy

These definitions point to the broad scope of social policy. They point to a broad understanding of the meaning of welfare, the broad responsibility for the achievement of welfare, the broad range of disciplines required for the analysis and development of social policy, and the interconnections between social policy and other areas of policy.

While *welfare* may be interpreted in a narrow way, meaning the services that are provided to people who are in need, we take the broad definition articulated in the Alcock definition of 'Actions aimed at promoting social well-being'. Social well-being encompasses how individuals and groups fare in a range of domains or spheres of life such as living standards (or material well-being), access to information, social participation, family relationships, and overall life satisfaction (Western et al. 1995). In Part Three of this book, we cover the key policy areas that contribute to the welfare of different groups in these domains of life. We cover employment and wages, income support, housing, health, education, community services, and financing and taxation. Policies in these areas are central to the level and distribution of material well-being in Australia, and most have an impact, either directly or indirectly, on people's relationships and capacity to participate. Policies related to financing and taxation directly affect the distribution of income but also have an important indirect effect as they can determine whether certain social policies are adopted.

This broad definition of welfare also points to a shared responsibility for welfare. While social policy is mainly concerned about what governments do (public policy), it also covers the market, the operations of local communities, non-government organisations and families, *as all influence social welfare*. For example, the market affects social well-being through the production of goods and services and also through its capacity to provide employment at wage levels and conditions that provide reasonable living standards and quality of life. Through self-help and the exercise of choice, individuals promote their own living standards and usually those of other family members through sharing material resources and providing social and emotional support. Community organisations have traditionally played a strong role in the provision of a wide range of services in Australia from nursing homes for older people to employment assistance for unemployed people, and this role has increased in recent years. Social policy is concerned with how governments intervene to change the operations of markets, families, and community organisations, but also about how policies are made in these other spheres of society.

The scope of social policy is also broad in the sense that it covers a range of disciplines as no one discipline has sufficient knowledge to enable us to understand how welfare is produced, distributed, and consumed. We need to draw on the understandings of a range of disciplines including sociology, economics, psychology, philosophy, political science, and history. Sociology helps us to understand social relationships, including the relationships between different groups. Economics helps us to understand the resource allocation aspects of social policy, the need to allocate resources efficiently and also how to improve aggregate material well-being, while psychology is important in understanding how individuals behave and the factors that influence their development. Debates about values and goals are also informed by philosophy. In addition, given the central role of government action in social policy, knowledge about political science and the factors that influence the actions and decisions of governments, is also important, as is some understanding of past policy approaches.

The interrelationships between economic policy, social policy, and public policy are especially salient. Economic policy affects critical aspects of well-being central to social policy such as the level and distribution of employment, the price of goods and services such as housing, and the finances available for government expenditure. Well-being is best promoted when public policy integrates economic and policy considerations in decision-making, but over the past few decades social policy has become very subservient to economic policy. As government action is a critical feature of social policy, there is also a strong relationship between public policy and social policy. Public policy can promote social policy considerations but this is not necessarily the case. Finally, with a deepening concern about environmental sustainability, environmental policy has become a more influential area of policy. Policies to promote the environment can have strong social policy implications. They can influence the costs of essential goods and services (such as electricity or water) and also levels of employment (related to debates about the environmental impact of woodchipping industries or the need to change agricultural practices to conserve water). There is increased recognition of the *triple bottom line* meaning that policy-making needs to integrate social, economic, and environmental considerations.

Finally, the scope of social policy is also broad in the sense that there is a broad range of influences on social policy. As policies do not operate in isolation, in order to explore the impact of particular policies and to understand how polices are developed, we need to understand their broader social, political, historical, economic, and ideological contexts. The social context is important as the roles and relationships of different groups influence the expectations of behaviour and the supports that should be provided by family members or other community members. This in turn affects the adoption of particular policies as well as their impacts. For example, the expectation that parents will financially support their children until a certain age has influenced the adoption of a parental income test to determine the level of support that should be available to young Australians. The political context influences the political acceptability of different policies and the economic context affects the resources available to pursue certain actions as well as the living standards of different groups, as already explained. The historical context is important for understanding the impact of previous policies and for understanding the limits that historical choices may place on the present. The international context is important because the international environment, such as interest rates in other countries, especially in the United States of America (USA), impacts on the choices available in Australia, and this influence has become more marked with increased globalisation. However, the extent of the limitations posed by globalisation on national choices is much contested. The ideological context, and the prevailing values and beliefs, will affect the goals of social policy—for example, the value placed on pursuing equality versus individual freedom. It will also influence the actions that are understood to be effective in improving welfare—for example, through placing emphasis on individual behavioural change or on changing societal structures.

SOCIAL POLICY AND THE WELFARE STATE

The introduction and development of particular social policies, such as the aged pension, assistance with the cost of health care, or the expansion of child care, is intimately related to the development of welfare states. Welfare states provide the institutional context for social policy and for particular policies. Welfare states have developed in advanced capitalistic societies alongside the development of the responsibility of governments for societal well-being. The form and operation of particular welfare states influences the outcomes of particular policies and also affects the capacity to introduce policy change. Social policy has also developed as an area of study in response to the need for systematic knowledge to inform the way we understand and change our welfare states. And so social policy contributes to the development of welfare states and is also influenced by welfare states. In general, the scope and focus of welfare states has considerable overlap with the scope and interest of social policy as the definitions in Table 1.2 illustrate.

Table 1.2 Definitions of welfare states

A society in which the state intervenes within the processes of economic production and distribution to reallocate life chances between individuals and/or classes.	Pierson 1998, p. 7
The range of state interventions that aim to protect individuals from unimpeded market processes and their outcomes.	Cass 1998, p. 40
A type of state predominately concerned with the production and distribution of societal well-being.	Esping-Andersen 1990, p. 1

Some key points about the relationship between welfare states and social policy arise from these definitions. First is the concern of welfare states with *well-being*, and therefore the broad ambit of what we understand by the welfare state. It includes a range of areas and is not confined to a narrow view of welfare. The idea of the welfare state includes systems such as the employment, education, and housing systems, and not just, for example, what welfare departments do. As mentioned, social policy also has a broad ambit. Second is the focus on the distribution of well-being—distribution is also a key focus of social policy and the production of aggregate well-being is also of concern to both. Third is a particular focus on the role and responsibility of the state for ensuring well-being as reflected in the idea of social citizenship, which is also a key idea in social policy. Fourth is the importance of the role of the state, but also the increased importance of the roles of individuals, families, the market, and community organisations. The increased role of other sectors (apart from the state) in promoting welfare has led some to talk about the welfare mix, rather than the welfare state. It is particularly important to understand how these different sectors interact and how these interactions influence the welfare of different groups.

The development and operation of welfare states is affected by the combined operations of economic, social, and public policy. And, as mentioned at the beginning of this chapter, these polices are informed by dominant values and assumptions. The next chapter goes on to explore values, ideologies, and concepts, and their influence on social policy and on welfare states in some detail.

SUMMARY AND CONCLUSION

Social policy matters and past social policy activism have significantly altered the nature of Australian society in a number of important ways. Policy activism can be required for a number of reasons including:

- changing policies that are causing harm
- articulating different values and beliefs
- responding to changing needs.

We can understand social policy in a number of ways. Social policy can be an output—that is, the expression of intent or purpose. This expression may be in the form of a very detailed policy statement, a series of related statements, a very general statement of values, or an informal agreement. Social policy is also reflected in the institutional arrangements that assist people's welfare and in the impact of those arrangements on people's lives. Social policy is also an area of study involving knowledge and analysis that helps us understand the aims of social policy, the context of policy, and the impact of policy on people lives. If we want to develop good policy and effective policy practitioners, we also need to understand the process of social policy development that is most likely to lead to good policy.

Social policy is about purposeful activity to improve societal well-being, and as such has a broad scope, utilises a range of disciplines, and overlaps with economic policy, public policy, and environmental policy. It is particularly concerned with the distribution of well-being and with social relationships. Social policy involves rational analysis and action but also political contest about different values and the position of different groups. Social policy has developed alongside the development of welfare states and the responsibility of governments for societal well-being, but is also concerned with the operations of markets, families, and community organisations.

2

VALUES, CONCEPTS, AND SOCIAL POLICY DESIGN

Alison McClelland

Ideas and values are important influences on social policy, as

> Policies are fashioned and refashioned through the interplay between
> ideas and events, between political commitments and the experience
> of administration, and between values and the exigencies of office and
> electoral politics.
>
> (Deacon 2002, p. 9)

Some pivotal ideas (or concepts) in social policy include need, desert, rights, social justice, and efficiency. But the interpretation of these ideas, and the value placed on them, depends on broader frameworks and ideologies about what works (that is theories about how humans and societies behave and develop) and what ought to be (key values). This chapter explores some of the value and ideological differences that have historically influenced the development of social policy as well as the different frameworks that play out in contemporary debates. It then canvasses some of the key concepts, and how their meaning and priority is affected by different values, and how in turn they influence the design of social policy.

VALUES, IDEOLOGIES, AND FRAMEWORKS OF WELFARE

As Teles argues, 'welfare raises fundamental questions about the rights and obligations of citizenship, and about the scope and purpose of public policy' (in Deacon 2002, p. 8), which is essentially 'about our responsibilities one for another' (Williams in Deacon 2002, p. 9). The tension between the principles of community responsibility towards others and that of personal responsibility towards one's self represents one of the key value tensions in welfare. The priority given to the principle of community responsibility over the principle of personal responsibility and private provision varies between different societies and over time. According to Deacon (2002), the priority given to one over the other depends on the value given to reducing dependency or to promoting equality. Others see the conflict as being between the promotion of individual freedom (negative freedom from coercion) and the promotion of equality.

Dalton et al. (1996) identify four different political philosophies based on different views about the desirable relationship between the individual and society. First is the libertarian tradition based on writings of English philosophers such as Hobbes and Locke, championed more recently by Hayek and Nozik. This tradition assumes individual self-interest and individual (negative) freedom are paramount, places high value on the market, and is hostile to government action. Neo-liberal economics and the new-Right political philosophy draw on this tradition. They have been exemplified in the ideas and policies of the Thatcher government in the UK and the Reagan government in the USA.

The second tradition is the social liberal tradition, drawing on utilitarian ideas of Jeremy Bentham and the philosophies of thinkers such as John Stuart Mill. It is said to have been very influential in Australian social policy. This tradition still holds individual freedom highly but would value positive freedom (freedom to achieve certain goals, such as economic well-being) as well as negative freedom (freedom from coercion). Social liberalism is also based on the utilitarian ideal of the greatest good for the greatest number and, therefore, is interested in the pursuit of social goals and intervention in the market towards that end as well as individual self-interest.

Third is the egalitarian tradition articulated by English writers and activists such as Paine and Tawney. This tradition is reflected in the social democratic philosophy. An important view underlying this tradition is that all are born equal and, therefore, have equal rights, and that these equal rights go beyond civic and political rights to encompass social rights. Redistribution is therefore justified in the pursuit of equality, which is important for the development of individual freedom, where freedom is seen in the sense of positive freedom and in a social context. Society also benefits through greater equality, although equality does not mean that everyone should be equal or the same in every way, rather that all should have equal opportunity to develop fully to their full potential. The following quotation from Tawney illustrates the social reasons for equality and the kind of equality to be sought.

> It is these simpler and more elementary considerations that have been in the minds of those who have thought that a society was most likely to enjoy happiness and good will, and to turn both its human and material resources to the best account, if it cultivated as far possible an equalitarian temper, and sought by its institutions to increase equality…'Equality'… may either purport to state a fact, or convey the expression of an ethical judgement. On the one hand it may assert that men are, on the whole very similar in their natural endowments of character and intelligence. On the other hand, it may assert that, while they differ profoundly as individuals in capacity and character, they are entitled as human beings to consideration and respect, and that the well-being of a society is likely to be increased if it so plans its organisation that, whether their powers are great or small, all its members may be equally enabled to make the best of such powers as they possess.
>
> (Tawney 1931 cited in Tawney 1964, pp 46–7)

The fourth tradition is the communitarian tradition, which places high value on individual and social development through social relationships, cooperation, and the promotion of community. It therefore provides for some restrictions on individual freedom to allow for community and social development. This tradition encompasses a variety of philosophies including Marxism, the Catholic ideal of community, family, and subsidiarity, as well as other non-Marxist communitarians who emphasise the social and political nature of human beings (Dalton et al. 1996). A modern expression of communitarianism, as advocated by writers such as Etzioni, has strong moral overtones and is explored later in this chapter.

To these four traditions, we would add a fifth, the conservative tradition, which while perhaps somewhat related to the social liberal tradition, is distinguished by a strong respect for the support and continuation of social institutions such as the family, community, religion, and private property (Pinker 1998). It has a strong preference for order and authority, with the ideas of Edmund Burke being very important in the development of the tradition. It has been reflected in the policies of the Conservative Party in the UK and the Liberal Party in Australia, especially in the social policy focus of Prime Minister Howard, who has been described as a social conservative.

These traditions generally reflect two important differences. The first is the difference between the liberal ideology of individual freedom and the social democratic or socialist ideology of social relationships and social equality. The second difference is between the liberal ideology of individual freedom and a more conservative ideology of respect for authority (and for community in some cases). Richard Titmuss, one of the seminal social policy thinkers of the twentieth century, saw these differences reflected in different models or frameworks of welfare and social policy differences between capitalist countries as they developed welfare states from an early reliance on charitable provision.

According to Titmuss (1974), the *liberal ideology* with its values of individual freedom and responsibility is reflected in a *residual welfare* model with welfare provided through private provision (the market) and by the family, with a limited safety net for those unable to provide for themselves in this way. The USA is a current example of the residual welfare model and Australia is frequently also seen in this way, although this is contested (as will be covered in more detail in Chapter 6). The *conservative ideology* places less value on individual freedom and more value on authority, status, and the promotion of social inclusion. This ideology is reflected in the *industrial achievement performance* model, which has a greater role for government but also preserves the status of different groups and values group identification and performance. The European welfare states, especially countries such as Germany, are exemplars of this model. The third ideology is the *social democratic* or *socialist* ideology, which according to Titmuss is reflected in the *institutional/redistributive* model. This model values equality and community responsibility, and therefore has a strong role for the state, with universal provision of income support and services based on citizenship. The Scandinavian countries are exemplars of this model, which was seen by Titmuss to be the most advanced and preferable model. A similar breakdown has been developed by Esping-Andersen (1990) who has clustered countries into welfare state regimes. These are the *liberal welfare* regime, the *conservative corporatist* regime, and the *social democratic* regime. He concluded that the social democratic regime performs best according to criteria such as the extent to which welfare states allow people to meet their needs without reliance on the market, that is the extent to which welfare is *decommodified*.

However, this idealised typology of models or regimes has also been criticised, first on the basis that the arrangements developed by individual countries in pursuit of values such as equality do not fit neatly into these models and regimes. Australia is one example of a country that does not neatly fit into one of these regimes. The regimes are also said to be irrelevant to the emerging models of welfare in areas such as Asia, South America, and the transitional countries (from communism to capitalism). This is followed up in more detail in Chapter 6. The second criticism is that these regimes do not reflect the key value differences around the position of women, the preservation of the environment, racial and ethnic divisions, and other concerns of the new social movements (Manning 2003a). Feminist analysis places much greater importance on understanding how social policy deals with issues of reproduction and caring responsibilities, and how citizenship and dependence is understood. These criticisms apply more generally to the philosophical traditions associated with the development of social policy in Western countries, which are generally developed from the perspective of Western males in industrial societies.

More recently, Deacon (2002) has drawn on current debates and ideas about welfare (in the more narrow sense of government income support and services) to identify five different perspectives based on different values or ethical ideals. These perspectives are not mutually exclusive, but they do have a different understanding and articulation of the role and purpose of welfare. The first places priority on acting against inequality, the remaining four are more concerned with welfare dependency (that is, on state payments and services). These are:

- *Welfare as an expression of altruism* as articulated by Titmuss drawing on the ethical understandings advanced by Tawney. This presents the ethical case for a more equal and socially cohesive society. Redistribution enables the expression of altruism and also the development of human and social potential. This is also compatible with the social democratic or socialist ideology identified above. Titmuss's ideas about altruism are further explored later in this chapter.

- *Welfare as a channel for the pursuit of self-interest* based on the notions of the rational person acting to secure their own welfare. This understanding draws on libertarian ideology and is compatible with neo-liberal economic thinking. Welfare provision needs to have a system of incentives (such as very low levels of income support) to enable the expression of rational self-interest, especially through increased work effort. Currently Charles Murray (1994) is the well-known advocate of this view of welfare and he recommends reducing income support entitlements to encourage self-provision.

- *Welfare as the exercise of authority* based on the view that people are not always capable of acting in their own self-interest. The New Paternalism advocated by Laurence Mead (2000) is the contemporary articulation of this view, which was very influential in welfare reform in the United States of America and, to a lesser extent, in the United Kingdom and Australia. This is more compatible with the conservative tradition with its respect for authority and its lower value placed on individual freedom.

- *Welfare as a transition to work*. This view really arises from the previous two perspectives, although it can also be compatible with the communitarian perspective identified next.

■ *Welfare as a mechanism for moral regeneration* based on the view that a key task of welfare is to develop our sense of community responsibility and membership. Communitarianism, as advocated by Etzioni (2004), is an expression of this view. According to Deacon (2002, pp 70–1) 'Communitarianism seeks a "new moral order" in which members of society share common values and there is a "moral infrastructure" based around "the family, the school, the community and the wider community or communities"'. Reciprocity (also explored later in this chapter) is a strong value of communitarianism, but communitarianism also supports the conditionality of welfare payments. The case for the conditionality of welfare rests on the moral case for compelling community responsibility. This is also reflected in the conservative ideology of some European countries, which place great value on family responsibility for welfare and for the role of local communities, as well as requiring some responsibility by employers. A different version is contained in the arrangements of a number of Asian countries. Japan provides an interesting example, with a strong social role for employers (though lifetime employment and welfare benefits through work) as well as for the family in the provision of welfare support.

Deacon claims that the last four perspectives are having the most influence on public policy in the United Kingdom and in the United States of America (and, some could add, in Australia).

CONCEPTS AND SOCIAL POLICY

These different frameworks and perspectives are important because they influence how the ends (purpose or goals) and means of social policy are understood and the priority accorded to some ends over others. These in turn can influence the design principles of welfare.

Table 2.1 identifies key concepts relevant to the ends, the means, and the design principles of welfare.

Needs, rights, desert, and risk

Social policy is essentially concerned with meeting *social needs*. We can think of basic human needs for survival (such as food and shelter) but also social needs, such as the need for health care, housing, income, education, and so on.

By terming needs as social needs, we understand that we do not just experience needs in isolation, but that they arise from our social relationships and from social arrangements, including social values and norms. Social needs are the goods, services, and relationships we require to satisfy our basic needs. There are different views about whether we can identify common basic needs against which our social policies can always be measured. Maslow outlined a hierarchy of human needs from very basic physiological needs through to the need for self-actualisation. Doyal and Gough (1991) identify the two universal basic needs as the need for some physical capacity to participate and the need for personal autonomy. Our social needs, such as the need for economic security, a basic standard of living, and the capacity for community involvement arise from the need to ensure that these more basic needs are met.

Table 2.1 Concepts, welfare, and design principles

Concepts and the ends of welfare	Concepts, the means and design principles of welfare
Need, rights, desert, risk, capability	Efficiency and effectiveness
Equity, social justice, equality, and redistribution	Universalism versus targeting
Altruism and reciprocity	Occupational, fiscal, or state welfare

Manning (1998) distinguishes between *needs* and the related concepts of *wants and preferences*. We may want things we do not need (for example, an expensive item of clothing) and we may need things that we do not want (such as a visit to the dentist). The concept of preference is used more than want and need in economic analysis. The concept of preference also implies that we give priority to certain wants over others (for example, the preference for fast food implies that it has priority over home cooking or over a restaurant meal). Preference therefore evokes the idea of choice and opportunity cost, meaning that if we choose to use resources in one way then we sacrifice their use in other ways. This is a cost that must be measured against the benefit we receive from the choice we have made. We need to choose because of the notion of scarcity—that is that there are insufficient resources to meet all our wants.

In attempting to better understand needs and how we can identify priorities in meeting those needs, social policy frequently involves the collection and analysis of information about different perspectives on needs. According to Bradshaw (1972) information about needs can be obtained in four different ways. Needs may be:

- *felt*, as indicated by a subjective judgment by those who have the need
- *expressed,* meaning that the need is revealed in some way that indicates a choice has been made to give that need a priority (similar to the economists' concept of revealed preference—for example, by spending money on medical care rather than some other need or preference)
- *comparative*, as indicated by comparing the situation of one person or group against others—for example, the needs of the Queensland population for health care compared with the needs in other Australian states
- *normative,* with experts judging that the need is real and has priority.

It is arguable that too little attention is given to felt needs in the development of social policy, with much social policy informed by expert analysis and quantitative information about the situations of different groups. Information about felt need requires more attention and listening to ordinary people about how they understand their needs, as well as to the recipients of welfare services about whether services are adequate and appropriate in meeting their needs.

However, the extent to which there is community responsibility for the meeting of needs will also critically depend on whether it is determined people have a *right* to have certain needs met or whether community responsibility can be modified according to whether an individual *deserves* to have assistance. Rights are a legal concept referring to the legitimacy of a person's claims (Taylor-Gooby 1998). The idea of social rights has developed as the legitimacy of people's claims on the state to have social needs met has also developed. Marshall coined the term *social citizenship* to illustrate the expansion of rights based on citizenship status, from civil rights in the eighteenth century, to political rights in the nineteenth century, to social rights in the twentieth century (Manning 2003a). Social citizenship refers to the acknowledgment of social rights, which are granted on the basis of citizenship and are not conditional on status (who you are) or the way you behave. Such conditions, however, will apply when desert or merit, and not social citizenship, become the reasons for welfare. Welfare is then less entitlement-based and more conditional.

Most countries have some mix of welfare claims based on social citizenship and on notions of desert; however, the priority given to desert-based claims is much higher in countries where the liberal ideology dominates and needs are meant to be met through market-based activity. For example, the social security arrangements of all countries aim to ensure that people in work have a higher income than people who are unemployed and are reliant on the state for income support. In this sense, some desert-based notions exist in all industrialised welfare states and are, at least partly, based on the idea that people who work deserve to have a higher standard of living that those who do not. However, in the USA, the exemplar of the liberal welfare state, a single, unemployed person has no basic entitlement to income support or to basic health care, reflecting the strong belief that even basic support from the state needs to be deserved and earned through work.

In a number of countries, including Australia, the priority previously given to meeting rights has recently been questioned, with the view that greater attention must be given to notions of responsibility and obligation. Income support has become more desert-based and less rights-based. This is reflected in the extension of more conditions for the receipt of income support, such as requirements to take part in training programs or programs such as Work for the Dole for unemployed people and some sole parents. It is also reflected in a higher payment being available for people who are on an aged-pension than single, unemployed people, the idea being that older people deserve more support. Desert- and merit-based claims for welfare are also a feature of some European countries where community responsibility and authority are important values. This is also compatible with the communitarian philosophy outlined earlier, which emphasises the need for people to be responsible members of their communities. Welfare can be denied or reduced when this responsibility is not exercised. 'Third Way' writers, such as Anthony Giddens (1999) and Tony Blair in the UK and Mark Latham and Noel Pearson in Australia, talk about 'no rights without responsibility' (Latham 1998; Pearson 2000a) and aim to change the balance between rights and responsibilities in modern welfare states. In this sense, the 'Third Way' is a path between the more unconditional citizenship rights-based approach to welfare associated with social democracy and socialism, and the excessive reliance on the market and residual welfare associated with liberal welfare thinking. The 'Third Way' became prominent as a welfare state model in the mid 1990s and will be discussed in more detail in Chapter 7.

Amartya Sen (2001) has developed the concepts of *capabilities* and *agency freedom* as important ideas when thinking about the end or purpose of welfare and economic and social development. Sen sees the purpose of welfare (in its broad sense) as the achievement of *agency freedom*. Agency freedom is the substantive opportunities that people have to pursue their own goals. These goals can include an improvement in the well-being of others and also need to be understood in a social context. The aim of development (and welfare) is therefore to help people develop the important capabilities they require to meet their own goals. Sen (2001) identifies a number of such capabilities or freedoms, such as political freedoms, the capabilities (or opportunities) to use economic resources to improve material well-being, social opportunities (with health care and education as key examples), and protective security—the importance of an effective safety net.

Another recent change is a focus on risk. Social policy has always had a role in limiting people's exposure to foreseen and unforeseen risks of harm, and of not having basic needs met. For example, the development of social insurance programs in European countries represented ways of dealing with the known risk of reduced income in old age and the more unknown risk of insufficient income through unemployment or disability. However, these days, as we shall see in later chapters, risk is now understood differently and risk management approaches are also said to have changed. Writers such as Kemshall (2002) claim that the changed focus of social policy is from meeting needs to risk management approaches that minimise the exposure of organisations and governments to risks, such as financial risks and reputation risks. Through policies that limit services more stringently and that limit the goals of government (for example, by moving away from the goal of full employment), the exposure to risk is transferred downwards to more vulnerable people who are more likely to be at risk of not having basic needs met.

Equity, social justice, equality, and redistribution

As social policy is concerned with *the distribution* of welfare, the concepts of equity, social justice, equality, and redistribution have special salience. Ideas of equity and social justice are concerned about who gets what and under what circumstances. However, equity does not necessarily mean the achievement of equality. What is regarded as fair or equitable will differ according to different ideologies and philosophies about social justice; about the end of welfare and the priority accorded to needs, rights, and desert. For example, some may understand fairness to mean that people receive benefits in relation to their contribution rather than in relation to their need for assistance. Taylor-Gooby (1998) discusses two very different approaches to social justice (or distributive justice) that have been influential in recent years. This first is from Nozick (in Taylor-Gooby 1998) who argues that one's labour is the basis of a just claim and it is unjust to take away from an individual's income derived from labour. This argument has been used to justify low taxation, especially income and wealth taxation, and, consequently, low levels of government spending on welfare. It is compatible with the libertarian tradition outlined earlier in this chapter. In contrast, Rawls's (1972) philosophy of social justice argues that a measure should be judged according to whether it benefits those in society who are worse off. Such a philosophy would give priority to taxation and spending to reduce poverty and disadvantage, but would not necessarily be concerned with taking action to make everyone equal. This is more compatible with the social liberal tradition (see earlier discussion).

Rawls's ideas suggest that there are different aspirations for equality. Promoting equality can mean:

- The achievement of some kind of *minimum standard*—beyond that we are not concerned about the extent of inequality. For example, we may say that it is acceptable to have very wide variations in wages and salaries, so long as there is an acceptable minimum wage.
- The achievement of *equality of opportunity*. This goes beyond the minimum standards approach to the achievement of an equal opportunity for all to achieve the same degree of well-being. For example, we may wish our educational and health systems to operate in such a way that we have all an equal opportunity to have a high standard of health care or a high quality education. The Australian notion of a *fair go* seems to embrace this idea of equality.
- The achievement of *equal outcomes*. The goes beyond minimum standards and equality of opportunity aspirations to the goal of the achievement of equality on certain levels of well-being—for example, the achievement of the same health status or level of education of different groups around Australia.

Generally, when we assess equality we are more concerned with equality between different groups (for example, between men and women, different ethic groups, different regions, or different socio-economic status) than between each individual. This is because we would expect some differences between individuals based on natural endowments, although we still often try to limit some of the inequalities arising from such differences. We are also often more concerned about equalities that are widespread and mutually reinforcing than those that may have a more limited impact. This is illustrated in two different ideas of distributive justice. According to Walzer (1997), justice is compromised if one's standing in one spheres of life dominates one's standing in another sphere (for example, if having a low standard of living affects one's capacity to have meaningful relationships or to exercise one's political rights). Similarly for Sen (1999), social justice requires the achievement of substantive freedoms relating to political and civil rights, economic and social opportunities, the transparency of arrangements and institutions, and protection from misery.

Such views influence the priority given to redistribution, the kind of redistribution that is pursued and the domains of welfare within which redistribution is considered important. Redistribution is often categorised in the following way:

- First is vertical redistribution by which we mean redistribution according to need or capacity to pay—for example, from rich to poor. This justifies a progressive taxation system or services where access is based on need rather than capacity to pay.
- Second is horizontal redistribution, by which we mean redistribution such that people in similar situations are given equal treatment. This is frequently used to justify equal assistance to people in similar stages of the life cycle or with similar needs. For example, assistance to all families with children or to all people with disabilities.
- Third is life cycle redistribution, which is very related to horizontal redistribution. Life cycle redistribution justifies policies to assist people achieve a reasonable level of well-being regardless of their particular stage in the life cycle. This can involve taxing people more at stages in their life when they are doing well so that they can receive benefits at times when their needs are greater, or their earnings capacity is lower (for example, during old age).

Altruism and reciprocity

In his seminal book, *The Gift Relationship*, Titmuss (1970) saw altruism as an important justification for community responsibility for the welfare of others and a concern about equality. By altruism, we mean the concern for others, including for *The Needs of Strangers* (Ignatieff 1984). The important point is the belief that people are motivated by more than self-interest but are also altruistic. Titmuss also believed that people and societies develop best when altruism is able to flourish (Deacon 2002).

Families are important sites for the expression of altruism and for reciprocity. By reciprocity we mean the sense of interdependence we have with others, which is built up over time and gives rise to expressions of mutual support. Land quotes Finch and Mason as arguing that reciprocity is developed, 'through contact, shared activities and particularly through each giving the other help as it is needed. This process of reciprocity—accepting help and then giving something in return—is the engine which drives the process of developing commitments' (Land 1998, p. 51). For these reasons there is a strong role for families and communities in social policy. However, while reciprocity is experienced within families and communities, at the societal level we can also have some sense of reciprocity for people we do not know. Such reciprocity is very important for the development of social solidarity. Concepts such as social capital and social cohesion, by which we mean our sense of connectedness with others, networks of support, and the extent of trust we have in others and in society's institutions, are very related to reciprocity. As Ritzen says, 'The objective of social cohesion implies a reconciliation of a system of organisation based on market forces, freedom of opportunity and enterprise, with a commitment to the values of solidarity and mutual support which ensures open access to benefit and protection for all members of society' (Ritzen cited in Healy & Cote 2001, p. 13).

Some are worried that the current focus on deregulation and market forces, and a growth of individualism and increased inequality, may be undermining the shared contact and understandings that are important for reciprocity. They can lead to the sense that we only 'owe to the community in proportion to what we obtain from it and have no claims upon the resources which others have deservedly earned for themselves' (Fitzpatrick 2005, p. 18). There is also a feminist concern that the role of families as an important site for the expression of altruism has in the past been largely based on the altruism of women. There has been limited reciprocity between men and women in the undertaking of caring activities, which has meant that women's caring activities have often been at the expense of their economic well-being.

THE MEANS AND DESIGN OF WELFARE

Social policy also draws on concepts and design principles relating to the means of welfare—that is, how we can achieve the kinds of ends reflected in concepts such as need, rights, and altruism. Efficiency is a critical concept relevant to the means of welfare. Design principles, such as targeting and universalism, and the choice of various forms of welfare (occupational, fiscal, and state), are in turn influenced by our understanding of the interaction between the ends and means of welfare.

Efficiency

As mentioned, efficiency is a concept relating to the means of welfare (how we achieve given ends) and to the assessment of our use of resources. It is slightly different from the related concept of effectiveness. Policies or programs are *effective* if they meet their intended ends or goals, and *efficient* if they meet these goals with least use of resources. Efficiency is very important because of the scarcity of resources in relation to ends. Generally, at any point of time, we do not have enough resources to achieve all of our ends. And so we need to make choices as to the best and most effective and efficient use of resources in our everyday lives, in our organisations, and also at the community and societal level. Because resources are scarce, the less we use on one policy or service, the more are available to meet other policy objectives. For example, we wish to have effective health services, but we also want to use our resources in such a way that sufficient resources are also available for other purposes such as quality education, improved housing, more child care places, and so on. Even within these broad areas there are also choices to be made about how to best use resources. For example, within the health system should we spend more on hospitals or medical services, or on preventative health care rather than on treatment?

Different versions of economic thought have different ideas about how best to promote efficiency and therefore how such choices should be made. Neo-liberal economics, the current dominant form of economic thought (commonly known in Australia as *economic rationalism*), considers that efficiency is best achieved through the unimpeded operation of the market rather than through public action. The market is where resources are exchanged for goods and services. Through the market, people's preferences can be expressed through their demand for goods and services. These preferences can then be met by firms, through the supply of goods and services. People buy and sell for a certain price, and the price mechanism allows the efficient allocation of resources. If the price is higher than people's preferences, supply will exceed demand, firms will be unable to sell all of their goods, and the price will drop to more accurately reflect their preferences. If the price is too low, the reverse occurs. (See Stretton 1999 for a more detailed but still simple explanation of this theory and Argy 2003 for a conventional economic critique of neo-liberalism, which he terms *hard liberalism*).

Neo-liberal economics is criticised on a number of grounds. They include the fact that people do not always have the knowledge to be able to buy at the lowest price or at the best quality, that firms do not always operate competitively, and that people do not behave in the rational self-interested manner anticipated by neo-liberalism. However, beyond these criticisms are two critical problems with the narrowness of the way that efficiency and economic development are understood in conventional economics. These problems are especially relevant to social policy. The first is that economics tends only to measure and value activities that are traded in the market. This ignores most environmental degradation (or improvement); non-market activities such as home production and caring for children or disabled family members; volunteer activities in a range of areas; and changes to our quality of life, especially the amount of leisure at our disposal and including time to spend with our families. Therefore, conventional measures of efficiency omit aspects of welfare that are of great interest to social policy. Such narrow measures also mean an undervaluing of activities performed by governments, leading to policies that reduce government expenditure and that privatise public activities. The second problem is that the *distribution* of well-being and of economic growth is often explicitly rejected as fundamental to economic analysis. Yet, the way growth is pursued, used, and distributed is critical to personal and societal well-being and is a central concern of social policy.

Targeting and universalism

Targeting and universalism are concepts relevant to the way we design social policies. Targeting implies policies to direct or restrict services to those at greatest need. In contrast, universalism implies the availability of welfare assistance to all who may benefit. Targeting is seen as a way of meeting need efficiently. All welfare systems use some form of targeting. In this sense, the debate about targeting versus universalism is less about targeting per se and more about the extent of targeting and the use of targeting in particular policy areas. Targeting can be undertaken by limiting access to services or income support on the basis of characteristics seen to reflect need, such as age, disability, or income.

Much of the debate about targeting concerns the use of means tests—that is, the use of income and assets as targeting criterion. Australia has a means tested income support system. The means test requires the level of income support to be reduced when an individual or family's income and wealth increases. This is to ensure that most income support is directed to those with least income and wealth. In contrast, the principle of universalism would mean that payments should go to all citizens regardless of their income and wealth. Medicare is a more universal policy, as all people are required to pay the Medicare levy and all are eligible to the basic benefits, regardless of income. However, as explained earlier, under the Howard Coalition government, Medicare has become more targeted and less universal—for example, through the introduction of incentives for doctors to bulk bill certain groups the government considers more in need and through incentives for people to take up private health insurance. Residual welfare systems use means tests as a way of limiting welfare to those unable to provide for their own welfare through private provision. Means tests can be directed at the level of the individual, couples, or the family. Where there are strong assumptions and values placed on sharing and reciprocity within families, rather than on the rights of individuals, social policies may be premised on the expectation that families will provide care or income support to other members. In these cases, the amount of income support may be varied according to family income, rather than just the income of the individual.

Advantages of targeting include its lower cost and its capacity to assist those in greatest need more efficiently. Disadvantages include the stigma that can apply to those receiving the service, low take-up rates (thus undermining effectiveness), poorer quality service applying to the targeted program, an undermining of social solidarity, and the fact that the community may be less inclined to pay taxes for services that do not benefit all. Means-tested services can also create problems of incentives and poverty traps, as assistance is reduced as family earnings from work increases. Richard Titmuss was a great advocate of universalism, which he saw as overcoming the disadvantages of targeting through 'making services available and accessible to the whole population in such ways as would not involve users in any humiliating loss of status, dignity or self-respect. There should be no sense of inferiority, pauperism, shame or stigma in the use of a publicly provided service; no attribution that one was or becoming a "public burden"' (Titmuss 1968 cited in Fitzpatrick 2003, p. 336).

Occupational, fiscal, or state welfare

When designing social policy, we need to decide how assistance should be provided. Another very important contribution made to social policy by Richard Titmuss (1976) is his clarification of the three different forms of welfare: occupational, fiscal, and state welfare. We generally think of welfare as state welfare—that is, the benefits directly provided by governments in the form of direct payments or services. Titmuss's point is that people's well-being (or welfare) can be enhanced through benefits that are provided in other forms, namely through employers and through the tax system, which we do not always understand as welfare. Table 2.2 gives examples of these different forms of welfare in Australia.

Occupational welfare is welfare that is provided through work. In one sense the most important form of occupational welfare is the wage that people receive from work. Wage earnings make the most significant contribution to the incomes of most Australians, with approximately 60 per cent of Australians having wages and salaries as their principal source of income (ABS 2003a). Reliance on an equitable wages system to sustain living standards has historically been a feature of Australia's welfare state, which consequently has been called the *wage-earners'* or *workers' welfare state* (Castles 1985). We cover the development and characteristics of Australia as the workers' welfare state in more detail in Chapter 5. However, most commonly, occupational welfare refers to the contribution to welfare provided through a range of employer-provided benefits in addition to wages. Occupational welfare can be mandatory (such as the 9 per cent employer superannuation contribution) or discretionary (such as paid maternity leave). Occupational welfare is only accessible to those in work and is less open to stigma, but, depending on the way it is provided, can be inequitable. It can include a range of benefits such as employer-provided child care, the provision of a car, shares or share entitlements, and the payment of personal expenses.

Table 2.2 Examples of different forms of welfare in Australia

Occupational welfare	Fiscal welfare	State welfare
▪ Employer superannuation contributions	▪ Private health insurance rebate (offset)	▪ Family tax benefits payable to families with dependent children (these can be both fiscal or state welfare as they can be paid in the form of direct payment or tax forgone)
▪ Employer-provided or assisted child care	▪ Superannuation tax concessions	
▪ Company cars for private use	▪ Senior Australian tax offset	
▪ Other fringe benefits such as share options, assistance with payments such as private health insurance, school fees, or other educational expenses	▪ Tax rebates (offsets) for excessive medical expenses, living in a remote or isolated area, and maintenance of an invalid relative.	▪ Centrelink payments such as aged pension, disability allowance, unemployment allowance, and parenting payments
▪ Leave arrangements including sick leave, long-service leave, and parental leave.		▪ Child-care assistance
		▪ Free public hospital care.

Fiscal welfare is assistance through the tax system—assistance in the form of reduced tax than would otherwise be paid. It is a popular form of welfare, but it can have similar problems to occupational welfare in that it can be inequitable. It can provide greatest assistance to higher income earners, depending on whether it is provided through a tax deduction or through a tax rebate (offset). Those who are in greatest need may also miss out because they are not paying sufficient taxes to benefit or because they cannot afford to make payments that are eligible for tax assistance (such as private health insurance payments). Fiscal welfare can be very costly. The private health insurance rebate cost well over $2 billion in 2003 and superannuation tax concessions are worth approximately $10 billion (in gross terms). However, because fiscal welfare is less visible, it is less open to scrutiny and debate than state welfare. Occupational and fiscal welfare benefits can also be problematic as they can encourage two-tiered systems of welfare, with private provision for the better off and public welfare for the more needy, possibly leading to poorer quality services for those with fewer resources, and also possibly undermining social solidarity.

State welfare is welfare through direct government spending, is usually targeted to those most in need, and is often means tested and subject to more stringent conditions than the other forms of welfare. It is very visible and can be stigmatising. The debates about welfare dependency in Australia refer to people who receive state welfare rather than those who receive fiscal or occupational welfare. However, many Australians are very dependent on a continuing basis on assistance they receive from employers and from the tax system.

SUMMARY AND CONCLUSION

In this chapter, I have examined some of the important social policy-related concepts. Social policy is faced with a fundamental challenge in the development of policies to meet needs. A number of sometimes competing aspirations must be reconciled. Generally, we are trying to combine the following imperatives:

- providing adequate assistance
- providing coverage for all who need help
- providing assistance equitably
- not undermining individual incentives and responsibility
- fostering social solidarity and reciprocity
- ensuring sustainability over time and maintaining community support
- using resources efficiently at an affordable cost to the community.

Social policy is essentially concerned with meeting needs; however, the priority given to meeting needs, how they are met, and how they are understood and measured, is very dependent on values and ideologies. Value differences about individual freedom and responsibility, collective identification and responsibility, and authority and equality, are associated with different models of welfare and different priorities placed on the right to welfare as compared with freedom and responsibility. However, social policy must also be cognisant of the scarcity of resources in relation to needs, and efficiency is important. One of the enduring social policy debates is about targeting versus universality. Should programs be available to all or should they be directed to those most in need? Another debate is about how assistance should be provided—through employment-related help, through the tax system, or through government payments and services.

3
A FRAMEWORK FOR UNDERSTANDING AND ACTION

Alison McClelland

This chapter covers frameworks for understanding and action. It presents information and ideas about how to analyse policy and how social policy is made. This is so readers can understand, debate, and engage in the policy process and be effective policy practitioners. A *policy practitioner* can operate in different settings, and be activated by different situations (see Table 3.1).

Policy practice applies to people in addition to those in designated policy positions. Policy practitioners are people who wish to understand policy and contribute to social change and policy development. They can be policy workers. They can also be workers with individuals, families, or communities, who use their practice experience to contribute to policy change through their 'on the ground' appreciation of the impact of policy on people's lives. Intervening in the policy process is an 'essential part of professional responsibility' with 'the expectations that workers will intervene beyond the individual level of experience' (Dalton et al. 1996, p. 20). O'Connor et al. (1998, pp. 181–91) identify occasions when professionals such as social workers should be policy active. One occasion is when there is systemic discrimination against a group—for example, the way in which our institutional arrangements have discriminated against women, people with disabilities, or Indigenous Australians. Another is when there are gaps in services—for example, the absence of sufficient community supports for people with a mental illness in the context of deinstitutionalisation. It can also be when a policy adversely affects people in need (for example, the impact of breach penalties for failing to comply with activity tests on people dependent on government payments). Generally, it is when the structures of society cause difficulties, especially for people who are vulnerable.

Table 3.1 The scope of policy practice and situations requiring policy practice

Scope of policy practice	■ Anyone concerned about certain aspects of society they would like to better understand, and possibly change. ■ Local community activists and members of social movements who wish to improve their community or change society's response to their issue. ■ Health and community workers interested in understanding how social policies affect the lives and choices of those with whom they work. ■ People in designated policy positions in government, community organisations, or peak bodies.
Common situations requiring policy practice knowledge and skills	■ A community health centre worker sees large numbers of people unable to get access to dental care without waiting for long periods of time. The worker wants to understand why the current policy creates long waiting lists and if something can be done. ■ A carer of an older child with an intellectual disability is worried about what will happen to the child when the carer is no longer there, and joins a local group to improve services. The group wants to lobby the state government for better services, but needs to know how to develop relevant proposals, who best to lobby, and how to gain their attention.

Other names are used to describe policy practitioners, such as *policy activists* (Yeatman 1998) and *policy actors* (Considine 1994). Considine says a policy actor can include, 'any individual or group able to take action on a public problem or issue' (1994, p. 6). This opening up of the scope of policy practice contributes to a democratisation of the policy process (Parsons 2002). It reminds us that policy is not just the preserve of the 'expert' and that good policy usually comes from the incorporation of a variety of groups and perspectives into the policy process.

In this chapter, I consider some of the different ways of understanding how policy is made and the influences on social policy. I then present two frameworks: a framework for analysing policy and a framework for the development of policy and policy advocacy.

DIFFERENT VIEWS ABOUT HOW POLICY IS MADE— MODELS OF THE POLICY PROCESS

How did Australia come to accept Medicare in 1983 or the Goods and Services Tax (GST) in 1999? There are different theories and models that explain how policy change occurs. It can be seen as mainly the result of puzzling and analysing (a rational exercise); the result of contest and struggle (a result of power and politics); or as learning and networking (a result of institutions and systems).

Policy as a rational exercise

As Howlett and Ramesh (1995, p. 140) say, 'The rational model is rational in the sense that it prescribes procedures for decision-making that will lead to the choice of the most efficient means of achieving policy goals. Rationalist theories are rooted in enlightenment rationalism and positivism, schools of thought which seek to develop detached, scientific knowledge to improve human conditions.'

The critical elements for good policy in the rational model are ordered thought and objective analysis. Policy change and policy evaluation should be the result of the ordered sequencing of:

- a careful identification of the problem
- a definition of the objectives and goals to be sought
- a comprehensive analysis of all available alternatives according to agreed criteria and known consequences to determine the most cost-effective option.

The process involves comprehensive analysis, the use of objective knowledge, and a search for the optimal solution. The comprehensive rational model was popular in the late 1960s and 1970s, and exemplified by the development of related decision-making frameworks, such as program budgeting or PPBS (Program Planning Budgeting Systems). According to these models, all activities of government are regularly analysed and evaluated (preferably in the annual budget cycle), to ensure that they are the most efficient use of resources in meeting the government's objectives. A less comprehensive but more current application of the rational approach to policy is the use of evidence-based policy making—for example, by the Blair government in the United Kingdom (see Parsons 2002).

Rationality has benefits in policy making. According to Dalton et al. (1996, p. 18), the benefits include attention to information about the distributional consequences of policies, the identification of key stages in the process, and the provision of some order to a complex and messy process. The rational model can help to make decision-making more informed, but will not ensure good decisions. It can assist by providing some structure and logic to the policy process and by identifying the types of information that will be important. Welfare organisations, such as the Brotherhood of St Laurence in Melbourne, and the peak welfare body, the Australian Council of Social Service (ACOSS), have used relevant information and rational policy analysis to influence policy in a number of policy areas over the years, including tax reform, income security changes, and labour market programs.

There are also serious limitations to the rational model. Dalton et al. (1996, p. 18) identify some as:

- the neglect of power and politics, and the role of values in the policy process
- the rational model does not reflect real world policy decision-making, which is not systematic and linear
- the cognitive limits to people's capacity to comprehensively examine all alternatives and their consequences, as required by comprehensive rationality
- the need to compromise when decisions have to be made quickly (see also Howlett & Ramesh 1995).

Other important limitations include our inability to predict the consequences of various alternatives, and the difficulty of having information in a form that allows for an objective comparison of the consequences of different alternatives (Howlett & Ramesh 1995).

Herbert Simon (1972) proposed an alternative to comprehensive rationality based on the idea of *bounded rationality*, which retained an aspiration to some kind of rational analysis, but that was more limited and realistic than the comprehensive approach. Simon developed the criterion of *satisficing*. Satisficing means that, given limitations to human rationality, rather than seeking the optimal solution (and therefore having to examine all possible options in detail), we should attempt to reach one that is satisfactory. Etzioni also developed a less comprehensive model called *mixed scanning* that involves a broad identification (scan) of a number of alternatives, with a detailed analysis of only a limited number, seen to be the most promising (Howlett & Ramesh 1995).

In a more substantial critique, Charles Lindblom (1959) argued that public policy decision-making is significantly different from that assumed by the comprehensive rational model. First, decisions usually lead to limited change. They are *incremental*, with most change occurring in small steps rather than by great leaps. Bureaucracies tend to stick with existing policies rather than promoting significant change. Second, decision-making is characterised by 'bargaining and compromise among self-interested decision-makers', with considerations of political feasibility being more important than considerations of the best option (Howlett & Ramesh 1995, p. 141).

Analysis often considers a limited and familiar range of alternatives and only some consequences, focuses on solving problems rather than meeting goals and objectives, is fragmented between different parties, and does not always distinguish between means and ends. Hence, policy decision-making means *muddling through* (Lindblom 1959) and involves politics and power as much, if not more, than rational analysis.

According to Donald Schon, muddling through also occurs because of the limitations of our knowledge about how to respond to many critical contemporary problems. The most important problems and issues are characterised by uncertainty, and are a 'swampy lowland where situations are confusing "messes" incapable of technical solution … and require methods of inquiry that involve "experience, trial and error, intuition and muddling through"' (Schon 1983 cited by Parsons 2002, pp. 4–5). Policies about critical issues such as child protection and Indigenous welfare have some of these characteristics. And while Schon may overstate the extent of confusion, one relevant conclusion is that the development of solutions to these kinds of problems requires much more than technical analysis and objective data.

Policy as the result of politics and power

A key limitation of the rational model is its inability to explain causation; why some policies are adopted and others are not (Dalton et al. 1996; Howlett & Ramesh 1995). Policy making is also a political process. In contrast to the rational model, where the dominant influence on policy is the objective analysis by the policy expert and power is understood as a constraint, the power model of policy understands policies as being mainly determined by the political contest between different groups, with the groups that have the most power determining policy outcomes. This is another explanation for why critical issues such as child protection and Indigenous welfare remain as unsolved problems—because the political imperative to find solutions that are effective and enduring is limited.

One definition of power is the 'ability to implement plans of action and persuade or coerce others to follow suit' (Manning 2003b, p. 35). It is frequently invested in governments because of their capacity to regulate the conduct of others, and through the legitimacy they receive from elections. Weber saw government power ultimately as 'rational-legal authority' that arises because there are 'clear and explicit rules understood by all citizens as the basis for a government's claim to have power' (Manning 2003b, p. 35). However, the power of modern governments is limited by a number of factors, including the inability of the state alone to direct the kind of activity required to respond to critical problems and issues such as unemployment, drug abuse and addictions, violence, and poverty. Also relevant is the limited knowledge of bureaucracies about contemporary issues and how to respond (Adams & Hess 2002).

Power is exercised at all stages and activities in the policy process; in how problems and issues are defined and acknowledged, in what options are considered, and during the decision and implementation stages. The exercise of knowledge in the policy process is deeply affected by power, and this power contest includes a contest of the different values of different groups. An early influential writer of public policy, Harold Lasswell, saw that policy making 'took place in conditions of power inequalities and recognised that knowledge is utterly embedded in power and value contests and relationships' (Parsons 2002, p. 11). Considine says that 'the battle to enact policy involves a struggle to fix a definition of the facts which is consistent with the values of those who have a stake in these problems' (1994, p. 29). Different models of power relationships have different explanations of what power relationships exist and how they influence policy. The models most frequently identified include the Marxist model, the elitist model, the corporatist model, and the pluralist model.

Marxist model: policy power is concentrated in those with economic power: the owners of capital. In contemporary terms, neo-liberal globalisation has increased the power of capital, which can now be moved between countries with few restrictions from national governments. It is accompanied by a policy orientation towards deregulation and small government. This affects social policy through its influence on policies about taxation, industrial relations, employment and unemployment, overall government expenditure, and welfare expenditure.

Elitist model: policy power is concentrated in a few elites. Policy making is closed to all but a few, such as influential academics, journalists, senior bureaucrats, and leaders of powerful lobby groups and think tanks. They come from similar backgrounds, have similar world-views (which currently includes support for competition and deregulation), and either move between the top of different sectors or spend time with each other. Michael Pusey's (1991) study of the similar backgrounds and ideas of senior public servants in Canberra is one illustration of the elitist model of decision-making in Australia.

Corporatist mode: policy power is distributed between business, unions, and the state—the organised blocks of power. Policy is determined by bargaining between these three power blocks. Some European and Scandinavian countries have used corporatist-type models. In Australia, the Hawke and Keating governments used a modified corporatist model, with successive Accords with the Australian Council of Trade Unions (ACTU), through which agreements to policy packages were negotiated. These packages combined changes to wages, taxation, and social expenditure (the social wage), and were accompanied by negotiations with business groups and the development of forums such as the Economic Planning Advisory Council (EPAC), through which the three blocks, alongside other groups, debated current policy issues.

Pluralist model: policy is developed as part of the democratic process and power is shared between different groups. This model is frequently regarded as more an ideal than reality. The organisation of political parties, the dominance of the major parties in parliament and governments, the growing power of the executive over parliament, and the declining membership of the major political parties are all factors seen to limit the practical expression of the ideal of the pluralist model. Advocates of pluralism recommend changes to promote participatory democracy. These changes include increased requirements on governments to consult when developing policy changes and the development of policy-advising structures outside of the executive, such as Senate committees or independent commissions (Marsh 2003), which would be responsible for policy advice to the executive after independent analysis and the active involvement of a range of interest groups and perspectives. Another option is the increased use of networks involving people and organisations from different sectors and organisations. Networks can be used for not only policy advice, but also for policy decision-making and implementation. The interest in networks arises from the view that the government's power to solve all problems is limited and that responsibility needs to be shared (Considine 2002). A related consideration is that the objective quantitative information about issues and options available to public servants is too limited. Such information needs to be supplemented by a focus on policy through learning and knowledge that is acquired from a range of sources outside of government and that involves active engagement of all parties (Adams & Hess 2002; Parsons 2002).

Power and discourse

A different and important understanding of power is provided by Foucault and post-structural thought (Fitzpatrick 2005; Healy 2000). Power does not necessarily involve an action (of coercion) on someone or some group and is not necessarily held by individuals. It is exercised through a 'technology of disciplinary norms', and discourse is central to the development of these disciplinary norms (Fitzpatrick 2005, p. 38). Healy (2000, p. 39) quotes Parton to explain the meaning of discourse in the following way.

> Discourses are structures of knowledge, claims and practices through which we understand, explain and decide things. In constituting agents they also define obligations and determine the distribution of responsibilities and authorities for different categories of persons such as parents, children, social workers, doctors, lawyers and so on … They are frameworks or grids of social organisation that make some actions possible while precluding others.
>
> (p. 13)

People take on their views of the world, their understandings of what is right and true, through structured language or discourses. As Healy (2000) says, discourses influence what is written and what views are portrayed in the media. They are produced by 'rules and procedures', which means that we can say some things in one time or place that would not be said in other contexts (Healy 2000, p. 40). Discourse is therefore context dependent—for example, how we discuss and understand poverty varies between cultures, between different groups, and at different times.

Such discourses can be extremely powerful because they can govern our own behaviour as we take on these norms and truths as applying to our own conduct. Discourses influence the way we understand different groups (the unemployed, the 'battlers', terrorists, workers), and issues and problems (welfare dependency, social capital). Therefore, discourses influence the adoption of particular policies—for example, the application of mutual obligation because of the discourse around welfare dependency and self-reliance, or action against family violence due to a feminist discourse about violence. How we come to understand things is 'governed by power relations' and so dominant discourses can reflect the view of those with material power (through, for example, their capacity to have their views articulated in the media). There is no one discourse but many and this also means that power is dispersed.

Drawing on Foucault's analysis of power, other theorists (Rose, O'Malley) have developed the idea of 'governmentality', (the 'conduct of conduct' and the development of regularity regimes) as an important way that power is exercised in modern welfare states (Fitzpatrick 2005). One way governments exercise power in this way is through the devolution of risk and responsibility to individuals and organisations. For example, in Australia we need to contribute to and monitor our own superannuation in order to have a reasonable retirement income. Non-government organisations are increasingly responsible for delivering outcomes that were previously the responsibility of government, such as the role of Job Network organisations in the application of mutual obligation requirements because they receive government funding to help people obtain paid work.

Policy arising from institutions

Institutions also influence the adoption of policy. Government departments are very influential institutions because of their key role in advising ministers about policies, their possession of information and knowledge that has developed over time, and their role in policy implementation. A state-centred view of policy making gives government departments a central role in initiating policy change and places priority on understanding how government departments operate in the policy process. This includes the structure of departmental responsibility, the key personnel and their links within and outside government, the rules within the government and department relevant to the policy area, the departmental and government decision-making processes, and the institutional policy knowledge that has developed over a number of years. Chapter 4 provides more discussion about the institutional nature of policy decision-making in Australia.

Bureaucracies are likely to exercise a conservative approach to policy change for two reasons. The first reason is that change may have a negative impact on them—existing roles and relationships in which people can have a stake are threatened by significant change. The second reason is because the policy understanding—the knowledge about what may work—partly depends on past experience, policy advisors are reluctant to recommend change in the absence of substantive information about its impacts. The concept of 'path dependency' refers to the way that past experience exercises a limit on the change that can occur in the present.

Policy systems and policy development

Policy systems are another way of understanding the development of policy. Considine (1994, p. 22), whose work on policy systems is used in this section, defines them as 'groups of actors engaged in continuing, *interdependent* activity'. Policy systems involve patterned relationships and key participants are 'linked through institutions, groups, networks, and other continuing relationships' (Considine 1994, p. 8). According to Considine, policy systems have two dimensions. The material dimension is the generation and distribution of resources within the system, and the intellectual dimension is the development and sharing of ideas and values. Policy systems therefore have a political economy and a policy culture, both of which must be understood and used to influence policy development. The political economy dimension directs our attention to understanding the relationship between producers and consumers, how governments intervene, and what techniques are used in order to get things done. For example, if our interest was in policies for aged services, we would need to understand the profile of service providers, the relationships between the services, and between the providers and the users of services, as well as understanding what kind of activities are used and are possible if we wish to make changes. The policy culture directs us to the importance of the key values and ideas that are held or are emerging within the policy system—the policy discourse (Considine 2005). For example, in the area of aged care services, is the value of increased private provision becoming more prevalent? Who are the key promoters of powerful ideas and values in this policy area?

According to Considine (1994, p. 103), policy systems contain actor networks, which are 'informal and semi-formal linkages between individuals and groups in the same policy system'. Some actor networks can be more powerful than others and monopolise the policy area by having the ability to control the way the problem or issue is understood and debated (Baumgartners & Jones cited in Howlett & Ramesh 1995). In the 1980s, the issue of child poverty was placed on the policy agenda, with policy change occurring as a result of a network that included key academics such as Bettina Cass; policy activists from the welfare sector; key policy analysts inside government, including Meredith Edwards; researchers from the Australian Institute of Family Studies; and politicians, in particular the Minister, Brian Howe. However, in the 1990s a change of government and ideas, and a different network of people and organisations came to influence policy discussion around welfare reform.

Considine stresses the importance of participating in networks over time. Policy change occurs when people work together, often across different sectors and disciplines, as actions and policies are the product of 'group achievements which reflect the character of received wisdom and negotiations of interdependent individuals, none of whom have full control over the knowledge and resources needed to create programs, decisions, or other outcomes' (Considine 1994, p. 105). Change is unlikely unless it involves more than one actor (or organisation) in a network. For policy practitioners, it highlights the importance of understanding the structure, processes, and key actor networks in the policy system in which one wishes to engage.

A FRAMEWORK FOR UNDERSTANDING

Although the rational model has serious limitations, there is value in frameworks that clarify the kinds of information that will help in understanding a particular policy, as well as the kind of actions that are part of a good policy process. Policy frameworks are presented in two ways in the remainder of this chapter. First, there is a framework for appraising a particular policy. This is presented to help readers understand how to define a policy and how to understand the impact of that policy. Later we present a framework for action—how we may understand the key activities involved in policy change. Both are important and have overlapping areas of analysis.

A simplified framework

Policy analysis can be very complex as a range of factors need to be considered in order to be able to define the specific policy, clarify the key influences on the policy, and understand the impact of the policy on people's lives and on the nature of society.

Table 3.2 contains a simplified framework for analysis, which identifies the key aspects of policy definition, context, impacts, and options, and policy implementation. It is a modified version of a framework developed by Dalton et al. (1996). The subsequent, more detailed discussion illustrates how this framework could be applied to the policy area of aged community care.

Table 3.2 A simplified framework for analysis

General area of analysis	Meaning and specific actions
Policy definition	Clarify what the policy is, the key elements of the policy, the policy's goals, and the problem or issue the policy addresses
Policy context	Analyse historical, social and economic context, political values and assumptions, and institutional and welfare state context
Policy impact	Identify target group, outputs and outcomes, groups affected, costs and financing
Policy alternatives	Identify other possible options to existing policy
Policy implementation	Identify organisational/administrative issues, resource requirements, status and symbolic issues

Policy definition

Through policy definition, we are attempting to understand what the policy is, what it is trying to achieve (goals and objectives), how it is doing it (elements), and the problem or issue the policy is trying to address. We need first to clearly identify the policy in question. It may be a broad policy area, such as the policy relating to ageing. However, our interest is likely to be more specific—for example, with the policy for aged community care. As this is a policy area that contains shared and overlapping responsibility between Commonwealth and state governments, we need to clarify whether we are more interested in how it applies to one particular state or whether our interest is Australia-wide. In this case, we have decided to concentrate on the Commonwealth government's policy, *The Way Forward* (Bishop 2004).

The goals and objectives are what the policy is attempting to achieve. Policies can have multiple goals, which may be broad and sometimes unclear or unstated and may be in conflict. Some goals may have a higher priority than others. Objectives are meant to be more specific statements of purpose than goals and able to be measured, but not all policies clearly differentiate between goals and objectives. In the case of aged community care, the main goal is to assist older people to 'age in place'. A more implicit goal is to contain the cost of ageing through the lower cost community care (rather than institutional care) policy.

The policy elements are the actions; how the policy achieves its goals. They include the programs and services and the activities required within them, such as payments to organisations or individuals, regulations about how individuals or organisations can behave, or education and information in an attempt to change people's behaviour. For example, the Home and Community Care Program (HACC) is a key element in the Commonwealth government's aged community care policy, and particular services within that program include home nursing, personal care, meals on wheels, home help, basic home modifications, transport, and some allied health services.

The final aspect of policy definition is to understand the problem or issue that the policy is attempting to address. There may be more than one issue or problem. In the case of aged community care, the key issue is the imbalance between community care options and institutional care, with broader issues including the ageing of the population, the cost of institutional care, the pressure on relatives who are responsible for caring, and the lack of appropriate services to help people to remain in their own homes.

The policy context

The policy context includes the historical, social and economic, ideological and theoretical, and institutional context. The historical context is important as most policy change is incremental, and knowledge and interest in policy change is influenced by past experience. History constrains current policy choices and provides knowledge about what has worked in the past. In aged community care, it would be useful to understand, for example, the forces that led to the development of the HACC program, and factors contributing to its successes and problems over time. Especially relevant are the changes introduced from the mid 1980s onwards, which have attempted to change the balance of care from institutional to community care. The economic and social context helps inform the extent of the need or problem the policy is seeking to address, the economic capacity to resource the policy, and the social supports that are available. For aged community care this means understanding the economic and social implications of population ageing, the extent to which the problems associated with population ageing are affected by economic and social factors, and how these factors affect our capacity to respond. For example, economic factors influence the capacity to finance aged community care services, the extent of poverty and inequality affects people's capacity to finance their own community care services or the need for public support. Social factors include the increase in the number of people living alone and the increased pressure on carers who may wish to combine work with caring, especially given women's increased participation in paid work.

The ideological and theoretical context means attention to the key values and assumptions informing the policy. For aged community care, this includes values such as self-reliance or collective responsibility, and therefore the extent to which individuals are expected to pay for their own community care or that families (and especially women) are expected to provide the care. It includes assumptions such as the assumption that people's well-being and autonomy is generally promoted if they can stay in their own home rather than living in institutions or with other family members. The political context involves understanding whose interests are served by the policy, who is likely to support the policy, and how much power is possessed by those supporting and those opposing the policy. Support for aged community care can be expected to be widespread among older people and their families, and the providers of home and community care services. On the other hand, there is a powerful lobby group of private institutional care providers who would want to ensure that the funding of institutional care is not reduced.

The institutional and welfare state context is relevant as particular policies are likely to reflect the general social policy orientation embedded in different welfare states, as well as institutional capacity. Australia's more 'liberal' and targeted welfare state has always had a strong role for private provision and community organisations, alongside some expectation of government support for both, especially in areas of high need. In community care, this is reflected in a strong role for community organisations and a targeted approach to access, with little support for people with low care needs. It is also reflected in a role for co-payments (user pays) in the funding of community care. Also relevant is the historical reliance on institutional care in many policy areas, with community care being a more recent policy change. The federal nature of Australia's welfare state means that Commonwealth and state governments have overlapping roles in the area of aged care. Successful attempts to rationalise their respective roles have failed to deal with resulting problems of overlap and cost-shifting (see Chapter 4). This, alongside an incremental development of community aged-care policy, has meant a complexity of provision and a poorly integrated service delivery system (The Myer Foundation 2003).

Impacts and options

We need to understand the policy's impacts and compare them with other policy options. This involves clarifying the target group, the likely outputs and outcomes, costs and financing arrangements, the groups likely to be affected, the availability of different policy options, and the impacts in terms of effectiveness, equity, and efficiency. The target group is the group intended to be the main focus or beneficiary of the policy. For aged community care, the target group is frail aged people (especially those who otherwise would go into institutional care) and their caregivers. The outputs are the immediate product of the service, and for aged community care, it may be the number of meals delivered to x number of older people or hours of personal care provided. The outcomes reflect the longer-term impacts—for example, the extent to which people are able to remain in their own homes with a reasonable quality of life. The costs and financing arrangements depend on the extent and type of provision and government subsidy. This affects both overall costs and how they are distributed. For aged community care, financing is through a combination of co-payments, government subsidy, and the unpaid care of caregivers at home.

Having considered key elements of the policy, the target group, the likely outputs and outcomes, and the costs and financing arrangements, it is now possible to develop an understanding of who might be affected. In the case of aged community care, in addition to the target group and sub groupings of the target group (such as older people on different incomes, with different care needs, in different accommodation arrangements, and different geographical areas), this could include the families of the older people, providers of care (including institutional providers), and, depending on financing, those who are meeting the cost of the policy.

Next is the consideration of alternative policies. These can be very broad alternatives (such as much greater or lesser reliance on institutional care), or variations such as changes to the type of community care and the target group (for example, extension of services to people with lower care needs and a better integration of services). Alternatives then should be assessed according to key criteria, especially effectiveness (how well the alternatives meet the policy goals), efficiency (how much it costs to achieve certain agreed outputs), and equity (whether the policy meets the needs of all the target groups, or whether certain vulnerable groups miss out).

Implementation

Understanding implementation requires a more detailed examination of the elements of the policy to determine responsibility for delivery and the kinds of instruments to be used, the organisational and administration issues involved in the policy delivery, resources required, and the status or symbolic issues affecting the policy's acceptability.

Bridgman and Davis (2004, p. 69) define instruments as 'the programs, staffing, budgets, organisations, campaigns and laws giving effect to policy decisions'. They identify four categories as follows (see pages 71–7):

- *Advocacy: 'arguing the case'* using education, information campaigns, advertising, and consultation with key organisations. In the case of aged community care this could be information about available services. Other examples include advertising campaigns against smoking, drink driving, or dangerous work practices.
- *Money: 'using spending and taxing powers'* to influence individual or organisational behaviour through financial incentives and subsidies. This includes the general fiscal (budgetary) stance—for example, the level of government activity needed to influence economic growth, and tax incentives, such as the private health insurance rebate to encourage private health insurance take-up. In aged community care, the Commonwealth uses money as an incentive to state governments to fund community care. It provides $60 for every $40 contributed by state governments.
- *Government action: 'delivering services'*. Bridgman and Davis see this as mainly government provided services, such as income support payments, state schools, and public hospitals. For aged community care this would include payments to carers. However, through the HACC program it also includes government subsidies to other organisations or individuals to provide services, such as grants to community organisations to provide care for older people in their home. As they note, contracting out and privatisation have changed how this instrument works in Australia, with governments moving to act more through funding (within a policy framework that can be very specific about required outputs) than through direct provision.

- *Law: 'legislation, regulation, and official authority'* including specific laws— for example, the requirement to wear seat belts, or to adhere to certain occupational health and safety requirements. It encompasses *delegated legislation* that allows government departments to develop regulations—for example, regulations around activity requirements for recipients of income support. State governments are responsible for regulating providers who receive funding through the HACC program.

This classification is not mutually exclusive—for example, a subsidy for a community organisation could come under both government action and policy through money. However, it is useful for clarifying the actions that governments can use to implement policy goals. It is also useful to remember Titmuss's classification of welfare into occupational, fiscal, and state welfare, identified in Chapter 2.

Consideration of implementation also means identifying organisational responsibility. As mentioned, this includes identifying the level of government responsible for planning and funding, and the kinds of organisation(s) responsible for service delivery. The organisational and administration issues associated with these organisations, which can affect how well the policy works in practice, must also be considered. Organisations responsible for service delivery may have a culture and way of working that is very compatible with the policy, or they may have difficulty in accepting it. Coordination is another important implementation issue as organisations often need to work together for the policy to work. Lack of attention to incentives and barriers for coordinated activity are common problems with policy implementation. This is a particular problem for aged community care where policy has developed on an incremental basis and involves a very complex system with different levels of government, organisations, and services to overlapping target groups. Another common problem is lack of attention to resources, including insufficient funding and inadequate staff training for the new functions and approach required by the new policy in particular. Such a different approach can also be undermined at the implementation stage by status and symbolic issues—for example, the status accorded to the key functions staff need to perform.

A FRAMEWORK FOR ACTION

The second framework is a *framework for action*; those activities needed for the development and adoption of new policies. This is a framework for achieving policy change. It draws heavily on Bridgman and Davis's policy cycle and the key activities (or stages) of identifying (issue identification), consulting (consultation), analysing (policy analysis), deciding (decision-making), applying the decision (implementation), and asking if it works (evaluation). It is based on the understanding that such activities are a necessary part of a good policy process and a good process is more likely to lead to good policy, although this cannot be guaranteed.

As Edwards (2001) emphasises, these stages are not always linear. They can be understood as a *policy dance*, with actions associated with the key stages moving backwards, forwards, and sideways, rather than in a linear progression. And although consultation is presented as a separate stage, it should occur throughout the policy process. Advocacy should be seen in a similar vein. Further, while Bridgman and Davis also have coordination as a separate stage, here coordination as presented as a critical issue requiring attention throughout the policy process. Finally, although the framework involves rational thought and analysis, it also incorporates actions arising from ideas from other models, such as the importance of politics and power, and the role of institutions and systems in the policy process (discussed earlier in this chapter).

Issue identification

This is perhaps the most critical stage of the policy process and has two aspects. The first is obtaining a clear understanding of the issue or problem—what it is, its importance, and its scope. The second is placing the issue on the policy agenda, which means commanding the attention of policy decision-makers and understanding the factors and actions that will achieve this.

How the problem or issue is understood has a large impact on the kind of options considered for adoption in the policy analysis and decision stages. Many problems and issues are understood very differently by different sectors, and by people with different values and theoretical positions. This applies to many important current issues such as population ageing, unemployment, and drug abuse. Policy practitioners need to ensure that their understanding of the issue is clear, communicated to key actors in a timely way, and shared by those in positions of power and influence. For example, there were many different understandings about the problems with the tax system in the mid 1990s and, therefore, about the issues that needed to be tackled by tax reform (see Table 3.3). The welfare sector, through its peak body the Australian Council of Social Service (ACOSS), wanted tax reform to deal with problems of lack of revenue, unfairness, and economic distortions. ACOSS placed high priority on the removal of tax loopholes in the income tax system (such as negative gearing—see Chapter 13 on taxation). The business sector also had a different perspective of the problem, although there was some sharing of these different understandings through a dialogue between the welfare and business sectors. However, the Commonwealth government and Prime Minister Howard always saw the problem very differently, as a problem of high income tax rates requiring tax cuts that could be funded from the introduction of the Goods and Services Tax (GST). As a result ACOSS was very critical of the package released by Howard government in 1998. The package was seen to be based on too narrow a construction of the problem by the government, particularly in relation to income tax where it was seen as a problem of high rates only and not as a narrow and eroding base. The limited view of the problem by the government also reflected the closed nature of the Howard government's tax policy process. This process reduced the capacity of those developing the package to understand community views fully and to devise a more rounded package that more closely reflected these views as well as broader insights from a number of academics and research institutions. The final package was negotiated through the Senate with a broader consultation process.

Table 3.3 Different understandings of the problems of the tax system in the mid 1990s

Welfare Sector	Tax system generates insufficient revenue due to loopholes in income tax system and narrow consumption tax base.
	Tax system unfair because of income tax avoidance and high effective marginal tax rates facing welfare recipients.
	Economic distortions and insufficient investment due to income tax loopholes.
Business Sector	Wholesale Sales Tax leads to lack of overseas competitiveness by importers.
	High marginal tax rates lead to a lack of incentives to work.
	Gap between company tax rate and personal tax rate an incentive to avoid tax.
Government	High marginal tax rates facing average worker unfair and cause work disincentives.
	Income tax too high generally.

When defining the issue or problem, we need to consider the following factors as they will affect the interest and capacity to take action about the issue, as well as the options that will be considered in responding:

- the scope—how many are affected?
- who is affected, directly or indirectly?
- the impacts—personal, social, economic, and political
- the causal factors—what do we know about the causes of the problem?
- interest in the problem—who may be interested in taking action?

Accurate and sufficient knowledge about important social policy issues requires information from a range of sources. These include large-scale survey data about the extent of the problem, impacts, and groups affected; longitudinal data to inform changes over time and the understanding of causation; and case study and qualitative data to inform our understanding of personal meanings, impacts, and causation. However, a full understanding of the issue often also requires a dialogue about the different interpretations of the problem, as many problems are not easily defined. Bridgman and Davis (2004) distinguish between *well-structured* and *ill-structured* problems, and then further identify a group of *wicked problems*. Well-structured problems are 'open to solution' and an issue or problem will not get on to the policy agenda unless there is some prospect of solution. This means that ill-structured problems, such as poverty, unemployment, and ageing, which are broad and capable of different interpretations, need to be broken down 'into smaller well-structured issues' (2004, p. 43). However, some problems are not easily broken down in this way and are seen as intractable, as wicked, in the sense that the parties that need to take action are unwilling to compromise. And yet with a change in the understanding of the problem, particularly when it becomes so serious that it can no longer be ignored, and when a change in personnel in key policy systems enables some mutual interdependence and dialogue, action can be possible. Some of the actions taken by the Hawke government in relation to issues such as unemployment and child poverty had elements of preparedness to tackle wicked problems through the development of a consensus understanding of the problems and possible solutions.

It is not easy to get an issue onto the policy agenda. A government's policy agenda is crowded with many groups and issues clamouring for attention, and governments (and most organisations) do not have enough time or resources to deal with all the issues that come before them (Bridgman & Davis 2004). Bridgman and Davis (2004, p. 41) have four conditions that must be satisfied. The first is agreement about the problem. Second, it is very important that there is some prospect of a solution. Community campaigns that focus only on the problem and do not present solutions, may obtain some short-term attention but are not likely to command the kind of long-term attention and support needed to get the issue onto the policy agenda. Third, the issue must be an appropriate issue, that is an issue for which there is political support, which affects a group of political interest, or has significant impacts and consequences such that action is required. Fourth, responding to the issue needs to be congruent with the ideology of the party that holds office.

Issues can emerge from inside or outside of government but for them to be successful from outside of government, the capacity to gain media attention and support is very important, as is the capacity to gain support from a range of interest groups and sectors. According to Bridgman and Davis (2004), issue drivers are those factors or circumstances that may give policy attention to an issue or problem. They can be:

- political; changes to government, ministers, or party platforms
- external to government; changes to the economy, media attention, opinion polls, legal changes, international, demographic, and social changes, and technology
- internal to government; information from monitoring and reviews, budget problems, and audit reports.

Such drivers can present important opportunities to get an issue on to the agenda.

Consultation

Consultation can meet different purposes. It can provide useful knowledge about the issue, possible solutions, and the extent of political support for change, and act as a vehicle for gathering political support and limiting opposition. Consultation is also important for ensuring that issues of coordination are understood and dealt with during the policy process. The complex nature of many social policy issues means that effective action requires a coordinated response by different departments within government, between different levels of government, and between public sector and non-government organisations. Consultation can also contribute to participatory democracy by providing a vehicle for citizens to have their say about policy change.

To be effective, input needs to be as early as possible, before options are decided. Ideally consultation should start at the issue identification stage. Drawing on Uhr, May (2001) has three requirements for effective democratic participation in the policy process that are relevant for consultation:

- Ensure that there is time for those interested to have a say.
- Give sufficient publicity to those involved in the policy process and to the general public.
- Provide opportunities for debate, for a 'deliberative process which weighs options for action through debate over the merits of contending proposals' (Uhr cited in May 2001, p. 270).

Consultation processes are frequently criticised. Community groups complain about insufficient consultation, unrealistically short time frames, the costs of consultation, and the lack of clarity and openness of the process, and that often consultation is more tokenistic than genuine. Public servants and politicians complain about the delay in decisions created by the need to consult, the unrepresentative nature of some groups, the costs, and the lack of useful information provided. Bridgman and Davis stress the importance of being open and transparent about the parameters of the consultation, as well as having sufficient time. Policy practitioners, inside and outside of government, need to know how to operate effectively on both sides of the consultation process—how to consult and how to be consulted.

Table 3.4 gives examples of two very different consultation processes in the 1990s. The first, associated with the contentious tax reform of the 1990s (discussed previously) was relatively closed and tightly controlled by the Howard government. However, the government's subsequent package was not accepted by the Senate, and a revised package was developed and passed after a more open process by a Senate Committee. The second example, the development of *Working Nation*, was less contentious and involved generally well-regarded action to reduce unemployment, especially long-term unemployment, following the recession of the early 1990s and the unexpected election of the Keating government in 1993. The consultation process was more open, with an interesting mix of consultation forms. It is well documented by Edwards (2001), who indicated that it had a positive impact on the final policy adopted by the government, even though it occurred within policy constraints.

Bridgman and Davis (2004) see consultation instruments on a continuum depending on the extent of participation and control given to the participants. The usual forms of consultation include meetings (with key contacts, experts, interest groups, or the public), public hearings, surveys and submissions, and the circulation of proposals for comment. Advisory committees are another form of consultation. Governments have formal structures and processes to ensure that consultation occurs for coordination purposes. Such considerations include the need to ensure that a particular proposal fits in within the overall policy stance, that economic, social, and financial considerations are taken into account, and that the relevant departments affected by the proposal are able to comment. Chapter 4 provides more information on governmental structures and processes.

Table 3.4 Examples of two different consultation processes

Tax reform: GST package—ANTS (A New Tax System)—mid to late 1990s	Consultation very limited and process very closed.
	Much consultation informal.
	Public consultation through government-backed committee with very limited influence.
	Treasury taskforce, established to develop policy only formally accessible through Minister.
	Formal and informal consultation through meetings with Minister.
	ACOSS used networks with business and other sectors to discuss issues and ideas.
	Substantial consultation through a Senate Committee after legislation was blocked in Senate—consultation with Democrats (with balance of power) was very important (McClelland 2001).
Working Nation: policies to reduce long-term unemployment—mid 1990s	Establishment of Committee of Employment Opportunities—both avenues for consultation with experts and also role in conducting consultation with community groups.
	Use of submissions (1400 received) and face-to-face meetings with community groups (430).
	Informal and formal consultation, mainly within government prior to Green Paper, plus work with academics.
	Formal consultation after Green Paper with a wide range of community groups and sectors and using key questions about policy options for feedback.
	Policy proposals affected by consultation (see Edwards 2001, pp. 159–60).

Informal consultation is very important and can occur continuously, especially through the operation of the actor networks in policy systems. Effective policy practitioners, inside and outside of government, use these networks to give and obtain information about the issues and policy options, and also about the policy process. This means the development of ongoing linkages with relevant academics, public servants, consumer organisations and special interest groups, producer organisations, relevant peak bodies, and key journalists. Such links are also critical for effective advocacy and experienced policy practitioners know how to use both formal and informal consultation as opportunities for advocacy. Effective advocates are also very aware of the structures and processes for decision-making within their policy area, the people with key decision-making power, and those people and organisations who are likely to exercise influence on the decision-makers. They will also know how best to approach these people and organisations (through a meeting or written submission, for example).

There are a number of important issues and lessons for effective consultation and advocacy (see also Hewett & Wiseman 2000).

First, clarity of objectives is important whether it is a meeting with a Minister, or preparing a submission. Second is to obtain relevant information about the person or organisation you want to persuade, including their key values and beliefs, and their issues and interests. Third, present positive ideas and solutions, avoid merely restating a known problem, and provide information that is new and different— for example, about what is happening 'on the ground'. Fourth, develop personal contacts, become a member of an actor network, and make connections with people and sectors who may have ideas and policies that are different. Fifth, trust, respect, and credibility are very important for effective advocacy and consultation, as are good communication and negotiation skills. Sixth, consultation is more likely to occur with people and organisations who are not deeply antagonistic, who are representative of key interests, who have useful knowledge, or who have political power or influence. Organisational legitimacy can be very important. Seventh, effective use of the media is important, but as welfare is often not 'good copy' and advocates need to develop personal contacts with journalists, use the media strategically (some may be able to influence government decision-makers and opinion leaders, others to raise public awareness and support), and work at developing a reputation as 'good talent'—that is, able to provide useful information in a timely, clear, and interesting manner.

Finally, people can advocate in different ways—as a member of campaigns and special interest groups, through membership and involvement in peak bodies, through influencing the policy stance of one's work organisation, through membership of government advisory committees, and through the development of key contacts and relationships. Effective consultation and advocacy involves a variety of approaches.

Policy analysis

The policy analysis stage was covered in some detail in the previous section, a framework for understanding. Briefly, it involves the following (see Bridgman & Davis 2004):

- Undertake a further clarification and more detailed examination of the issue or problem in terms of the factors identified earlier, such as scope and impact.
- Clarify goals and objectives, including any conflicts between objectives, and identify those of highest priority.
- Clarify the decision parameters—that is, what is possible given government (or organisational) policies and priorities, the availability of resources, the time required for the decision, and the probability that change will occur. The type of decision is relevant, whether it is likely to be a minor adjustment or an opportunity for a significant policy shift. Views on how decisions occur and what influences change, as discussed at the beginning of this chapter, are also relevant.
- Identify options—ideas for alternatives are sought from a range of sources including consultations, policies implemented overseas or in other states, findings from pilot projects, the experiences of community organisations, and reviews, reports, and journals.
- Undertake an analysis of options according to key criteria, including effectiveness, efficiency, and equity (see discussion under framework for policy understanding). Other relevant criteria include acceptability (will the alternative gain the necessary political and administrative support), feasibility (are there available instruments to implement the option and are the resources available in the form required), and durability—that is, will the option be able to be sustained over time? To analyse the options according to these criteria, the impacts need to be identified. Potential impacts need to be predicted from assumptions about how people and organisations will behave under certain circumstances. Such assumptions should be open to scrutiny about the evidence that is available to support them.
- Propose solution, or a set of options and their likely consequences (Bridgman & Davis 2004).

Decision stage

Effective policy practitioners are well aware of how decisions are made in their policy area, and know where, how, and when to present their policy proposals. Having already covered issues about the types of decisions and key influences on policy change earlier in this chapter, this section concentrates on the public policy process for decision-making—in particular the legislative process, given that much social policy action involves decisions by governments. However, we need to be mindful that social policy change is also brought about by the actions of community organisations and, increasingly, by the actions of business organisations. The decision-making styles, structures, and processes in these organisations are also relevant. The allocation of decision-making power and responsibility between the legislature and the judiciary, different levels of government, and Parliament and the Executive, as well as the roles of government departments and Cabinet, are also relevant and are covered in Chapter 4.

Considine (1994, pp. 79–88) identifies four stages in the legislative process for decision-making in Australia. Some overlap with the stages of issue identification, consultation, and policy analysis identified above. The first is *Initiative*, the development of the proposal. Often this takes place within the government department, but often with substantial input from the Minister's office. Next is *Clearance*, 'the vetting of proposals' to gain permission to go further. Other relevant departments will be asked to comment and an inter-departmental committee may be established at this stage. Party and caucus committees may also be involved. The coordinating departments (Prime Minister and Cabinet at Commonwealth level and Premier's Departments at state government level) are frequently heavily involved here, as are the Departments of Treasury and Finance, especially when proposals have expenditure or other economic implications. *Consideration* is the detailed analysis of the impacts, usually with a heavy involvement of Cabinet. Considine says that undertaking formal consultation and ensuring that the proposal has sufficient support takes place at the consideration stage. Issues involving cost and coordination receive a great deal of attention. At this stage, a decision is made by the Executive to adopt the proposal and send it to be drafted as legislation. Understanding Cabinet processes and dynamics is very important (see Chapter 4 and Bridgman & Davis 2004, pp 107–18). The final stage, *Decision*, is when proposals are developed into legislation and presented to Parliament for acceptance. Depending on the political control of the Executive, the legislation may be passed unchanged, amended, or defeated. Prior to 2005, no Commonwealth government since 1981 had had control of the Senate. The detail of legislation is sometimes considered by Parliamentary Committees who may recommend changes. The legislative process can be an important opportunity for further advocacy as the final legislation may not always reflect the policy objectives or may contain unintended consequences. However, it is usually too late at this stage to question the basic intent of the policy.

Budget and election times are special opportunities for influencing decision-making (Considine 1994). Annual budgets reflect the government's priorities and budget decisions are far-reaching. They influence the level of economic activity and employment opportunities, the distribution of income, and the level and composition of government taxation and expenditure. Most governments in Australia at Commonwealth and state levels have expenditure review committees and policy actors need to know their composition. Policies involving changes to spending will need to gain the support of the relevant department and, therefore, be presented early in the budget process when departmental bids are being considered. They will also need the support of the relevant minister and, if significant in spending or political terms, the support of the Prime Minister, the minsters for Treasury and Finance, and other affected ministers. Proposals are more likely to be accepted if they can be financed by other spending cuts. Regardless, spending proposals need to have some indication of how they will be financed and the impacts of such financing arrangements. Decisions about taxation are usually made later in the budget process and are often very sensitive. The first budget of a new government presents an opportunity for decisions about taxation that may be unpopular with certain groups. Spending cuts are also more likely to be introduced in the first budget.

Elections present a different kind of opportunity for policy change. They are an opportunity to focus attention on alternative policy approaches and very different value positions, and they can provide a mandate for policy change. They can present a window of opportunity for obtaining political commitments. Welfare organisations can find elections very difficult times to have their voices heard. It is difficult often to get the attention of either the media or the political parties as their attention tends to be concentrated on others with more political power. This requires careful planning and action well before the election. The election campaign is usually far too late to attempt to persuade a party of the merits of a substantial change on policy. Work on this needs to take place well before the election campaign. It is possible, however, to use election campaigns to block policy changes of concern. For example, ACOSS used the 1996 election campaign to obtain a promise from John Howard not to reduce the level of income support payments. Policy activists need to be very clear about what they are trying to achieve from an election campaign as the strategies and tactics will differ according to whether the aim is to influence policy commitments and voting behaviour (very difficult for welfare organisations), or to increase community understanding about a particular issue or set of issues.

Implementation and evaluation

Implementation (how the policy is put into action) is frequently ignored as an important stage in the policy process and many policies flounder because of inadequate attention to the implementation details. The impact of a policy depends very much on how it is carried out. However, implementation is often very difficult. Issues relevant to implementation were considered in the earlier section, a framework for understanding. In brief, implementation issues include:

- how the policy is being enacted: the type of instrument being used (for example, an education campaign on drug use or the funding of community organisations to provide rehabilitation for drug users)
- the organisation accountable for the policy and the organisation responsible for delivery (these may be different organisations)
- the resources required in terms of money, training, and physical infrastructure
- the symbolic and status issues, including the emotional reaction of clients, service providers, or the community to the policy, and to their role in it
- coordination requirements, including the sharing of information and the dependence of one service on another.

As an example of the last point, in the Job Network (through which employment assistance is provided to unemployed people), the capacity of funded organisations to provide employment assistance to the target population was very dependent on timely and accurate referrals from Centrelink, the government agency that was the initial access point (see Chapter Nine). Coordination issues are central to many of the implementation problems facing complex social policy issues such as homelessness, unemployment, drug abuse, and child protection. These days the focus is on 'whole of government' responses that are meant to overcome a 'silo' approach to social policy and public policy that has prevented coordination in the past.

Table 3.5 contains a list of factors that contribute to policy failure in the implementation stage. Successful implementation requires attention to a number of factors of success. These include:

- clarification of responsibility
- attention to strategic marketing and communication to ensure that sufficient knowledge and support for the policy and its requirements are available to the relevant people and organisations
- a careful mapping of the possible consequences of the policy, distinguishing between transitional and longer term effects
- clarity of resource requirements and timing issues
- recognition of symbolic and cultural matters
- attention to coordination and collaboration (Bridgman & Davis 2004, pp. 125–7; Green 2002; Howlett & Ramesh 1995).

Table 3.5 Common implementation problems

Poor design	Failure to consider 'the real world' and unanticipated consequences. This is especially important in social policy where we are often dealing with problems that have a number of interacting causal factors and where understanding how behavioural change is achieved is an often unclear but is still a critical issue. Unanticipated changes in the social and economic context can also occur.
Problems with goals and objectives	Conflicting objectives, confused/unclear objectives, or changes in objectives during implementation.
Inappropriate organisation	Inappropriate organisation chosen to deliver service—organisation does not have sufficient expertise, commitment, or standing.
Transition issues ignored	Failure to consider transitional issues and consequences.
Limited competence	Inadequate attention to training and staff recruitment needs.
Symbolic issues ignored	Ignoring emotional, symbolic, and cultural issues that influence political acceptability and how key actors respond when asked to implement policies.
Communication failures	Inadequate communication of objectives and conflicting directives about procedures that need to be followed.
Incentive failures	Rewards and targets are not appropriate to the achievement of main objectives of policy and may be counter to them.
Resources	Insufficient or inappropriate resources allocated.

Source: Bridgman & Davis 2004, pp. 125–7; Green 2002; Howlett & Ramesh 1995.

Evaluation is designated as the final stage of the policy process, but it is an activity that can occur throughout—for example, during the issue identification stage where we are considering if existing policies are meeting new or current needs sufficiently, and at the policy analysis stage where the different options are evaluated against agreed criteria. The evaluation can be the evaluation of the policy or of the specific programs that are part of the policy.

Evaluation has two key purposes. The first purpose is accountability. The use of evaluation for accountability purposes has increased with the increased focus on managerialism and the funding of outputs. It includes the accountability of governments to their electorates and of organisations to their funding bodies and to a range of stakeholders. It involves different types of evaluation including evaluation of the continued appropriateness of the policy or program objectives, evaluation of the efficiency of the program, and evaluation of effectiveness, sometimes called outcome evaluation (see earlier discussion in the section, 'A Framework for Understanding', for more detail).

The second main purpose of policy and program evaluation is to contribute to policy learning so that those developing policies and programs can learn from experience and improve as a result of this learning. For this purpose to be achieved, the evaluation needs to be timely, involve a range of people with a stake in the policy or program, and have results that are widely available. Howlett and Ramesh (1995) say the capacity to learn and to change policy as a response is related to organisational capacity and expertise, and also to the nature of the policy subsystem, especially the links between system members. The use of actor networks in policy systems as a repository for ongoing knowledge can be an important source of information and relationships to contribute to policy improvement.

However, while evaluation can be understood as part of the rational side of policy analysis it is also has a deeply political aspect. Some programs and policies are more frequently evaluated than others and the results can be used to justify the policy's demise. The use of the evaluation of the Keating government's policy, *Working Nation*, by the Howard government, to justify substantial cuts to labour market programs and the introduction of much cheaper programs, such as Work for the Dole, has been criticised for this reason. Other policies involving substantial amounts of money but which benefit more powerful groups, such as the private health insurance rebate or tax concessions for superannuation, are much less open to evaluation and public scrutiny.

SUMMARY AND CONCLUSION

In this chapter, I have covered different models of how policy change occurs, a framework for analysing policy, and a framework for action. It is presented to help readers become more effective policy practitioners with an understanding that people can contribute to social policy from different positions and that the role of a policy practitioner is much broader than someone in a designated policy position. Here are some key points about policy practice that arise from this chapter.

First, the policy process is more than a rational exercise, it involves politics and power and is also limited by existing and past institutional arrangements. Policy practitioners need to understand who exercises power in areas of policy interest, the institutional arrangements, the key ideas and debates, and the limitations of history in creating change. In this, we need to remember that power is exercised through the capacity to dominate the policy discourse (as well as through the capacity to direct the conduct of others), thus influencing how problems and possible solutions are perceived. Effective policy practitioners are aware of the policy discourse in the area of interest and attempt to influence current ideas and understandings. It is also relevant to remember that policy change involves more than analysis but also includes actions such as influencing, persuading, negotiating, controlling, and commanding.

Second, while policy change can represent a major policy shift on certain rare occasions when dramatically different ways of understanding and responding to issues are accepted, most policy change is incremental, involving minor adjustments. However, over time, such small changes can build on each other and be part of a dynamic for major policy change. Effective policy practitioners are able to pick the prospects for such shifts by being able to link information about the detail of their individual policy area into a broader context of economic, social, and political change (Considine 1994). In particular, they are able to pick the long-term dynamics and prospects of the 'policy window'. The policy window is where the acknowledgement of the problem combines with ideas about how to respond and a political interest in responding—that is, when the problem, policy ideas, and politics all come together (Kingdon 1995). The policy window represents the opportunity to achieve policy change.

Third, good analysis is a critical aspect of the policy process and it is important to keep in mind the activities and information that can contribute. Understanding a policy and its impacts requires the identification and analysis of a number of features including the policy itself, the goals of the policy, the key elements, and the issue that the policy is attempting to address. The policy does not operate in isolation, and needs to be understood in context, including the relevant historical aspects, the social and economic factors surrounding the policy, how the policy relates to society's values and assumptions about behaviour, the political and power issues relevant to the policy, and how the policy fits into the broader social policy picture. To understand the impact of the policy, the target group needs to be identified alongside the actual or anticipated outputs and outcomes, viable alternatives, costs and financing, and analysis according to key criteria of effectiveness, efficiency, and equity. Finally, the key implementation matters of the actual instruments used, organisational responsibility, resources, and symbolic issues need to be considered.

Fourth, different types of knowledge are required in policy analysis and development. Marsh (2003, pp. 12–13) reminds us that policy change depends on being able to give positive answers to two very distinct questions. The first concerns the availability of ideas about solutions—that is, is there a possible course of action? The second concerns the acceptability of the policy proposal— will it work and how will it be accepted by those affected and by the public? Answering these two questions requires different types of information from a range of sources. Information for policy making is therefore much broader than objective data about the extent of the problem and the impacts of various alternatives, but also requires information about how problems and solutions are perceived from a number of perspectives, including from service providers and users.

Finally, most significant change requires action and agreement from a number of organisations and sectors, and policy practitioners need to work with other people and be receptive to different ideas and perspectives. Policy practitioners in welfare organisations with limited power need to consider how they can maximise their influence in the policy process through good analysis, the effective presentation of scarce 'on the ground' knowledge, and the development of linkages in the relevant policy systems.

4

THE INSTITUTIONAL CONTEXT FOR DECISIONS AND ACTION

Alison McClelland

Social policy has an institutional context. Institutions 'shape the aspirations and assumptions of those who work within them, structure the problems they meet and determine the values and solutions available for consideration' (Weller 2000, p. 4). They also determine 'the rules of engagement' (p. 4). The institutional context affects how change occurs, including the power relationships between different key actors and institutions in the policy process, and what is achievable at any point of time. This chapter first considers the roles and relationships of the different non-government groups and institutions relevant to social policy in Australia. It then examines the government-related institutional arrangements in more detail.

ROLES AND RELATIONSHIPS OF DIFFERENT NON-GOVERNMENT GROUPS AND INSTITUTIONS

Many groups and institutions contribute to decisions about social policy and its implementation. They include business, unions, community organisations and other special interest groups, and the media. Table 4.1 summarises their role and influence in social policy.

Business

Ultimately business is responsible to shareholders and is required to produce a rate of return on capital invested. Business influences social policy in three ways.

First, the actions business takes in relation to investment, employment, wages, and prices directly influences social well-being and its distribution. Economic globalisation alongside neo-liberal (pro-market) economic policies have intensified the capacity of business to influence well-being in this way. Second, business exercises a great deal of influence on government decision-making through its capacity to withhold or change the use of capital, and through the considerable resources it deploys to influence decision-makers and public opinion (Mendes 2003). Third, business is increasingly having a direct impact on the development and implementation of social policy through its increased representation on the boards of welfare organisations and the increased role of the private sector in welfare delivery. The Howard government has promoted *social coalitions* as a major social policy plank. Social coalitions mean the planning, funding, and delivery of welfare through partnerships that involve business working with community organisations and government. Prime Minister Howard has also urged business to be more philanthropic and has developed special forums and tax concessions to this end.

Given the political importance placed upon how well the economy is going and the pivotal role of business in debates about economic management, governments take the claims of business very seriously. John Dawkins, a former Minister and Treasurer, has identified the strong influence of business claims on fiscal (budget) policy during the Hawke/Keating Labor governments (Stilwell 2000). Influential peak organisations include the Business Council of Australia (BCA), the Australian Industries Group, and the Australian Confederation of Commerce and Industry (Marsh 2000). According to Marsh (2000), the BCA has at least two private meetings per year with the Howard government's Cabinet. At critical times, the peak business organisations have come together to resource their advocacy and policy work jointly and to speak on a united front. The development of the Business Round Table for Tax Reform, during the late 1990s tax reform debate leading up to the GST, is a good example of business working as a group to maximise its influence. The Round Table had membership from all peak business organisations and was well resourced.

The substantial resources of business therefore give them influence through their funding of political parties, their own policy and lobbying efforts, and also their funding of pro-market think tanks. Since the 1980s, a number of very influential think tanks have developed or grown in authority. They promote neo-liberal economic ideas and an anti-welfare social policy agenda and include the Institute of Public Affairs (IPA), the Centre for Independent Studies (CIS), and the Tasman Institute. Peter Saunders from CIS has produced reports questioning whether there is much poverty in Australia, and recommending changes such as the introduction of time-based welfare payments (Saunders & Tsumori 2002). As March (2000) indicates, these neo-liberal think tanks have been most influential in getting certain issues on the agenda, such as privatisation, cuts to government spending, and a behavioural/individualised approach to understanding poverty.

Table 4.1 Non-government groups: social policy role and influence

Grouping	Social policy/welfare role	Influence over social policy decisions
Business	Influence/provide welfare directly through decisions about jobs, wages and prices.	Strong influence on government through power to withhold capital, and capacity to deploy resources towards analysis and lobbying. Growing role on boards of community welfare organisations and government authorities.
Unions	Some limited benefits to members.	Influence through power to withhold labour, an institutional role in arbitration system, and, in the past, through the Accord with Labor governments. Partly depends on membership and government legislation.
Community welfare organisations (CWO)	Provide welfare through direct service provision and own decisions about this. Dependent on extent of government funding and conditions of funding.	Limited capacity to influence because rarely withhold services as a group. Influence through moral persuasion and quality of analysis, plus organisational cohesion on key issues. Also influences through demonstration of new ways of meeting need.
Social movements/ special interest groups	Some limited services to group membership.	Influence through moral persuasion (from past neglect and discrimination), community interest, and organising capacity, including effective campaigning.
Churches	Welfare mainly provided through support/auspice of CWOs and also some other services.	Influence through moral authority, membership, and media capacity of key spokespersons.
Media	No direct role (see business)	Influence on community opinion and understanding through communication reach; indirect influence on government decision-making.

Unions

Unions are responsible to their members for action to sustain employment, wages, and working conditions, and historically this has been their main focus. Unions exercise influence in the policy process in a number of ways. Their most significant weapon is their capacity to withhold labour, which in turn depends on the extent of union membership and the legislative capacity to strike. Union power is now more limited than in the past because of the decline in union membership from almost 60 per cent of the workforce in the 1950s to approximately 26 per cent of the current workforce (Marsh 2000). Structural changes to employment away from manufacturing and towards service industries, and the significant increase in part-time and casual employment, alongside the collapse of compulsory union membership, have contributed to this decline.

Australia's arbitration system has also historically given unions a strong voice in decisions about wages and working conditions in Australia by providing them with institutional legitimacy and with a forum (previously the Arbitration Commission, now the Industrial Relations Tribunal) through which their claims could be put and independently assessed. In this way, arbitration acted to somewhat redress the power imbalance between employers and employees. However, the introduction of enterprise bargaining and individual contracts, and recent legislative restrictions to the role of the Industrial Relations Tribunal and to the role of unions, have significantly weakened union power in this area.

Unions have also exercised power through their formal and informal relationship with the Australian Labor Party (ALP), thereby influencing the policies of Labor inside and outside of government. This influence was most pronounced in the 1980s and early 1990s through the successive Accords developed between the Hawke and Keating Labor governments, and the union movement through its national peak body, the Australian Council of Trade Unions (ACTU). The Accords were packages of agreed changes to wages, taxation, and the social wage. They included the agreement of unions to moderate wage claims in return for tax cuts, improvements to superannuation, and improvements to the social wage, including the introduction of Medicare, the expansion of child care, and increases in government payments to low-income families, including low-wage-earning families. The union movement is said traditionally to hold a laborist approach to social policy issues (Mendes 2003) with most attention paid to the wages and conditions of those in work rather than those without jobs. This has sometimes been a source of tension between welfare and union groups in social policy debates. Another concern has been the male-oriented policy focus of unions. However, in recent years, both limitations have been challenged with the unions taking on issues such as maternity leave, child care, and working hours.

Non-government organisations

There is an extensive range of non-government organisations (NGOs) apart from business and unions (which can also be regarded as producer organisations) (Marsh 2000), and there are also different terms used to refer to them, including the third sector, civil society, and not-for-profit organisations. These are organisations that do not exist to make a profit and that occupy a space between government and the market. They include organisations of varying degrees of size and formality. Such organisations contribute to social well-being and to social policy in a number of different ways. They can provide friendship, support, and opportunities for individual and group development, deliver services to meet social needs, promote the interests of members, and articulate the importance of certain issues and ideas for policy change.

NGOs have been categorised in different ways. Dalton et al. (1996, p. 67) categorise them as:

- *Charities*: established to assist people experiencing poverty and disadvantage (for example, St Vincent de Paul)
- *Social reform organisations*: established to take action against social issues by moderating the social and economic environment (for example, the Brotherhood of St Laurence)
- *Earlier self-help organisations*: established to achieve self-sufficiency through mutual organisation (for example, building societies)
- *Later self-help organisations*: established in recognition of new identities and the need for cooperative activity (for example, Nursing Mothers Association)
- *Community-managed service organisations*: established in recognition of the need for accessible and responsive community-based services, which should be publicly funded (for example, youth refuges)
- *Collective and participatory service organisations*: established to respond to the need for women-centred organisations (for example, sexual assault services)
- *Social movement organisations*: established because of the need to raise society's consciousness about the need for radical change in particular areas (for example, the Wilderness Society).

In the following discussion about their role in social policy, they are grouped more broadly as: community welfare organisations, other interest organisations, social movements, and churches.

Community welfare organisations

Community welfare organisations (CWOs) include the wide variety of organisations established to provide some kind of service. They range from large, traditional charities, such as the Smith Family; to locally based and community-managed organisations, such as community health centres; to self-help organisations based around the needs of often marginalised groups. Many of the larger CWOs are church-based. The decisions and actions of CWOs have been very important in shaping social policy in Australia over time due to their decisions about how to implement funded services on the ground and through decisions about what kinds of services to deliver. It is therefore important to also understand the processes of organisational decision-making in such organisations.

Community welfare organisations have always played a strong role in welfare-related service delivery in Australia. This has historically included the care of families in distress and substitute care of children, the care of people with disabilities, the accommodation needs of aged and homeless people, and child protection and custodial training of young offenders (until the mid and late 1980s).When welfare services were being developed in Australia's early years, Australia lacked a developed system of local government, and thus the early state administrations turned to the charities to take this role, especially in Victoria (Kewley 1973). Over time, the scope of services delivered by CWOs has increased in parallel with an increase in the demand for the state to take action in new emerging areas of need. In other countries, the expansion of the welfare state was more likely to be through direct state provision (Roe 1976a). The 1960s saw an expanded role for CWOs, which encompassed aged nursing home and hostel care, with government support through the provision of capital grants. During the 1970s and 1980s, there was an extension of CWO involvement in new areas such as home and community care, women's refuges, and community-based child care. It also entailed the growth of different types of organisations that were more self-help- and community-based, as well as being more participatory and critical. This led to the development of a strong, broadly based constituency and capacity in the community welfare sector. During the 1990s it included a significant expansion into employment-related services.

In addition to influencing social policy through the delivery of services, CWOs also influence the broader social policy context and the decisions taken by government in two ways (Lyons 2001). The first is through the development of new services or new ways of meeting needs, which are then demonstrated to be useful and important, and are taken up more widely. Lyons (2001, pp. 190–1) comments thus, 'To take two examples: the revolution in aged persons' accommodation in the 1950s and 1960s was pioneered by nonprofits seeking a better way of meeting the needs of poorly housed older people. Then, it was a nonprofit organisation that introduced the case management approach, helping older people with complex care needs obtain the services they needed while remaining at home.'

The second way to influence the social policy decisions by government is through direct advocacy and lobbying. CWOs have varied in their interest and capacity for advocacy. The Melbourne-based Brotherhood of St Laurence (BSL) is perhaps the most well-known CWO for advocating changes to society's structures and government policies in order to take action on issues such as poverty and unemployment. It has advocated for policy changes including improved housing, changes to social security payments, better employment services, action to reduce the cost of education for low-income families, improved health services including the introduction of family planning and better access to dental care, and improvements to wages. Important features of the BSL's advocacy approach have included:

- a traditional focus on social justice and an imperative to examine and respond to injustice arising from societal structures and processes
- a religious background and church links providing a moral authority to speak out
- a strong service delivery arm giving a legitimate 'on the ground' perspective
- a well-respected research and policy unit providing information and rational arguments to back the moral case
- service innovation assisting further with ideas for change and reinforcing the organisation's authority in social policy change
- the presence of key leaders able to articulate a case to the media and the community, and to negotiate with leaders from government and other sectors.

Community welfare organisations also use peak organisations for advocacy and lobbying. Their numbers increased during the 1970s and 1980s. Some are more concerned with advocating for the needs of the organisations that they represent, but many focus on advocacy for their client groups' needs. National peak examples include: National Shelter, Alzheimer's Association of Australia, Consumers' Health Forum, Council on the Ageing (Australia), National Association of Community Legal Centres, and National Council on Intellectual Disability. The umbrella peak body is the Australian Council of Social Service (ACOSS). Since its establishment in 1956 and especially from the 1970s onwards when, according to Mendes (2003), it changed from a charity model to a social justice framework, ACOSS has undertaken an advocacy role that is unique around the world.

The broad span of ACOSS's work has encompassed 'economic development and taxation; employment, education and training; social security and income support; community services; health, including mental health; housing and urban development; law and justice; and rural and regional communities' (ACOSS

2004a). Proposals are disseminated to decision-makers and the community though regular meetings with senior bureaucrats and Ministers, submissions to government, attendance at parliamentary and other inquiries, and special research and policy reports. ACOSS's Federal Budget submission is a regular method for presenting key priorities for the coming year and is also a source of information about social needs and issues for the welfare sector. A strong media presence is a particularly important means of dissemination, and past ACOSS Presidents, such as Merle Mitchell, Julian Disney, and Robert Fitzgerald, have been well known and articulate in presenting ACOSS's views to the public. Membership compromises the main national organisations in Australia and the eight state and territory councils of social service (COSSs). Small organisations are represented through the state COSS membership.

This diversity of membership has been important for ACOSS's legitimacy and authority over the years, as has its reputation for sound policy development by drawing on research, policy analysis and development, and the 'on the ground' experience of its membership. According to May (2001, p. 253), ACOSS's approach to policy has been both reactive and proactive. Its main strategies have been 'built around research and documentation, coalition-building, networking, lobbying and public campaigning', with its influence stemming 'largely from a traditional call to moral authority, together with an appeal for rationality, participation and representation in policy-making.' Mendes says that ACOSS's policy influence was very strong during the Hawke/Keating governments when it became a 'policy insider' and a member of the 'government's "policy network"' (Mendes 2003, p. 126). He comments that during this time, 'ACOSS's influence with government arguably reflected its adherence to a number of key strategies identified as crucial for lobbying success. These include the provision of well-researched case studies, professional expertise, speaking with a united and representative voice, topicality and timing in its interventions, moderate and considered recommendations, and an emphasis on broader national concerns rather than narrow self-interest'(Mendes 2003, p. 127).

Along with other peak welfare bodies, ACOSS has relied heavily on funding from the Commonwealth government. This funding of peak organisations by governments is a positive feature of Australian governance (Lyons 2001), but it means that welfare advocacy is more vulnerable with resources dependent on the current government's views. Criticism can also be limited in this way. A number of peak organisations either had significant funding cuts or ceased to be funded at all by the Howard government after a review in late 1996. They included the Australian Youth Policy Action Coalition (AYPAC), National Shelter, and the Australian Pensioners and Superannuants League (May 2001).

A number of factors weaken the policy influence of ACOSS and welfare organisations generally. First, welfare has limited economic power compared with business and unions. While welfare organisations could exercise some influence by refusing to deliver services, they have been reluctant to do so because of their moral obligation to assist people in need and because of their increased dependence on government for funding. ACOSS has attempted to reduce the impact of the limited power of welfare in various ways, including through the development of strategic relationships with other sectors on critical issues. During the period of the Hawke/Keating Labor governments, ACOSS worked with the ACTU to promote improvements to the social wage, and more recently has supported the unions' actions to obtain increases to the wages of low-wage earners. However, there have also been points of difference between the policies of ACOSS and ACTU, especially when ACOSS had considered that the ACTU did not consider the needs of non-wage earners and, at other times, around policies such as superannuation. Similarly, during the Howard government's term of office, ACOSS has worked with business to promote a joint dialogue and understanding around issues such as tax reform and unemployment. ACOSS has also attempted to increase its influence by bringing different welfare peaks and large CWOs together to speak with a united voice on key policy issues, such as the impact of penalties on welfare recipients. However, according to May, ACOSS is limited by its inability to ensure that its policies will be supported by its membership given its 'voluntaristic associational structure' (2001, p. 253). This may reflect the low value placed on solidarity in the culture of welfare organisations when compared with the union movement.

A second, more recent problem arises from the adoption of public choice theory, which understands government decision-making as captured by self-serving interest groups. In this view, ACOSS will not represent the real welfare needs of Australians but will be self-serving and only reflect the interests of its members, which are also self-serving. The increased public funding of welfare organisations, alongside the governments' adoption of the purchaser/provider model of funding, have reinforced such views. The funding relationships between community organisations and governments are now more at 'arm's length', tightly specified in terms of required outputs, and sometimes the result of some form of competitive tendering. Welfare organisations are often then seen to represent *provider* interests rather than being able to reflect on the needs of their clients. The special place accorded to CWOs in the provision of welfare and in understanding social needs is also challenged by the increased role of the private sector in the provision of welfare services funded by government in areas such as employment assistance, child care, and home and community care.

The reliance of welfare organisations on government funding, which is tightly specified, also threatens the capacity of welfare organisations to influence policy through innovation.

A third limiting factor may be the sense that people in welfare are difficult to satisfy and not willing to give credit to policy change that is an improvement but is not perfect. Welfare advocates sometimes have the reputation of being unwilling to compromise and having a 'yes but' approach to responding to positive change. This can mean that politicians do not see much political gain from attempting to introduce changes that are advocated by welfare groups as they do not consider that they will receive much political kudos as a result. Finally, welfare advocacy is also limited by the great difficulty in assisting user groups to speak out. While support for advocacy and self-help groups in areas such as health, disability, and sole parenting has provided forums for many user groups, two key groups around whom much social policy is formulated—people experiencing unemployment and people experiencing poverty—are still left out. The need for social policy practitioners and advocacy organisations such as ACOSS to be more effective in helping these very marginalised groups to organise and have a stronger voice in the policy process remains a very important challenge (May 2001; Mendes 2003).

Other interest groups, social movements, and churches

Social policy is influenced by other NGOs, in addition to CWOs. Professions can exercise influence by limiting entry into their profession, through the possession of expertise in the policy area, and through the support and legitimacy accorded to them by the community (Marsh 2000). Legal and health professional groups have tended to have a greater influence on social policy change than welfare professional groups. Factors that may limit the influence of social work professionals and its association, the Australian Association of Social Workers (AASW), include:

- the increased focus on risk management in welfare organisations and the diminution of professional discretion in welfare service delivery
- the limited resources provided by the social work profession for the development of social policy competence and social policy proposals
- the heavy concentration of employment within government, thus limiting social workers' perceived capacity to speak out
- the absence of a clear ideology within the AASW and the absence of representative clarity (see Mendes 2003).

Some interest groups are formed specifically to advocate for the interest of members. They may also provide some service to their memberships. Such groups include the Australian Consumers Association, the Country Women's Association, and various motorist organisations (Lyons 2001). Their influence depends on the extent of community support and interest in the people or issue they represent, and the organisational capacity of the group. At certain times, groups such as the Returned Services League have exerted considerable influence and war veterans have been able to secure superior benefits to other groups in similar economic circumstances due to the community's desire to repay them for service rendered. Other groups, identified by Lyons as 'public interest organisations' are formed to promote a particular cause or issue—for example, the Australian Conservation Foundation. Policy development and advocacy are key functions of such groups and their influence also varies not only according to community interest and organisational capacity, but also their research and policy development capacity, and the existence of effective spokespersons.

Public interest organisations overlap with social movements. Since the late 1960s, they have developed a special significance and political influence, and according to Marsh have formed around 'the women's, peace, environment, consumer, gay rights, animal liberation, ethnic, black rights and the "New Right" movements' (2000, p. 182). They have developed in recognition of the diversity of legitimate needs and lifestyles, and have often acquired a strong moral legitimacy because of the impact of past discriminatory structures and practices. Marsh says that they have organised very successfully in the following way, 'All the movements have access to adequate funding. All are experienced campaigners. All have capacities for networking, coalition building and outreach, particularly to the media—these being the essential ingredients for effective campaigning in the current pluralised political environments' (March 2000, pp. 182–3). While many if not most of these movements have dealt with issues and people who have suffered past inequality, they also run the risk of contributing to a neglect of critical social policy issues around poverty and inequality, particularly that of class and social solidarity. Again to quote Marsh (2000, p. 183), 'All the issue movements give primary place to identities that are less comprehensive than social class, shading—in the case of the neo-liberal movement—into individualism.'

Churches have mainly influenced social policy through their funding, auspicing, and delivery of welfare services, and church-based welfare agencies have been very active in welfare and social policy advocacy in Australia, although the church-based CWOs have varied in their capacity and interest in social policy and advocacy. However, the churches have an influence that is additional to their relationships with CWOs, and some church leaders speak out on issues such as tax reform, gambling, Australia's treatment of refugees, and poverty. While to date this has mainly involved Christian church leaders and organisations (such as the Anglican Archbishop Carnley, the Reverend Tim Costello (from the Baptist Church), or the Catholic Bishops and their statements on social justice), increasingly it is also involving non-Christian religions, including people from the Jewish and Muslim faiths (Mendes 2003).

The moral authority of churches has given them a special capacity to draw attention to social issues. Politicians therefore take the comments of senior church officials very seriously, although they are also prone to criticise church leaders for speaking out on issues that are deemed to be beyond their brief. While there are differences, generally the churches in Australia have tended to support social policy change that promotes collective responsibility, human rights, and an expanded role for the state. This contrasts with the experience in the USA, where the religious right has exercised a strong individualistic influence in social policy debates. This may be changing in Australia with the development of the Family First political party, which is said to have links with more conservative and fundamental Christian thinking. However, it is too soon to be sure whether this will be a growing and enduring feature of Australian political life, and how representatives from Family First will operate.

Media

Social activists can use the media to influence social policy by using it as a forum to influence decision-makers directly about a current issue and as a vehicle to influence public opinion and understanding, thereby indirectly influencing policy decisions. While there are different views about the influence exerted by the media in changing public policy, the media is seen to have a significant role in getting an issue onto the public agenda and the agenda of decision-makers (Howlett & Ramesh 1995; Mendes 2003). Social policy activists can therefore use the media to obtain publicity for their issue, thereby increasing community understanding and support, as well as obtaining a reputation with decision-makers as someone who has some influence through their capacity to gain media attention.

However, it is difficult to use the media to promote a social policy agenda to increase access to welfare, or to comment on social policy change in detail, for a number of reasons (Mendes 2003; Uhr & Wanna 2000). First, a number of very popular media forums such as tabloid newspapers, talk-back radio, and current affairs television programs are more likely to have an anti-welfare perspective than one that is sympathetic. Second, welfare issues are not generally regarded as newsworthy unless the issue is presented in a sensational manner. This represents a dilemma for welfare activists. How can they promote issues such as unemployment without stories that are likely to present people as victims, which are very negative and promote fear in the audience rather than a sense of hope for change? Third, the media's treatment of public policy discussions during such times as parliamentary debates, or elections, is more likely to focus narrowly on leadership and personalities than on the substantial issues involved. Finally, many social policy issues are very complex and need more than a few paragraphs in a newspaper or thirty seconds on the radio or television.

Successful policy activists who have used the media well include the Reverend Peter Hollingworth (when he was Executive Director of the BSL), the Reverend Tim Costello, and past ACOSS Presidents, Julian Disney and Robert Fitzgerald. The attributes that contributed to this success included availability, clarity, and knowledge, and a preparedness to engage positively, rather than in a hostile manner (see Chapter 3 for further discussion).

THE INSTITUTIONAL ARRANGEMENTS OF GOVERNMENT

In talking about the institutional arrangements of government, I am referring to the structures and processes that influence how Australian governments function and make decisions. Such institutional arrangements are important for a number of reasons. First, they affect the patterns of influence in relation to social policy decision-making. Effective social policy practitioners (within and outside of government) know the relevant arrangements for their particular areas and how best to use them to influence decision-making. Second, institutional arrangements affect what governments can do and the capacity of governments generally and at particular levels. As Howlett and Ramesh (1995) stress, governmental institutions are important in reinforcing or weakening the policy capabilities of governments and also influence the way different actors behave in the policy process. Wanna and Keating give a positive view of Australian arrangements generally as 'institutions provide the framework within which our system of governance operates. Their traditions and structures help shape our response as a society to current problems and challenges, and temper any tendencies to over-react' (2000, p. 229). The Australian constitution provides the legal framework for our institutional arrangements. In the following discussion, I first examine the constitution and then move to the role of key institutions. These are Parliament and political parties, the Executive and Cabinet, public servants and government departments, public enterprises and statutory authorities, and the courts and administrative reviews.

The Constitution and the constitutional framework

The Constitution establishes the legal requirements of governments in Australia. The constitutional framework influences their mode of operation and, according to Parkin and Summers (1994, p. 5), 'consists of the set of rules, understandings and practices that establish the basic institutions of governance, allow for the exercise of legitimate authority of governments and provide for some form of democratic accountability by governments to the Australian people'. The two important concepts here are authority and accountability—who has authority for certain decisions and actions, and how are they accountable for them?

The Australian Constitution was established at Federation and drew on both US and UK traditions of governance. As such, according to Hughes (1998), it represents a balance between liberal and collectivist traditions. From the UK it draws on elements of the Westminster tradition and the notion of 'responsible Parliamentary government' with the Executive selected from the elected parliament (Weller 2000, p. 1). Federalism was taken from the USA along with the formation of the High Court as the interpreter of the legal meaning and requirements of the Constitution and as the final court of appeal. Despite being created over 100 years ago, and thus representing the ideas of government of that time, it has been very difficult to change and only nine constitutional amendments have been made since its inception (Hughes 1998).

The Australian Constitution does not establish a set of human rights. Originally human rights were to be achieved through the UK tradition of common law rights; however, most countries, including the UK, now see this as inadequate and have moved to legislate for human rights (Hughes 1998). The absence of human rights legislation at a national level denies social policy practitioners a potentially useful weapon to promote rights-based social policy, although there are disagreements about the importance of this. The USA, with its Bill of Human Rights, still has a social policy stance with limited rights to welfare, which have historically been much more limited than the UK, although the UK did not have a Bill of Rights until recently. Over the years there have been several unsuccessful attempts to introduce human rights legislation in Australia. Currently, the Howard government is not interested and, as Hughes notes, appears so opposed that in 1997 it refused 'to sign a trade agreement with the European Union because it contained a standard human rights clause' (Hughes 1998, p. 235). The High Court has made some decisions about 'implied rights', which have denied the legality of government legislation on the grounds that it would have compromised rights to free speech. Other important legal decisions, such as Mabo and Wik, have established limited land rights for Indigenous Australians and, together with the implied rights decisions, have led to accusations of 'judicial activism' (Hughes 1998) against the High Court and complaints that it was usurping the proper authority of the legislature.

Federalism

One of the most important features of the Australian constitution is the division of responsibilities between Commonwealth and state governments—between two different levels of '"sovereign" government' (Parkin & Summers 1994, p. 10). The Constitution gives a specified division of power with some exclusive powers to the Commonwealth and others shared between the Commonwealth and the states. Local government has no formal constitutional authority but is governed by state government legislation. For social policy purposes, it is relevant that many important areas of policy, such as health, education, housing, child care, and so on, are 'residual' areas in the Constitution (Parkin & Summers 1994, p. 11). While they were supposedly intended to be (under the Constitution) the responsibility of the states, in practice responsibility for them is shared between the Commonwealth and state governments. Part Three of this book provides more detail about how these overlapping areas of responsibility play out in particular policy domains, with some examples provided in Table 4.2.

The greater financial powers of the Commonwealth have enabled it to take action in many areas previously that were the responsibility of the states. While the states initially had control of income taxes, during the Second World War this power was permanently ceded to the Commonwealth. Their capacity to levy taxes on consumption (the other key taxation base) has been limited by High Court decisions, which have made most such state taxes unconstitutional. And while the GST is a major source of revenue earmarked for the states, it is still a Commonwealth government taxation instrument. As a result there is 'vertical fiscal imbalance' in Australia with the Commonwealth government collecting more revenue (approximately 80 per cent of all revenue) than required in terms of its direct responsibilities, and state governments not collecting sufficient revenue and therefore being dependent on the Commonwealth for supplementation. There is also 'horizontal imbalance', as revenue is allocated to the states by the Commonwealth, according to a needs-based formulae developed by the Grants Commission, an independent statutory authority. States such as Victoria and New South Wales receive much less than they would on a per capita basis and states such as Tasmania and Queensland receive more. While this is important for equity between different parts of Australia, the application of the formulae is frequently criticised.

Table 4.2 Examples of social policies with joint Commonwealth/state responsibility

Policy	Responsibility
Disability	Commonwealth responsible for income support and labour market programs, states responsible for accommodation, personal services and education.
Health	Commonwealth responsible for medical fees and pharmaceuticals, states responsible for hospitals (with Commonwealth contribution towards funding) and community health centres.
Public housing and private rental support	Commonwealth traditionally responsible for funding states for public housing, but states required to make contribution since 1989. States responsible for development and management of housing stock. Commonwealth responsible for income support, including assistance for private rental costs, but states responsible for rental rebates in public housing.
Aged care	Commonwealth responsible for income support, nursing homes, and hostels (apart from Victoria where the state also has a role). States responsible for hospitals and joint responsibility for home and community care.

Federalism has some positive features. It enables government that is closer to the people, and hopefully government that is more responsive and participatory. Different state governments mean that governments are more likely to reflect the diversity within Australia and accommodate regional differences. Finally, federalism places limits on the concentration of power by one government.

However, there are also significant disadvantages, which are:

- A reduction of the capacity of government overall, thus having important ramifications for government responsibility for social policy and the welfare of its citizens, in particular the achievement of national citizenship rights. The evidence is that countries with federal systems of government have governments that are not as strong and have a reduced policy capacity (Hughes 1998).
- Inefficiencies from the gaps, duplication, and cost shifting arising when both levels of government intervene in a policy area, and the longer drawn out policy process that is the result of having to obtain agreements to act in areas of joint responsibility. Important areas of social policy, including health and housing assistance, are subject to such complex agreements (see Table 4.2).
- The lack of action and blurring of responsibility (Hughes 1998) that can be the result of dual responsibility.

There have been attempts to introduce a more cooperative approach to federalism in Australia to reduce these disadvantages. A number of policy areas with overlapping responsibility between the Commonwealth and the states have inter-governmental agreements. There is also a 'network of Ministerial Councils' (Saunders 2003, p. 231) that provides a structure for cooperative policy development. Following its re-election in 1990, and its view that problems associated with federalism in Australia were limiting positive action, the Hawke government instigated the Council of Australian Governments (COAG). Through COAG, Ministerial Councils and working groups were established. They included the social policy-related areas of 'child care, public housing, and health and community services' (Hughes 1998, p. 286). However, the main success of COAG was the establishment and implementation of National Competition Policy and national agreements in relation to a number of utilities, and, more recently, for water. In social policy terms, there were related cooperative reforms introduced by the Hawke and Keating governments in disability, mental health, aged care, such as Coordinated Care Trials, and also through the Better Cities project. Many of these projects were through the instigation of Brian Howe, at the time Minister assisting the Prime Minister on Federal–State Relations, and the minister responsible for areas such as health, housing, and aged care. However, the Howard government has pulled back from the use of COAG for cooperative federalism and left policy development involving Commonwealth/ state relations much more to individual ministers.

Parliament, Executive, and Cabinet

The Constitution nominally gives ultimate power to the Parliament to make legislation about social policy-related matters. However, in practice power is concentrated in the hands of the Executive (or ministers). The dominance of the party system, alongside majority governments, means that individual Parliamentarians vote in accordance with policy determined by the Executive and Cabinet. Caucus (the collection of elected Parliamentarians from a particular party) may have some influence on the Executive where policy change is very politically contentious and the government of the day feels politically vulnerable. Backbenchers can give the government an indication of the political feeling in their electorates on specific issues. However, policy change is rarely achieved by lobbying individual Parliamentarians alone. The dominance of the party system, alongside declining membership of major political parties, has given rise to concerns about the inability of governments to be sufficiently in tune with the diversity of interests and needs in the community. The effective control of Parliament by the Executive also raises concerns about the capacity of the electorate to hold ministers and governments accountable for their actions, and, according to Uhr and Wanna (2000), questions remain about whether majoritarian and adversarial parliaments can develop effective policies, particularly policies that require negotiated consensus.

The Australian Constitution requires that the Commonwealth Parliament has a lower and an upper house. The Senate is the upper house, with Senators elected from each state. The Senate has had a greater diversity of political representation than the House of Representatives and has been important, not for initiating policy change, but in blocking or amending legislation. Over the period 1981–2005, no Commonwealth government held a Senate majority, and the balance of power was exercised by the minor parties and independents. During the Keating government the Senate required changes to legislation (such as land rights and increases to petrol excise). Examples relating to the Howard government, in the period between 1996 and 2005, include changes to the GST and industrial relations legislation, and the blocking of legislation to tighten eligibility for disability payments. Senate Committees, set up to examine the consequences of contentious legislation, have often been useful vehicles for social policy practitioners promoting alternative policies. However, their influence arises from their capacity to amend or block legislation, and the recommendations of other Senate Committees (or House of Representative Committees) are often ignored. As at July 2005, the Howard government possesses control of both houses of Parliament and the power of the Senate obviously has diminished as a result. Policy changes previously blocked or significantly compromised by the Senate are being revisited by the government—for example, industrial relations and income support payments for people with a disability.

Ministers are responsible for setting the policy direction for their portfolios. Their power comes from their capacity to control the resources and activities of departments and agencies under their supervision (Bridgman & Davis 2004). Ministerial support for policy change is essential, and policy activists know the relevant ministers, make contact with their advisors (who have became increasingly influential), and are also aware of those organisations and individuals close to the relevant ministers and advisors. However, ministerial authority has been diminished by the increased complexity of government, ministers' workloads have grown, and, according to Weller (2000), it is now hard for ministers to be sufficiently informed. The growing complexity of government activity means that coordination is a very important task for policy development and implementation. In turn, this means increased power for the Cabinet (the meeting of senior Ministers) and to the Prime Minister (or Premiers at state level). Cabinet performs a number of functions but its most important role is as the coordinator of government policy (Weller 2000). Cabinets operate on the basis of collective responsibility, loyalty, and secrecy (Weller 2000). Their power depends on their capacity to provide a cohesive government agenda and to control the Parliament (Wanna & Keating 2000). The increased workload of Cabinet has given Prime Ministers and their Departments (and Premiers) more central roles in 'coordinating policies, anticipating future challenges and developing a sense of direction' (Wanna & Keating 2000, p. 238).

Cabinets have detailed procedures, which are well documented by Bridgman and Davis (2004). Policy practitioners need knowledge about Cabinet membership and procedures.

Government departments and related authorities

Government departments have a central role in initiating, developing and implementing policy (Howlett & Ramesh 1995). Policy practitioners need to know the particular bureaucrats in their area of policy interest, as they will have a key role in advising Ministers about the likely impacts and desirability of policy proposals. A number of factors influence the policy role of government departments. They include the increased use of contracts for senior bureaucrats, which is said to have politicised the public service and diminished its capacity to provide advice that is independent and unwelcome, and the *New Managerialism* and its focus on affecting policy through *purchasing* and *steering*, rather than *providing* and *rowing*. Together with privatisation, these changes have not only strengthened the regulatory and advisory role of government departments, but also have limited their exposure to service delivery and implementation issues, making it more important for departments to open up their policy development processes to outside input at an early stage.

One important development is the growth of institutions that act as watchdogs on the decisions and actions of government departments. The Administrative Appeals Tribunal (AAT) provides an avenue of appeal against incorrect decisions in administrative law, as do Ombudsmen and the various anti-discrimination and equal opportunity bodies. Other bodies and instruments, such as Auditor-Generals, freedom of information provisions, and the Human Rights and Equal Opportunity Commission, have a more general monitoring function in relation to the transparency and accountability of government departments and decisions. Such institutions and processes can provide useful avenues for outsiders to propose policy and procedural change (May 2001). This is very important for social policy in relation to vulnerable people. May (2001, p. 269) comments that, 'there is a real need for institutional structures and mechanisms that monitor public policy and other matters for groups with "little voice" to ensure that their interests are taken into account on significant issues.' The development of Welfare Rights Centres, mentioned by Ziguras in Chapter 9, is an example of the usefulness of such structures for people reliant on government transfer payments. However, given their potential to embarrass government, such institutions are always under threat.

The growth of QUIGS, 'quasi-independent government-created arm's length bodies or arrangements' (Wanna & Keating 2000, p. 233) such as the Productivity Commission, the Civil Aviation Safety Authority, and the Reserve Bank, represents another change. These are organisations responsible for policy advice or service delivery that are not under the immediate control of the Minister or Departmental head and are more independent. While, according to Weller (2000, p. 3), 'Australia has a long-tradition of developing and determining policy through bodies held at arm's length', with long-serving institutions such as the Industrial Relations Tribunal (previously the Arbitration Commission) and the Reserve Bank as key examples, the need to open up the policy process has led to an increased interest in expanding the role of such institutions. However, social policy is notable for the absence of any equivalent institution to the Productivity Commission or the Reserve Bank, apart from the Australian Institute for Heath and Welfare, which is restricted to the collection and dissemination of information rather than policy analysis and advice.

SUMMARY AND CONCLUSION

This chapter has examined the contribution of different groups and institutions to social policy in Australia. We have seen that the changing welfare state is giving business an increased role in the planning, funding, and delivery of welfare, and a relatively unrecognised, but still significant, influence on debates and decisions about social policy-related issues. In contrast, the influence of unions is threatened by a changing labour force, declining membership, labour market deregulation and legislation restricting their role. For community groups, there is an increasing role in the delivery of welfare services but there are still obstacles to their effective input into social policy development in Australia. Social movements and interest groups are now more important.

For government institutions, there are some important points to remember. First, the federal system of government and the problems associated with shared responsibility for critical social policy issues between the Commonwealth and the states. Second, the absence of a Bill of Rights can limit action to pressure government on social policy reform. Third, the concentration of power and authority within the Prime Minister and Cabinet means that effective decision-making is dependent on the way Cabinet operates and its processes could well be opened up for more input and scrutiny. Policy practitioners also need to be well-versed on Cabinet procedures. Fourth, the declining membership of political parties and their reduced capacity to represent the interests of a diverse electorate presents a challenge for the policy process and there is a need for different structures to allow the representation of different voices in the policy process. Finally, the changing role of government departments and the public service, alongside the development of a number of arm's length institutions, raises the question as to whether social policy is sufficiently served by the existing institutional structures.

These changing institutional arrangements in government, the economy, and society reflect the impact of broader forces of change, including technology, economic globalisation, a greater focus on the individual in society, neo-liberal economics, and changed thinking about the management of organisations, including public sector organisations. Chapter 7 explores these changes and their wider impacts in some detail. The important point to note here is that these changes have meant increased insecurity and uncertainty for some (in terms of work and relationships), and increased choices and opportunities for others. Similar changes have taken place in the way the institutions covered in this chapter operate and the balance of power between them. There is increased power for big business and also to those at the centre of government, who may not be in a position to understand the diversity of need and interest that social policy must accommodate. Wanna and Keating (2000, p. 234) summarise some of the main institutional challenges that have arisen as a result of these and other changes in the following way:

> In a democratic polity, we need an institutional structure that is capable of balancing the main political interests—for example between a powerful executive and the democratic expression of diversity, or between governments and citizens. We need institutionalised ways of mediating between antagonistic vested interests … and ways of achieving interest integration in order to promote social cohesion … We need to discover better ways of representing diverse societal interests in policy deliberations and encouraging a better appreciation of policy choices. And in our pluralistic democracy, where there is substantial power to impede new initiatives, we need actively to seek more participative forms of governance—to open up the policy process to respond to the tapestry of diverse interests and multiple political divides, while still maintaining the overall coherence of policy.

This chapter has covered the role of Australian organisations and institutions in social policy development in Australia. However, the impact of globalisation has increased the importance of international institutions and the challenge for government decision-making, and for social policy practitioners more generally, is also to understand and engage with international institutions both within our Asia-Pacific region and globally. The development of the international human rights system, including international treaties and conventions, provides another vehicle with which to promote social policy change at a national and a state level (see Antonios 2000 for further elaboration of the important area of international action).

Part Two

THE HISTORICAL, INTERNATIONAL, AND CHANGING CONTEXT FOR ACTION

The second part of the book covers the history of Australian social policy, putting it in comparative context and finishing with a chapter about its changing nature, including emerging issues and critical debates. A sense of history is vital for anyone concerned with effective social action. On the one hand, social policies are very much path dependent: once in place they can be difficult to alter. On the other hand, things do change and when we discover just how different social policy has been in earlier generations, it reminds us that choices are always there to be made and that we can 'seize the day'. Chapter 5 highlights some of these critical choices and developments, emphasising the need to have a sense of the pattern of social policy as a whole. It suggests that we would do well to revisit the very different approaches to economic management at the time of Federation and of the post-Second World War years where social protection was embedded in a larger strategy of social investment offering a much more integrated approach to economic and social policy than we see around us today. Other great struggles around gender, immigration, and reconciliation with the Indigenous owners of the land sound the deepest reaches of the national memory with enormous import for action in contemporary Australia.

Other countries display different path dependencies and have different options open to them. Like history, comparative analysis is also an enormous instructor and stimulus to action. Why is Australian social policy so different to that in other countries? What does this say about the menu of actions available to us? Chapter 6 shows how social policy comparativists have developed their trade, emphasising in particular the emergence of the understanding of 'regime types'. It looks at explanations of welfare state difference, focusing on Australia in particular, and moves beyond the traditional focus on European welfare states to include the Asian experience. Finally, the chapter challenges current demarcations between social development and comparative social policy, calling for a more integrated discipline.

The final chapter of Part Two will be concerned with key themes and issues at play in contemporary social policy and that are likely to be driving debates and events for the foreseeable future. It begins with a review of perspectives on the significance of globalisation for making national social policy, with a particular eye to developments under the Howard government. The chapter is determinedly positive about the future. It shows how, after years of dominance of policy discourse by economic rationalism, there is now a new inclination to think in terms of the potential benefits of social investment. This is especially the case when the investment is oriented towards promoting social inclusion by developing the capacities of individuals and communities to master the challenges and transitions of what is often called today, the 'risk society'.

5
THE HISTORICAL
CONTEXT FOR ACTION

Paul Smyth

INTRODUCTION

Social policy is no exception to the rule that while we can make our own history we do not do so in circumstances of our own choosing. This weight of history in our lives will be readily apparent from our chapter on comparative social policy. Each national social policy regime is inexplicable without reference especially to certain key periods when foundations were laid and 'historic compromises' struck. History teaches us that once in place, these key institutions change only with great difficulty. The turn of the millennium has, of course, been a time of deep social policy change in many countries as a concomitant of globalisation. Key institutions are changing and with that we are witnessing a series of 'history wars' as policy actors seek to justify their ways. An understanding of the historical context of our social policy action will always be vital to success.

The price people place on historical justification for their actions has been once again illustrated in Australia over the last decade in the debate over the 'Black Arm Band' version of Australian history. The term was coined by the Melbourne historian Geoffrey Blainey in 1993 to attack the so-called 'politically correct' version of Australian history and was taken up by Prime Minister John Howard in his campaign to refocus Australian historical interpretation. Blainey believed historians were dwelling too much on the wrongs done to a variety of population groups and not celebrating sufficiently great national achievements.

Conservatives associated this view, above all, with the historian Manning Clark and, from 1996, commenced an extraordinary public campaign to discredit him. The Foreign Minister, Alexander Downer, even refused to present Clark's monumental six volume *A History of Australia* to the Georgetown University, as had been planned. In explanation, he noted that 'history is a very, very powerful weapon' (Macintyre & Clark 2003).

Because social policy typically focuses on the key social questions of the day, we ought not to be surprised to find its history a battleground. In this context, it is important to note that history is no less value-laden and infused with theory and opinion than any of the other social sciences. Facts do not simply speak for themselves. But this does not mean that anything goes; history is a discipline, as Macintyre reminds us. Historians must demonstrate familiarity with and fidelity to all the relevant source materials, an appreciation and understanding of the sometimes competing and conflicting value of these materials, a knowledge and appreciation of the preceding historical writing on the subject, and an understanding of why others will inevitably take different perspectives on the same period.

CHANGING PERSPECTIVES ON SOCIAL POLICY

As we saw in Chapter 1, the field of social policy is diverse, and, in Chapter 2, that it is informed by different values and ideologies. In this chapter, I focus on general perspectives and questions. I will observe different ways of interpreting the pattern of Australian social policy as a whole. What have been the dominant sets of ideas and key institutions and interests that have set this pattern? How much continuity and discontinuity do we find with the present? What does this tell us about the state of social policy in Australia today? Throughout this process, it is important not to treat history like a second-hand shop. We do not go looking to pick policy solutions from different periods and different contexts off the shelf as though we could apply them automatically to our own very different social, political, and economic times. Nor should we court nostalgia in our policy histories: dwelling in the 'good old days' as a substitute for action in the present. What we should look for are insights into why social policy is what it is today. Who created it? What were the key choices? What values were at stake? Was there consensus? Or, conflict? The better we can answer such questions, the better placed will we be to press for change in our own times.

From sporadic beginnings in the 1950s (Cairns 1957; Mendelsohn 1954), social policy history developed in the 1960s and 1970s as a distinct area of historical writing as people like Kewley (1973), Mendelsohn (1979), and Dickey (1980) wrote accounts of the emergence of the Australian welfare state. On the whole, they demonstrated a benign view of the evolution of the welfare state; a viewpoint rapidly overturned by the so-called 'critical school' in the 1980s. This approach reflected the influential 'new left' Marxism of the period and emphasised the way in which welfare progress was inevitably undermined by certain structural features of capitalism that guaranteed continued exploitation of the working class and persistent poverty (Kennedy 1982, 1985; Watts 1987). Other histories focused more on the way the wage system had operated as an alternative form of redistribution (Castles 1985; Macintyre 1985) and developed into a distinctive 'Australian way' of doing social and economic policy (Smyth & Cass 1998).

By the end of the 1990s, social policy history writing was in decline. In the vacuum that resulted, social policy history was reduced to the recycled clichés of journalists and political sociologists. In particular, Kelly's (1992) notion of an 'Australian settlement' created at Federation and ending with globalisation in the 1980s, became a pervasive interpretation in the non-historical literature. His perspective was heavily shaped by the context of economic deregulation in the late 1980s and early 1990s. The deregulation of the economy appeared to clash with a range of time-honoured social policy values and institutions. Kelly believed these had formed a pattern of 'protection' designed to create a 'fortress' shielding Australia from a hostile world. The pattern created at Federation had five 'pillars': White Australia, tariff protection, wage arbitration, state paternalism, and imperial benevolence. The 'settlement' metaphor was in fact a poor guide to what was often an 'unsettled' history. As we shall see, it took no satisfactory account of the 'social investment' or 'developmental state' (1900s), nor of the 'Keynesian economic state' (1940s); and, as Stokes (2002) identified, omitted the dimensions of race (the doctrine of *terra nullius*), religion, and gender. Their inclusion (and we will add here, the role of civil society) points not to a static settlement but to a constantly evolving and contested 'Australian way' as the real context for thinking about the general historical context for social policy action.

THE NINETEENTH CENTURY

Recapturing a sense of the diversity and complexity of this history is helped by a widening of the usual chronology (typically beginning in 1901 with Federation) to take in key features of the nineteenth century policy landscape. In particular, we can better appreciate the sorry history of race relations, the importance attached to civil society and especially religious organisations, as well as the rise of those egalitarian and democratic social movements that gave rise to those social policies that once earned us a progressive social reputation.

Indigenous people—still no 'settlement'

Although estimates can vary, the Aboriginal and Torres Strait Islander peoples had occupied their lands for approximately 40 000 years. The invasion/settlement by white people from 1788 led to a varied history of destruction, dispossession, and bloodshed across the colonies, leaving policy conflicts that remain unresolved to this day. By the end of the nineteenth century, and not without a significant history of humanitarian and missionary welfare work, a policy of protection and assimilation had come to prevail. Based on conceptions of the racial inferiority of the Indigenous peoples, this policy led to their removal to settlements, loss of control over their children, loss of control over their savings, and even loss of the right to freely marry the person of their own choosing. Ravaged also by diseases introduced by white people, the Aborigines and Torres Strait Islanders were regarded by the white society as a disappearing race—a 'dying race'—for whom the policies of protection would 'smooth the dying pillow'. At Federation, the Constitution omitted them from the census and excluded them from the definition of the Australian peoples for whom the new Commonwealth government would govern (Stokes 2002).

By the 1930s, it was apparent that the Indigenous population was growing and this led to an intensification of control and segregation in settlements of those who were 'full blooded' and a policy of racial intermarriage for others in the hope that their dark colour would be 'bred out'. From this time also there was a reinvigoration of Aboriginal political activism that was to culminate in significant victories three decades later. After the Second World War, however, there was a new emphasis on assimilation. In 1948, Indigenous people were formally accorded citizenship but because this was compromised by a variety of state-based legislation (voting in Western Australia, for example, was not allowed), it remained largely an empty shell. A 1967 referendum finally reversed the omissions of the Constitution and paved the way for a series of legislative changes that overcame former barriers to the exercise of citizenship rights. Indigenous social policy action at this time was distinguished by public protest with the freedom bus ride across New South Wales, the Aboriginal tent embassy in Canberra, and street marches. However, achieving a formal equality of citizenship rights still did not lead to a substantive equality of livelihoods and life chances. Indigenous people in Australia today remain vastly unequal in terms of all the social and economic indicators (Chesterman & Galligan 1997; Hunter 2001).

Alongside this quest for equality has been the equally important theme of recognition of Aboriginal and Torres Strait Islander difference. For all those years that Indigenous peoples were considered outside of white political society they carried on in their own traditional cultural and political domain. They continued to regard themselves as the owners of the land and held a special attachment to it. Accordingly, they fought to have these land rights recognised by the non-Aboriginal society and to have their own wider sovereignty as a people to be recognised in a treaty of reconciliation. Some recognition of land rights did begin in the 1970s, reaching a high point in the Mabo decision of the High Court in 1992, which overturned the doctrine of *terra nullius*. By this legal fiction, Indigenous peoples had been held to have had no inherent rights to their land pre-existing the white invasion (Wilson et al. 1996). Since that time, there has been slow progress on the realisation of land rights and little action on a broader treaty acknowledging traditional sovereignty. The lack of improvement in social and economic well-being has in fact created a certain crisis around the future of social policy in relation to Indigenous peoples. So-called 'welfare dependency' is often blamed for this, but in reality a better future is unimaginable without more, not less, investment in the socio-economic opportunities of the Indigenous peoples. Moreover, after such a history, it is equally difficult to imagine a lasting 'settlement' without some treaty of reconciliation that affirms and respects the special rights of the Indigenous people as the original owners of the land.

An age of charities

The nineteenth century was also the 'age of charities', especially church-based charities in Australian social policy (Dickey 1980). Most of the welfare histories written in the 1970s and 1980s consigned their work to a dark age of welfare residualism before the twentieth century development of the welfare state replaced the charity system with one based on the social rights of citizenship. In the 1990s, however, with the eclipse of the welfare state, we have seen a revival of interest in the role of civil society and, with that, the term 'charity' has re-emerged as a popular term to describe the role of the community welfare sector.

The term charity is, of course, layered with many meanings that no doubt contribute to its mercurial adaptability and survivability in social policy discourse. Within the Judeo-Christian traditions alone we soon distinguish biblical, medieval Catholic, and evangelical protestant versions among others. In most writings about nineteenth century Australian social policy, much is made of the so-called 'protestant work ethic'—about which the great German sociologist Max Weber wrote—and that informed the construction of the role of charities in the nineteenth century. This ethic challenged earlier medieval views of poverty as an unavoidable presence ('the poor will always be with you') and even a state to be emulated by religious communities as a reminder of the need for reliance on each other and on God. The new ethic saw nothing inevitable or desirable about poverty at all. It was to be eliminated. A new emphasis on individual responsibility led to poverty being associated with bad moral behaviour. At the same time it suggested that the individual achievement of wealth was a sign of God's favour (Garton 1990).

This protestant emphasis on the spiritual importance of individual economic achievement coalesced with the new economic understanding that the free market not the mercantilist state was the real source of national wealth (Adam Smith). Also contributing was the political ideology of laissez-faire liberalism, which was all about releasing the individual from that dependency on Church and monarch that had characterised medieval society. These sorts of ideas created the policy context for the 1834 *Poor Law* amendments in the United Kingdom, whose spirit informed practices in the Australian colonies. Here the aim was to end charity as it had been known in its medieval forms and institute in its place a regime of what we popularly call today 'tough love'. Only the 'truly deserving' were to receive assistance. In the United Kingdom, work houses—whose horrors were exposed in the writings of Charles Dickens—were set up. These were meant to stigmatise the receipt of charity or welfare so that no-one would want it. You had to work for your assistance and the assistance was designed on the principle of 'less eligibility'—that is, whatever you received should be less in value than the lowest wage available in the free market.

These were the kinds of ideas that were influential on the development of charities in nineteenth century Australia—although it should be noted that mainly because of sparse and spread-out populations, the new *Poor Law* scheme was never formally established in the colonies. Governments typically had to provide the funds to maintain the charities that simply could not survive on free giving (Dickey 1980). It should also be noted that the world of colonial charity was in fact much more diverse than our older standard histories would have it. Other Christian communities associated with people like Sister Mary McKillop of the Catholic Sisters of St Joseph, and later Father Gerard Tucker of the Anglican Brotherhood of St Laurence, held very different attitudes to the poor, avoiding in particular the kind of severity of judgment associated with the evangelicals. Moreover, this charitable work needs to be put into the context of the widespread operation of Friendly Societies (Oddfellows, Foresters, Hibernians, Australian Natives, etc.), cooperatives, and other forms of mutual assistance that also reflected a popular desire to create what we might call today a 'welfare society' rather than a welfare state (Lyons 2001). Certainly in terms of being willing and able to insure themselves for health and welfare, Australians led the world in the early period (Roe 1976b).

This charitable activity carried on into the twentieth century, with a new layer of organisations added in the interwar period with business sector service clubs such as Rotary. At the same time, the direct role of government in welfare provision grew across the twentieth century and especially in the 1970s when the achievement of a welfare state brought a flourishing of community-based welfare groups. Indeed, of the 60 000 groups counted in the early 1980s, almost one-half had been established in the 1970s when programs like the Australian Assistance Plan sought to open up government in new partnerships with the community (Garton 1990). In this welfare state development the basis of welfare provision shifted decisively towards a universal, social-rights-based model. Reflecting this shift, the welfare sector now styled itself in terms of 'non-government organisations' rather than charities to reflect a new relationship with government based on the idea of welfare as a matter of rights and justice not of charity. Subsequently, with the return of economic rationalism in the 1980s and 1990s, a re-emphasis on the market not the state as the real source of wealth has led to attacks on welfare and 'welfare dependency' that are very much in the spirit of the nineteenth century. This economic libertarianism has also coalesced with a resurgent Christian fundamentalism, which some see as presaging a return of religious values as significant factors in early twenty-first century social policy development (Maddox 2005). Certainly we have seen a dilution of social rights to welfare, which has led to the rebirth of practices designed to sort out the deserving from the undeserving poor and so re-stigmatise the receipt of welfare. Curiously, old-fashioned charities such as the Salvation Army, the Benevolent Society, and Mission Australia have returned to the fore of a sector that is once again popularly labelled as a charity with little apparent sense of the ironies so incurred.

A democratic and egalitarian temper

The third defining feature of nineteenth century social politics was its democratic and egalitarian temper. It was the rise of this social radicalism and the accompanying conservative reaction that produced the intense class conflict of the 1890s, which then led into the social policy 'historic compromise' of the federation period.

Australia is styled as a 'settler society' that was 'born modern'. Unlike the old countries of the United Kingdom and Europe, there was no aristocracy against which to rebel. A self-styled gentry who had monopolised the pastoral lands in the first half of the nineteenth century were easily pushed aside by the ascendant middle and working classes. Pastoral lands were 'unlocked' and the gold rushes ushered in new populations and opportunities. The Eureka uprising symbolises the democratic temper of the colonies where most males had the vote by 1859—long before most comparable countries. Extensive industrial legislation, including an eight-hour working day, was way in advance of most (hence the tag 'working man's paradise'). The late nineteenth century witnessed a remarkable unionisation of the workforce and the creation of the Australian Labor Party (ALP), which led to the world's first Labour government in the state of Queensland in 1899. The ALP came to enjoy a level of electoral support unrivalled in any other country before the Great Depression (Smyth 2005).

The 1890s was a period of intense economic depression, when trade union protests were put down with considerable state force. With Federation, a politics of compromise developed that was aimed at knitting together the interests of labour and their conservative\liberal opponents. In fact, at this time much of the impetus for social and economic reform came from the non-labour side of politics. Here the ideas of a new liberalism developed in the United Kingdom by people like J.S. Mill and T.H. Green found champions in Australia in leaders like Alfred Deakin. Theirs was not the negative liberty of libertarian laissez-faire (freedom from), but the positive liberty of social liberalism (freedom to) (Beilharz et al. 1992). Emphasis was placed on the real world barriers to self realisation that citizens can face on the uneven playing fields of capitalist societies, and on the obligation of the state to remove these obstacles. With Federation, a political compromise was effected with the labour movement that would last until the Great Depression of the 1930s and the Second World War. A dynamic of conflict followed by compromise was established that was to be played out several times across the twentieth century, thus lending the 'Australian way' of doing social policy its key ideological features. So what was the social policy achievement at Federation?

FEDERATION AND THE SOCIAL INVESTMENT STATE

Although the nineteenth century social policy was closely linked to the era of laissez-faire capitalism, it would be a mistake to think that colonial economic policy was strictly ordered around Adam Smith's model of the free market. In fact, unlike America, colonial economic development was very much government-led. Until the 1930s, Australia had proportionately, the largest public economic sector in the world. There were many reasons for this, but by Federation it reflected the prevailing view in economic thought that an active 'developmental state' was needed if Australia was going to do more than simply rely on its natural resource advantages and develop a more diverse, competitive industrial base. This 'nation building' approach was, of course, well-adapted to the new consciousness of nationhood. It also set the tone for social policy where what we might call today the 'social investment state' played a complementary role in ensuring that everyone had fair and reasonable opportunities and rewards. This social investment approach encompassed a range of policy areas including early childhood and public health, but there were two policies in particular that had a special impact on the future development of Australian social policy: the introduction of the old age and invalid pension, and the minimum wage (Smyth 2004).

The Constitution gave the Commonwealth responsibility for old age and invalid pensions, which were enacted in 1908. It represented the first major welfare policy to depart from the ideological principles that had informed the 'age of charity' (Dickey 1980). Income support became a matter of statutory right for Australian citizens, even though initially there was a 'good character' test and the Indigenous populations, Asians, and aliens were defined out of entitlement. In an albeit limited way, what Dickey called the 'age of rights' had begun. Interestingly, public debate reflected a sense of what we might call today 'mutual obligation'. The pension was not seen as 'something for nothing', but rather as an entitlement because of the services the aged had rendered to the community throughout their working lives (at this point most did not pay income taxes). All citizens were thought to have contributed to the Commonwealth, not just government officials and armed service people as in the past. As the New South Wales parliamentarian, E.W. O'Sullivan said, 'We do not want anything in the nature of outdoor relief, or in the form of a dole'. Rather the pensioners were to be seen as people with a 'right to come to the State that they have so well served and claim this pension just the same as a soldier or a sailor would' (Kewley 1973, p. 4).

The pension was not, nevertheless, universal. Rather than institute a national insurance scheme in the manner of Germany under Bismarck in the 1870s, which to some extent was seen to be impractical with such a dispersed population, the Australian pension was to be targeted to those who most needed it. It had a means test. It has also been described as categorical—that is, it is a right assigned to a statutorily defined population group. This can be a positive design feature in that it gives flexibility: statutorily defined groups can be more easily modified by parliaments when circumstances dictate. At times, eligibility for the old age pension has been near universal, while at others it has been more restrictive. Third, the pensions were to be paid for from general tax revenue. These three features of means tests, categorical, and general revenue financing were to define the future pattern of the Australian welfare system.

The other major social policy development in the federation period was the institution of the minimum wage. The Commonwealth had the power to legislate in industrial disputes and it established an Industrial Arbitration Court. In 1907, Justice Higgins established the 'living wage' in handing down the Harvester judgment. This minimum wage (then 42 shillings a week) was meant to be 'fair and reasonable', an amount sufficient for a worker to satisfy 'the normal needs of the average employee regarded as a human being living in a civilised community'. Reflecting the times, it was of course implicitly a system for white, male breadwinners. However, as Dickey noted, no other policy did as much as the minimum wage 'to transform the lives of a whole sector of the community whose welfare in the nineteenth century had so often been a problem of selective charity' (Dickey 1980, p. 125). Sawer (2003) shows that it was much in keeping with the principles of the 'new liberalism', which acknowledged that inequalities of economic power vitiate the apparent freedom of contract between employers and employees in a market society. A similar influence on the Harvester judgment derived from the Catholic social teaching found in the encyclical *Rerum Novarum* of 1890. Castles (1985) later coined the phrase a 'wage earners' welfare' to underline the fact that, in Australia, the system of wage regulation developed as a form of social protection by other means.

It is important to note that the new social policy model forged at federation was meant as a safety net to underpin the welfare society. It was not designed to create a welfare state. The preference remained for individuals, families, and communities to meet their income support and health needs through friendly societies and other forms of private insurance. Through recognition of a working life, the old age pension underlined the productivist values at the heart of the Australian way. Likewise, wage justice was meant to make work pay. The system nevertheless remained informed by the nineteenth century optimism about the free market as the source of national wealth. The social investment state aimed to work with the market not against it, enabling all citizens to be effective participants. This productive orientation of Australian social policy continued through till the 1970s, when, reflecting a trend throughout industrialised countries, social policy became identified not with production but with redistribution, even to the point where the criterion of welfare state success was taken to be 'decommodification', which implied the removal from rather than insertion of people into productive activity. Reinventing this productive dimension of social policy is a central challenge for policy makers in welfare states today.

SECOND WORLD WAR: EMPLOYMENT AND IMMIGRATION

The next major phase of social policy development came in two instalments: the 'economic state' in the 1940s and the 'welfare state' in the 1970s. The first was concerned more with securing the economic foundation of social security through full employment and the second with a belated transition from the welfare society model to a welfare state. Both phases shared a common policy framework in the shift from a free market to a 'mixed economy'. In the new, Keynesian 'mixed economy', the market remained a key source of economic organisation, but only within an overarching policy framework in which macro social and economic goals were established through the political process.

The history of this reassignment of the role of the market from master to servant of the common wealth is one of the great dramas of the twentieth century. Against the background of the Great Depression of the 1930s—in Australia, the economic stagnation showed up in an official unemployment record of 30 per cent—the state came to be pitted against markets as an economically and socially superior basis of organisation. Communism and Fascism emerged as serious working alternatives to liberal capitalism. During the Second World War, the Keynesian-style 'mixed economy' emerged as a compromise. Markets and individual freedoms would remain where possible but would be overridden where necessary in the interests of the common wealth. In policy terms, this was expressed in the commitment to maintaining full employment in the White Paper of 1945. A new optimism about what could be achieved through the 'mixed economy' was also expressed in ambitious plans for public works— for example, the Snowy Mountains Hydro Electric Scheme—and for mass immigration (Smyth & Cass 1998).

In a Keynesian-style 'mixed economy', the volume of investment (which determines the amount of employment) was to be moderated by the government in order to maintain the economy in a state of full employment. This in turn required that employers and workers would moderate wages and prices to prevent inflation. It also required a Reserve Bank with full employment as well as low inflation in its charter. In addition, taxpayers had to agree to higher (and for the majority it was first time) taxes in order to ensure a sufficient investment fund. Accordingly, the Commonwealth took over responsibility for income taxation from the states. These were all significant new policy instruments allowing for a new social framework around market activity. In these new ways, individuals had to abridge their self-interest if governments were to achieve and maintain full employment. For social policy more generally, it was important because it underwrote a wide range of social investment as economically efficient as well as socially valuable. Australia was a strong advocate of full employment on the world stage, ensuring that it was included in the objectives of the United Nations as well as the rules and norms of the postwar multilateral trade system (Smyth 2004).

While not ignored in Australia at this time, welfare reform did not achieve the priority accorded in other countries. The British welfare state, for example, emerged with a national health system and a range of measures to combat what William Beveridge (1942) called, the five 'giant evils' of 'Want', 'Squalor', 'Ignorance', 'Disease', and 'Idleness'. In Australia, by means of a successful constitutional referendum in 1946, the Commonwealth took up powers for 'the provision of maternity allowances, widow's pensions, child endowment, unemployment, pharmaceutical, sickness and hospital benefits, medical and dental services (but so as not to authorise any form of civil conscription), benefits to students and family allowances'. Each of these areas witnessed the creation of new benefits and services in a way that continued the pattern established with the old age pension: means tested, categorical, and paid from general revenue (Kewley 1973). The safety net was extended rather than replaced by the systems of universal rights as developed in Europe.

More dramatic in this period than welfare reform was the change to migration policies. Matching the expansive approach to economic investment under Keynesianism was the plan to radically increase the supply of labour (and, it should be noted, defence capabilities, following the extreme national insecurity of the war). A program of mass immigration led to more than 3 million new arrivals in three decades from over 100 different countries. In social policy terms, this program began under the shadow of the White Australia policy established at Federation. Thus only Anglo Celts and some racially similar groups from Western and Northern Europe had been admitted before the war. While postwar demand pressures opened the way to greater diversity, the older policies of paternalism and assimilation dominated until the end of the 1960s. Accordingly it was believed that new arrivals should shed their former cultures and become more or less indistinguishable from the host population. In the 1960s, this began to give way to the policy of integration, whereby it was recognised that the process of 'blending in' would take much longer than thought so that in the interim there should be some tolerance of difference. The first relaxation of the White Australia policy in relation to Asian immigration was witnessed in 1966, and by the 1970s Australia had officially embraced the ideal of a multicultural society. It has been attacked from the Left for being more about lifestyles than life chances and by the right for endangering national unity. Nevertheless, multiculturalism has proved a particularly durable framework for successfully settling newcomers.

Full employment was thus laid down as the 'royal road to social security' in postwar social policy and it went hand in hand with the massive increase in immigration so as to rapidly expand the Australian economy. Even more than the Harvester judgment, it demonstrates the productivist values that have characterised Australian social policy historically. As Mishra has observed of Japan, we can say of Australia: in this period, full employment was our primary 'welfare' policy (Mishra 2004; Smyth 1994). Today the social policy problem is often presented as the issue of 'welfare dependency'; as though the introduction of unemployment benefits somehow led to the problem of high unemployment. The fact is that take up of benefits never became a policy issue until governments abandoned their 1945 obligation to ensure paid work for all those who want it.

THE AFFLUENT SOCIETY AND THE WELFARE STATE

By the 1970s, it looked as though the economic problems had been solved. Social welfare issues took centre stage. The 'welfare society' model appeared to be breaking down and it was Australia's turn to adopt the 'welfare state' approach. A range of social problems had emerged in the 1950s and 1960s to do with immigration, women's entry into the workforce, poverty among the aged, and suburbanisation, together with the rise of new social reform movements around land rights and gender issues in particular. John K. Galbraith's book, *The Affluent Society*, captured the new reformist agenda based on the facts of public squalor amid private affluence. Moreover, the escalating costs of services such as education and health simply proved too expensive and complex for the old networks of non-government organisations to meet. Increasingly they began to work in a new mixed economy of the 'welfare state' mirroring the mixed economy of the Keynesian 'economic state' (Smyth & Wearing 2002).

The principles behind this worldwide shift in social policy had been captured by Wilensky and Lebeaux in the USA (1965) and by Marshall and Titmuss in terms of the move from a residual (charity model) to an institutional (universal, welfare state) social policy regime. The new approach flowered in the period from 1972–75 when the Labor Party, under Prime Minister Whitlam, was in office. A national health service was implemented along with local area development programs (Australian Assistance Plan), free universities, and an aged pension extension to all people over 70 years of age. Major steps were taken towards the recognition of land rights for Indigenous peoples and multiculturalism informed immigration policy. It was as though the circle of social rights initiated at Federation was now widening to include all Australians.

This was especially the case for women. The Harvester judgment had been based on a male breadwinner model. A shift began towards a dual breadwinner model with policies to give equal pay and the abolition of the family element of the male wage; child care provisions; and affirmative action and antidiscrimination legislation (Bryson 1992; Edwards & Margery 1995). As with Indigenous issues, this was also a period of very public advocacy and protest. Associated with the women's liberation movement, this phase of radical action gave way in the 1980s to a different approach to policy action that focused on gaining power within the institutions of government. These reforms were incomplete in that women continued to take home less in wages because they were employed more in jobs at the lower end of the pay scale, such as retail and hospitality, and because they still undertook most of the unpaid domestic work, including caring, and therefore were less likely to be in paid work. Reforms to the income support system were longer in coming. However, beginning with the creation of the sole parent pension and its extension to males in 1977, older polices based on assumptions of gender difference (and dependency on males) have been replaced by the assumption of sameness between the sexes. In particular, there is still inadequate recognition of the responsibilities of caring (still female-dominated) and an absence of services and entitlements (such as paid maternity leave) that allow women to combine caring with full labour-market participation.

Many of the social welfare reform ideas that surfaced in the 1960s and 1970s were to define the social agenda for the rest of the century. However, the social policy framework of economic activity provided by the full employment objective came unstuck with the worldwide economic instability of the 1970s. The remainder of our story concerns the undoing of the economic policy tradition based first on 'developmental state' and then the Keynesian 'economic state', and the way these developments in economic policy have acted back on social policy to undermine the legitimacy of the 'welfare state'.

WORLD RECESSION AND THE ACCORD

The 1980s is synonymous in English-speaking countries with that political triumph of neo-liberalism associated with Thatcher and Reagan. In Australia, Labor governments faced the challenge of developing a progressive social policy while accomplishing the kind of economic restructuring that was required with the end of the postwar economic boom. Unemployment was at 10 per cent in the early 1980s, in an economy over-reliant on commodity exports such as wool and minerals at a time of rapid decline in their prices. Policy options took two forms.

The postwar boom had been carried along by a flood of private investment, so much so that little of the active government role in investment and indus-try policy envisaged in the 1940s had been taken up by the conservative Men-zies government (1949–66). According to Capling (2001), this left Australia ill-prepared for the kind of international competition in manufacturing that it had to face in the 1980s if it was to restore its export income. Labor had either to strengthen the role of government in the economy (refurbish the 'mixed economy') or to rely more strongly on free market forces (economic rationalism).

Labor began with the first alternative: an agreement known as the *Accord* (1983) was reached between the government and the unions. The government would pursue full employment while unions would exercise the wage restraint needed to prevent inflation. Tax cuts and a 'social wage' of social services, pensions, and benefits were offered to workers in compensation for lower wages. Such bargaining was established practice in Europe and especially in the Scandinavian countries, which were seen as a model. However, the venture ultimately unwound as 'economic rationalist' ideas took an increasing hold on economic policy. Economic policy became increasingly libertarian and deregulated, while social policy was left to carry the equity burden.

There were significant social policy achievements—for example, universal health care was re-established through Medicare, child care was expanded, university places increased (but with the introduction of HECS), and an expansion of spending on 'active' welfare as the prospects for re-inclusion in the labour market for the unemployed and single parents was becoming increasingly dependent on training and education. Nevertheless, the goals of social policy were increasingly redefined and expectations minimised in a policy pattern dominated by the market-based approaches to restructuring. Indicative of the narrowing space occupied by social policy was the controversy accompanying the increased targeting of welfare. For example, the Labor government made the universal Family Allowance payment income-tested and introduced a generous but targeted Family Allowance Supplement in 1988. Critics attacked the retreat from universalism, arguing that it would end up stigmatising recipients, creating poverty traps, reducing welfare state electoral support, and leading to an overall reduction in the resources available for welfare. Others defended targeting as a strategy suited to a time of economic constraint, a remaking of the 'Australian way'. This 'refurbished wage earner welfare' model came to be accepted by many as a viable social policy model to underpin the economic policy challenges presented by globalisation (Smyth & Cass 1998).

These Labor experiments left an ambiguous legacy. Some saw them as an end of the 'nation building' tradition of the seven decades since Federation (Beilharz 1994; Pusey 1991). Others have constructed them as an exercise in the politics of the 'Third Way'—that is, a new mix of economic neo-liberalism and social democratic social policy. Questions remained as to the long-term electoral sustainability of such a regime in Australia where productive values had been central to social policy for so long. The ever increasing resort to targeting invited that decline in legitimacy specified by the critics, a decline that accelerated at the end of the century.

LOOKING FORWARD, LOOKING BACK

The social policy impact of the Howard years will be taken up in Chapter 7, when we will consider current and future social policy trends. What do these key themes and perspectives suggest about social policy action in Australia today? Most commentators have observed a break down of the forms of social intervention and protection that had been built up across the twentieth century in an approach that is more free market oriented than any seen in earlier periods. They have queried the long-term sustainability of such an approach. Do we face now a period of social policy rebuilding? What forms might it take?

There are, of course, many ways of making sense of the historical developments alluded to in this chapter. One key interpretation that has been offered highlights the achievements of social rights in the 1970s and their subsequent abridgement. In this regard, some see in current approaches to welfare reform a recandescence of the 'welfare paternalism' of the nineteenth century, and a creeping privatisation of health care and education that further unwinds earlier citizenship entitlements. Others focus on the impact of labour market deregulation, declaring the end of the era of 'wage earners' welfare'. Clearly there is a 'crisis' in the tradition of the 'Fair Go', while even supporters of the neo-liberal thrust of Australian economic policy in recent decades now argue that the subordination of social to economic policy has gone too far (Dawkins & Kelly 2003).

The conclusion of this chapter is that it has been a mistake to interpret the Australian tradition in a way that has pitted the demands of economic reform against social policy as has the dominant interpretation associated with the 'Australian settlement'. It is historically wrong to think of the twentieth century Australian social policy project as an exercise in protecting Australians from the global market place. Both the 'social investment' and the Keynesian 'mixed economy' were more about overcoming market failures in the quest for more productive and sustainable economies than they were about restricting market forces. Likewise, the welfare state experiment of the 1970s had nothing to do with shielding Australians from global markets and everything to do with tackling public squalor amid private affluence. Other historical perspectives in this chapter remind us that public policy cannot simply become absorbed into the quest for economic success. There are the ongoing struggles around gender, immigration, and reconciliation with the Indigenous owners of the land. Together they reveal not only that social policy history is very much a contested terrain, but a knowledge of that terrain is indispensable for action today.

6

AUSTRALIAN SOCIAL POLICY IN AN INTERNATIONAL CONTEXT

Paul Smyth

INTRODUCTION

Social policy analysis is taking on an ever increasing international and comparative character. Interest in comparative social policy emerged in the early 1980s, several decades after the great postwar expansion of welfare states in industrialised countries, and this left its mark on the early literature. The focus of early comparative research was very much European and Anglo-American, and reflected a concern first to put together statistical evidence of expenditure growth in welfare states that had become so central a feature of postwar political life. Initial studies tended to be less developed in terms of theory. A second phase of comparative research was more preoccupied with classifying particular national experiences within a welfare state typology. Today we witness an explosion of comparative social policy. In part, this is driven by the concentration of nation states into regional blocs such as the European Union. It also reflects the rise of social policy in rapidly industrialised Asian countries. Beyond that, everywhere there is a much more global discourse around welfare and development. Earlier, artificial distinctions between the study of 'social policy' as a study confined to industrialised countries and 'social development', which is reserved for developing economies, are breaking down. All of this makes comparative social policy analysis an exciting and essential item for the research and study of social policy today.

Comparative social policy data can have a jolting effect on many taken-for-granted assumptions regarding national social policy performance. Many Australians, for example, have an ingrained belief that their country has an extravagantly high level of social expenditures and a correspondingly heavy burden of taxation. The data invariably comes as a shock. Table 6.1 provides a summary of how Australia compares with selected OECD countries (for which most comparable data is available) according to some key indicators. It shows, for example, that in the early 2000s, compared with most other countries we had a low level of taxation and of government social expenditure, but that we target our payments much more heavily than most towards the bottom third of the population. And while a number of countries have higher levels of poverty than we experience, we are certainly not one of the countries with very low levels of poverty or inequality.

Such data gets us thinking. How did these differences happen? Does high spending translate into more well-being for the people? Or, perhaps, less? And what about policy transfers? Can policies that work in one country be easily imported by another? Such questions become increasingly urgent as globalisation intensifies comparative scrutiny. Can social policy generosity coexist with economic efficiency? What are the optimal welfare arrangements that should be recommended by international organisations with a responsibility for raising living standards across the globe; organisations such as the United Nations, Organisation for Economic Cooperation and Development, World Bank, and International Monetary Fund? Such social policy comparisons arise with increasing urgency around the globe as economic internationalisation proceeds apace.

COMPARATIVE SOCIAL POLICY RESEARCH

The first wave of comparative analysis was at a very general level. It focused on identifying the broad aggregates of social spending in the newly developed welfare states (Flora & Heidenheimer 1981). Explanations of welfare state growth were of a functionalist or structuralist type. There were two rival interpretations: the 'industrialisation' account and the Marxist (structuralist) version; a rivalry that broadly reflected the dominant sociological paradigms of the time. Some viewed welfare states as the more or less logical outcome of the industrialisation process. Pre-industrial societies were much more rurally based, with longstanding traditional arrangements for meeting social need via extended families, larger civil society groupings, churches, and other social forms encouraging reciprocity. Industrialisation brought not just new productive technologies but a wider transformation of social life characterised by urbanisation, individualisation, and an increasing dependency on the market to meet socio-economic needs. In this view, it was more or less inevitable that some groups would be excluded from the market, such as the aged, disabled and sick, and those for whom there were no longer the traditional support systems in place. A 'welfare state' inevitably evolved to cater for these groups (Cutright 1965; Wilensky 1975).

Table 6.1 Indicators of economic and social difference across selected OECD countries in the late 1990s/early 2000s

Country	Relative Poverty %	Child Poverty %	Income Inequality Gini	Public Social Spending % GDP	Proportion of Government Transfers to Bottom Three Deciles	Taxation Revenue % GDP	Employment to Population Ratio: Males	Employment to Population Ratio: Females
Australia	11.2	11.6	30.5	18	37.2	32.6	76.4	62.2
Austria	9.3	13.3	25.2	26		48.5	76.0	61.5
Canada	10.3	13.6	30.1	17.8	22.0	39.2	76.5	67.7
Denmark	4.3	2.4	22.5	29.2	36.1	52.2	79.7	70.5
Finland	6.4	3.4	26.1	24.8	31.3	48.4	69.0	65.7
France	7.0	7.3	27.3	28.5	27.6		68.9	56.7
Germany	9.8	12.8	27.7	27.4	22.3	43.5	70.4	58.7
Greece	13.5	12.4	34.5	24.3		41.8	72.5	44.0
Italy	12.9	15.7	34.7	24.4	14.1	44.1	69.7	42.7
Japan	15.3	14.3	31.4	16.9	15.7	29.9	79.8	56.8
Netherlands	6.0	9.0	25.1	21.8	29.8	41.9	80.2	64.9
New Zealand	10.4	16.3	33.7	18.5	31.2	39.1	79.3	65.8
Norway	6.3	3.6	26.1	23.9	43.8	56.3	78.8	72.9
Sweden	5.3	3.6	24.3	28.9	29.5	54.6	75.6	72.8
UK	11.4	16.2	32.6	21.8	34.7	38.3	79.3	66.4
USA	17.0	21.7	35.7	14.8	17.6	29.8	76.9	65.7

Source Keating 2004a; OECD 2005

Notes: Exact year for individual country may vary and for Australia is generally for 1999.

Countries selected are those for which comparable data is available.

Poverty rates are proportion of population in relevant households with less than 50% of median equivalised disposable income at around 2000.

Child poverty is proportion of children in households with less that 50% median income.

The Gini coefficient is a way of measuring the overall inequality in a country. A Gini of zero indicates equality and the higher the Gini, the greater the overall inequality.

Public social spending and taxation is as a proportion of GDP.

Social expenditure figures are for 2001 and tax for 2002.

Employment to population ratios are the proportion of the working-age population in some form of paid work in 2003.

The Marxist (structuralist) interpretation saw the evolution of the welfare state less as a natural evolution and more a product of a fundamentally conflicting set of class relations at the heart of capitalist pathways to modernisation. In this view, welfare states did not arise as a natural, rational, or inevitable response to meeting social need. Rather they arose as a way to resolve or contain the class conflict created by the adoption of a capitalist mode of production and the need to reproduce labour. On the one hand, governments were compelled to guarantee and promote the capital accumulation of the ruling class in order to drive forward the development process. On the other, if the system was to survive, the working class had to acknowledge it as legitimate and in their interest. With the development of the prototypical welfare state in Germany in the 1870s by Chancellor Bismarck, for example, the growth of social policy was thought to follow this logic of legitimation (O'Connor 1973).

Parallel to this early accounting for welfare state development was an ever increasing comparative literature looking at particular social policy areas or particular social groups, and doing so from a diverse range of disciplinary perspectives. By the late 1980s, comparative social policy had become a distinctive field of both social policy research and teaching (Clasen 1999).

The second wave of comparative social policy developed in the 1990s. Attention began to shift from comparing broad aggregates of social spending to understanding the different purposes of such spending within the overall pattern of public policy. Gross spending figures do not differentiate between how money is spent. For example, a conservative welfare state may be a big spender but in ways that simply reinforce existing social relations in terms of equality, access to services, etc.

The functionalist/structuralist explanations of welfare state development also came under criticism. They implied an inevitability about welfare state development that was not matched by evidence. For example, they did not account for the different time frames for welfare state emergence, nor for social policy diversity within similarly industrialised societies. New explanations began to focus on the political agency that had produced these differences. Most influential was the particular approach that highlighted the role of the working class as political agent (the so-called 'power resource' school) of social policy development. Here working-class strength was seen as a precondition of welfare state strength. Studies focused on correlations between left-wing political strength (evidenced, for example, in periods of left party government, or in voting behaviours) and welfare state advance.

Of particular note in these studies was the importance of historical beginnings of welfare regimes often interpreted in terms of 'historic compromises' or 'historical settlements'. This emphasis on the apparent long-term durability or immutability of original institutions once set in place gained increasing influence in the 1990s as observers such as Pierson (1994) pointed out that in spite of all of the rhetoric of welfare state dismantling in the 1980s especially, the institutional substance had remained largely intact. Only recently has this focus on institutions as the key to understanding welfare state formations been challenged by scholars seeking to put new emphasis on the power of ideas and the way new ideational paradigms can in fact produce long-term change at the most fundamental level, even in institutions of long standing (Hall & Soskice 2001; Kingdon 1984).

TYPES OF WELFARE REGIMES

Besides these concerns with accounting for different developmental pathways, the major preoccupation in comparative studies has been with developing typologies of welfare states. Decades earlier, researchers like Wilensky and Lebeaux (1965) had written of the difference between a residual and institutional phase of welfare state development, a distinction later taken up into comparative social policy by Titmuss (1974). Titmuss observed that there was no linear historical sequence from the residual to the institutional but that both forms could be found in countries of otherwise similar economic development. His concern with taxonomy was reinvigorated by the very influential Swedish comparativist, Esping-Andersen (1990). His approach to welfare state classification reflected an understanding of social expenditure as expressing the achievement of the social rights of citizenship. In line with T.H. Marshal's understanding, people's citizenship status is thought to compete with their class position. A strong welfare state in this view is one where there is a high level of decommodification and also reduction in class stratification.

An important if difficult concept, commodification refers to the way in which a capitalist economy turns people's labour into a commodity to be bought and sold in the market place (indeed everything becomes 'for sale' in a fully marketised society). The granting of social rights, by contrast, decommodifies people by giving them access to resources through the state on the basis of their citizenship. To this extent they become able to live without relying on the market, thus allowing people's welfare to be less dependent on their market value. From this point of view, Esping-Andersen observed that in some welfare states, such as the United States of America, social policy functioned as a mere safety net of last resort, offering little by way of decommodification and in fact compelling people into the market in order to satisfy their needs. Others, like Germany, involved all citizens in compulsory social insurance, but the benefit payments closely mirrored market earnings so that little decommodification actually resulted. A third type of welfare state, Sweden for example, was high on decommodification. Here Esping-Andersen pointed to the policy ideal of enabling citizens to freely opt out of work when they thought it necessary, without losing their employment or diminishing their welfare.

Esping-Andersen's second criteria understands welfare states to be also in conflict with social stratification. Again comparative analysis highlighted fundamental differences of approach. The safety net model was designed in fact to reinforce stratification and stigmatise those who did not attempt to climb the social ladder. The reward structure of the social insurance model was also designed to reinforce traditional distinctions among professional, labour, church, and other social organisations. Government contributions to such schemes were also meant to cement loyalties to the state. A third type of welfare state had had uniform benefits for all citizens as a basic goal. Where attempted, this equalising objective had been modified over time, with a need to satisfy the growing middle classes. Different combinations of flat rate and second tier models had resulted with varying commitments to reducing class stratification.

These criteria led Esping Andersen to a three type classification of the 'worlds of welfare capitalism'. The first was called the 'liberal' welfare state. This was low on decommodification and high on stratification. Countries usually included in this category are Australia, Canada, Ireland, New Zealand, United Kingdom, and the United States of America. Here we find:

- payments and services are means-tested
- a clientele comprised of low-income earners
- strict entitlement rules creating a social stigma for recipients
- governments encouraging private provision as the ideal even with expensive state subsidies.

The second world of welfare is called the conservative model and includes Austria, France, Belgium, Italy, Japan, Switzerland, and Germany. In Europe, Christian democratic politics was a strong influence on many countries, giving a characteristic emphasis on families and civic associations ahead of the state through the very influential principle of subsidiarity. This regime emphasised:

- universal social rights, unlike the liberal model
- preserved status differences to which rights attach
- benefits favoured the preservation of traditional family type
- services provided as of right but delivered through non-state organisations where possible.

The third regime was called the social democratic regime and included countries such as Denmark, Finland, Norway, and Sweden. It was called social democratic because of the social democratic politics that had been its driving force. High on decommodification and equality, it ideally aimed at:

- benefits that were universal not selective
- social services designed to offer an equality of the highest standard
- a socialisation of the costs of family (encouraging men and women equally in work).

This threefold typology has proved markedly resilient as a focal point for comparative social policy research for more than a decade. Over that time, of course, significant critiques have emerged. Some related to the emphasis on class-based inequality at the expense of gender and race. Others were more concerned with national policy experiences that did not obviously fit the three types. Very recently, this latter critique has been fuelled by the discussion of the relevance of the typology to countries with developing economies.

CRITIQUES OF WELFARE STATE ANALYSIS

Esping-Andersen's use of decommodification as a criterion for welfare state differentiation, as well as his focus on working class, social democratic politics in the development of welfare states, alerts us to the emphasis placed on class in his analysis. Other comparativists have sought to give greater attention to the ways national social policy systems have dealt with issues of gender and race. In this regard, the Australian feminist literature on the place of citizenship in the development of welfare states provided a useful platform for an instructive critique of Esping-Andersen's work.

Writers like Pateman (1989) and Cass (1995) drew attention to the ways in which it was assumed that the social rights of citizenship—which T.H. Marshall and others linked to the formation of welfare states in the 1940s— were universal, when in fact they were not. They argued in particular that this liberal conception of citizenship purported to be gender neutral when it in fact privileged the male, public realm of paid work and ignored the private worlds of family, caring, and unpaid work. With its central focus on decommodification, Esping-Andersen's typology was also found to be gender blind. First you have to be in the labour market before you can be decommodified! In this vein, Shaver and others (O'Connor et al. 1999) examined a variety of liberal welfare regimes to see how much they enhanced or reduced women's autonomy. This autonomy, they found, was heavily circumscribed where child care, maternity leave, and parental care were not legal entitlements but left to private purchase. With the trend in these countries to treat men and women as the same when they are not because of women's greater involvement in the private sphere, the opportunities for autonomy for women were reserved for only the higher-income earners (Ginsburg 2004, p. 208; O'Connor et al. 1999).

Other writers have now developed different typologies in order to take greater account of gender by making 'defamiliasation' a key criteria. In the postwar period, different welfare states created different policies in relation to the traditional male breadwinner model. These authors examined the extent to which women's presence in the paid labour force had been encouraged, what proportion of welfare entitlements had been granted on an individual or a family membership basis, and the extent to which caring had become socialised (Lewis 1993; Sainsbury 1994). In these studies, the United Kingdom, Netherlands, and Germany were seen to be still heavily oriented to the male breadwinner model; some of the Scandinavian countries—Denmark, Finland, and Sweden—had become more effectively dual breadwinner models; while others, such as France and Belgium, were in between, as was Australia (Cass 1998). These findings highlighted that gender issues play out differently from class so that there is no straight correspondence with Esping-Andersen's typology. They alert us in particular to the dangers for women of liberal welfare regimes that purport to treat men and women as the same. Instead of the two adult workers as the ideal, where neither are assumed to have caring and family responsibilities, some authors now point to the 'one and a half worker' household as the basis of constructing more satisfactory work and family combinations.

Much less attention has been paid to race in comparative social policy research. Ginsburg (2004) reports on some seminal works on welfare state policies in response to race that are suggestive for future analysis. He draws attention to three types of policy response across countries in the postwar period: the settler, exclusionary, and post-colonial. Australia was an example of the settler model (along with the United States, Canada, and Sweden) in which the permanent settlement of immigrants was assumed without difficulty and typically managed through a range of policies from assimilation, integration to multiculturalism. Examples of the exclusionary model were Germany and Japan, where racially strong conceptions of the nation led to policies that allowed for 'guest workers' but did not assume their long-term settlement. The United Kingdom and France illustrate the post-colonial approach. Many people entered these countries especially from former colonies that had achieved independence in the postwar period—although they often achieved only a second-class status, becoming the occasion of civil unrest in the 1970s. In the 1980s and 1990s, both the post-colonial and guest worker models were wound up as a result of rising unemployment and racial violence. These countries embraced policy approaches closer to the settler model. Today, however, this policy area is once again fraught. A 'settler' country like Australia, for example, has been torn apart by divisions over refugees and asylum seekers. Alongside the growing cosmopolitanism associated with an overall heightened international population mobility, an overtly racist politics shadows the presence of immigrant workers, refugees, and asylum seekers in many countries (Castles & Miller 2003).

NATIONAL DIVERSITY IN WELFARE STATE ARRANGEMENTS

Clearly we need to significantly augment if not modify Esping-Andersen's typology if we are to understand, in a comparative way, the different policy configurations around gender and race. A further area where the typology has been found limited is in accounting for the diversity of nations. Over time an increasing number of exceptions to the schema have been identified and these began very early with the Australian case.

Historically Australians had prided themselves on their egalitarianism (the 'Fair Go') and, up until the 1970s, at least had regarded themselves as something like front runners in terms of social justice for ordinary citizens. Indeed at the beginning of the twentieth century, Australia was internationally regarded as something of a laboratory for progressive social policy experimentation. According to Esping-Andersen, however, Australia was to be considered within the liberal world of welfare! This was something of a paradox, a paradox that the Australian comparativist, Castles, sought to explain.

Castles' (1989) notion of Australia's 'wage earner welfare state' has been discussed in some detail in Chapter 5. Reckoning on Australia's relatively modest levels of tax and social transfers, he had originally been critical of Australia as a 'welfare laggard'—on these terms, well behind the social democratic regimes of Scandinavia. Over time, however, certain features of Australian social policy persuaded Castles that Australia was not so much a laggard as different. Australia's social policy regime had developed along quite different lines to those familiar in Europe. The wage system, not the tax-transfer system, had developed as the primary means of achieving social policy goals. This was what he dubbed 'welfare by other means'. The tax-transfer system was of course the primary focus of Esping-Andersen's analysis and here Australia did indeed have a residual, 'safety net' system of social assistance. Even here, however, as Castles and Mitchell (1992) pointed out, coverage of the population in some benefits was very broad. Indeed the vast majority of Australia's aged remain eligible for the aged pension today. In these circumstances, at least in the case of old age pensions for example, in the 1970s and 1980s there was none of the stigma Esping-Andersen associated with the liberal model.

Moreover, although lower than the social insurance systems for people on average earnings, the level of benefits was higher than that normally associated with social assistance or safety net schemes for low-income people in Europe. When this broadly based system of social protection was placed alongside Australia's progressive taxation system and social regulation of the wage system, the result according to Castles and his colleague Mitchell (1992) was actually a 'fourth world of welfare'. They called this the 'radically redistributive' model. Others have had different ways of naming the Australian system.

Jill Roe (1993) notably referred to it as the 'Australian Way' drawing attention to the fact that after the onset of globalisation in the 1980s, the Australian approach had proven very resilient when social policy in comparable English-speaking countries—notably New Zealand, the United Kingdom, and the United States of America—had suffered significant de-legitimation. Around the same time, it seemed indeed that the 'Australian way' was being refurbished to meet the demands of the more flexible labour market and dual breadwinner households. The timing of this assertion of the value of the national system is notable in itself. Up until the 1960s and 1970s, Australian social policy was very much embedded in the British tradition, although with an increasing United States influence. With the United Kingdom having joined the now European Union by the 1970s, Australia found itself alone on the world stage just as the period of globalisation was beginning (Finer & Smyth 2004). As we shall see in Chapter 7, the impact of the Howard government—building on trends set in place by his predecessor—has radically reoriented the Australian regime. Certainly the very progressive character of the tax-transfer system remains a distinctive feature of the Australian regime today; but not so the social policy role of employment and wages.

However, the targeted system has become more conditional and other comparative research should caution us against assuming that the targeted approach exemplified in the Australian model might be an example for other countries. Other scholars have argued that targeting does not in fact lead to more effective redistribution and poverty reduction; certainly when compared to the countries in Esping-Andersen's Social Democratic model. And we can see in Table 6.1 that Scandinavian countries have the lowest levels of inequality and poverty, with Australia tending towards the higher end—with only approximately five to six similar countries having higher levels of poverty or inequality.

Thus Korpi and Palme (2004, p. 165) conclude 'the Australian experience indicates that targeting by excluding the better off citizens is not highly effective in reducing poverty, and that it is relatively inefficient in reducing inequality'. A key factor here is the size of budgets available for redistributive purposes. This is a particularly significant finding given that international agencies have been promoting the 'safety net' as the model most suited to countries now developing welfare states. If there is an aspiration to reduce poverty and inequality then the lesson of the Australian experience appears to be that more encompassing models are to be preferred. However, as we shall see in the final chapter, the very notion of Australian exceptionalism is now clouded with uncertainty. As Smyth (1998) has argued, the use of the wage system as 'another means' of achieving social goals always depended on maintaining a system of full employment. With the disappearance of full employment and the overall loss of full-time jobs in the 1990s, together with significant deregulation of the wage system, the Australian model has been eroded substantially (Mishra 2004). What the future might hold for Australian social policy is a subject we return to in Chapter 7.

The Australian example of social protection by other means was not the only example of a diversity of national experience that proved difficult to accommodate within Esping-Andersen's three types. Southern European countries like Spain, Portugal, Greece, and Italy were found to have characteristics warranting a distinct category, one that became known as the 'Southern Model' (Ferrera 1996). These countries had systems of income maintenance that were fragmented in coverage although often quite generous to some—the aged for example. They placed greater obligations on families in relation to caring, but typically had national health systems if only partial in their coverage. Services were characterised by clientelism and patronage. So diverse is the national social policy experience, according to some, that the very concept of welfare regimes is flawed (Kasza 2002). Nevertheless, most would argue that the diversity is not such that analytically useful modelling based on national policy similarity and difference cannot be constructed. However, the exceptions to Esping-Andersen's three types may now be such that a new approach may be required.

More recent research in fact questions the principles on which Esping-Andersen based his typology. Here it is important to note that this was composed at a time when social policy research focused centrally on the role of the state and the tax–social transfer system. Today there is a less exclusive focus on the role of the state and more emphasis on the total 'welfare mix' created by the state, the private sector, and the family/community. Some now argue that Esping-Andersen's approach actually obscures the full welfare picture. They say we need a different starting point based on including all three 'pillars' if we are to avoid a narrow welfare statist preoccupation (Goodin & Rein 2001). A particularly illuminating critique in this vein was the work of van Kersbergen (1995) on what Esping-Andersen referred to as the 'conservative' welfare regime. Van Kersbergen highlighted what we might call the 'pro-Scandinavian' assumptions of Esping-Andersen's framework. It implied that the conservative regime had failed to achieve the 'successful' working-class social reform embodied in social democratic Sweden, for example. Van Kersbergen questioned this assumption and pointed to the Christian Democratic political tradition that had informed the development of the so-called 'conservative' regime. He showed that this was simply a different social vision to the social democrats; one that sought to limit the state through the principle of subsidiarity. According to Van Kersbergen, the social democratic presumptions of Esping-Andersen's analysis ought to be relaxed so that this different outcome was not ascribed to working-class political failure. This whole question of the appropriate principles or criteria upon which to construct comparative typologies has become particularly acute in the case of the Asian welfare state experience and also in relation to the new emphasis on social policy in developing economies.

THE 'EAST ASIAN MODEL'

The recent development of interest in comparative social policy research in the Asian region is of particular importance for Australia. Until the latter 1990s, comparative social policy was very much an occupation of Western scholars talking about the advanced industrial nations of Europe and the Anglo-American sphere. This ethnocentric bias was especially notable in Australia, where scholars were extremely well informed about how Australia compared to Sweden or the United Kingdom but knew nothing about how it compared with nations in our region. More generally, of course, the long shadow of 'white Australia' had meant that Australians had tended not to identify with their own geographical region. Moreover, with the notable exception of Japan, Asian countries were thought of as economically developing and not advanced enough to have 'welfare states'. In the 1990s, however, after the Newly Industrialising Countries (NICs as they were known) such as Taiwan, Korea, Hong Kong, and Singapore burst on the scene, this picture quickly changed. Scholars soon began to ask if there was in fact a distinctive 'East Asian welfare state'? (Goodman et al. 1998). For Australia this development has been of special interest following our increased economic integration in the region.

Indeed before the financial crisis, which hit the East Asian region at the end of the 1990s, many saw positive lessons for welfare states like Australia in the parsimonious approach to welfare that seemed to characterise the Asian social policy style. During the 1980s, national leaders like Lee Kuan Yew of Singapore and Mohammed Mahathir of Malaysia loudly distanced themselves from the welfare state trajectory of the West, declaring that they preferred to 'look East' (i.e. to Japan) for their inspiration. On a visit to Singapore, the British Prime Minister Tony Blair congratulated his hosts on their approach to social policy, finding in it the principles of the 'stakeholder society' that he hoped to promote in his own country (Finer & Smyth 2004). The key point to emerge from this first East–West encounter over welfare was the terminological confusion. While these countries criticised Western 'welfare' (at a time when conservative leaders in the West such as Thatcher and Reagan were doing the same), they also gave high priority to social expenditures that also enhanced economic growth, in areas such as education, health, and, certainly in the case of Singapore, housing (Gough 2001). In short, the East Asian approach to social policy was distinctive for the emphasis placed on what Holliday (2000) referred to as its 'productivist values'; values that had somehow slipped from Western usage, especially in frameworks such as Esping-Andersen's, which constructed the role of social policy in terms of social protection, redistribution, and decommodification.

Even in the case of social protection, however, we ought not conclude too quickly that East Asian states have been averse to developing programs for income security. Hort and Kunhle (2000) have reviewed the development of such systems in the East and South-East Asian countries. They remind us that when the economic miracle took off in these countries, only a few decades ago, they had low taxes, low wages, and often an absence of labour rights and democratic structures. Hort and Kunhle conclude, in fact, that given their late industrialisation, these countries have moved more quickly down the path of social protection development than did the Western countries at similar stages of economic development. In some places, the economic meltdown of the 1990s quickened rather than retarded this momentum. As Lee (2004, p. 151) writes, 'The Asian financial crisis has exposed fundamental weaknesses in [the East Asian social policy model]. Simply emphasising Confucius values, work ethics, family obligations and supportive/directive state institutions cannot ameliorate social ills, particularly during an acute economic downturn'. Following the downturn, Korea, for example, implemented an extensive system of unemployment insurance.

Explanations of East Asian social policy difference were first cast in terms of culture. Thus Jones (1990) referred to a shared Chinese cultural base of what she called the 'oikonomic welfare states'. Here, Confucian values were thought to lead to an emphasis on the family and the community as the pillars of care rather than the state. These emphases have led some to consider whether these states might fit within Esping-Andersen's 'conservative' model. Kwon (1997) concludes that in spite of certain similarities, the differences are such to constitute a separate 'East Asian' welfare regime type. He highlights the relatively small volume of welfare transfers and the different politics driving policy change. In Europe, social policy reforms followed working-class pressure, while in Korea, for example, the 'developmental state' drove the program of modernisation and industrialisation with which welfare legislation became associated.

Thus far the literature on Asian social policy has been mainly concerned with Japan and the NICs. The Asian social policy experience is bound to capture increasing attention as the dramatic economic developments in China and India bring rapid social policy change. Research will also have to address the cultural variety in ways not achieved until now; giving weight, for example, to cultures other than the Confucian, including Buddhism, Islam, and Taoism.

SOCIAL POLICY AND DEVELOPMENT

A most recent development in comparative social policy and one with radical implications for the future, has been the coming together of social policy and development studies. As Hall and Midgley (2004) recount, both these research areas emerged after the Second World War with social policy being the study of the welfare state in the industrialised economies and development being the study of economic growth in the non-industrialised economies of what was called the 'Third World'. The latter focused not only on the broad issues of the determinants of economic growth, but also on small-scale community development processes that might 'trickle up' into growth. This separate development began to unravel in the late 1990s and early 2000s. The World Bank and IMF began talking of the need for strong 'social capital' and sound social policy as a basis for economic development, just as welfare state countries were looking for new ways to 'strengthen communities' and find a more productivist rationale for social spending.

Unlike social policy, which became more and more exclusively concerned with redistribution and decommodification, the development research tradition has always been closely linked to economic policy. The Bretton Woods institutions, the World Bank, and the International Monetary Fund were set up under the influence of Keynesian economic ideas (Higgins 1968; Myrdal 1972). What was sought was a kind of international welfare state, whereby the economic power imbalances between rich and poor countries could be modified in ways to allow developing countries to build up their production capacities before full exposure to market competition. As Hall and Midgley (2004) note, unexpectedly good growth rates of 3.4 per cent were recorded in developing countries in the 1950s and 1960s. However, in the following decade radical critiques emerged on the political left, arguing that the development was not evenly spread among populations and that the system of international capitalism would in fact maintain these countries in a relatively underdeveloped condition (Frank 1971; Mandel 1975). By the end of the 1970s, development policies along with welfare state policies in industrialised countries were plunged into a crisis by a global economic recession.

The separate but parallel history of social policy and development continued into the 1980s, with the impact of economic neo-liberalism represented in the work of Hayek and Friedman. What became known as 'welfare reform' in the industrialised countries was called 'structural adjustment' in the emerging economies. Development was said to be impeded by public spending 'crowding out' the private sector, distorting market signals generally, and weakening incentives for unemployed people to engage with the labour market. In relation to development, this neo-liberal economic package enforced by the Bretton Woods agencies became known as the 'Washington consensus'.

Critiques of this consensus focused on the fact that far from sparking high growth rates, the policy regime proved deflationary with low growth rates. Particular interest centred on the need to develop the 'social capability' necessary for market activities. Initially the emphasis was not on what governments might do but on how communities might be strengthened through Non-Government Organisation (NGO) activities. Here building social capital was identified as a key objective (Fine 2001). Added to this emphasis on community strengthening was a reassessment of the role of the state as a result of 'new growth theory' or endogenous growth theory that emphasises the economic value of sound investments in social infrastructure such as education and health facilities. Moreover, evidence had mounted that neo-liberal assumptions about a necessary trade off between growth and equity were unfounded. In 1997, the World Bank, for example, drew attention to the way economic development in the NICs had been helped not hindered by egalitarian redistribution.

A key commentator on these post 'Washington consensus' developments, Mkandawire (2004, pp. 4–5) emphasises its breach with the neo-liberal assumption that social policy ought to act only as a residual 'safety net'—or, as is often said, an 'ambulance at the bottom of the cliff'. 'Social policy, he continues, 'should be conceived as involving overall and prior concerns with social development, and as a key instrument that works in tandem with economic policy to ensure equitable and socially sustainable development'. That is, once the state is involved in reviewing and deciding about the overall pattern of economic investment, it becomes possible to allocate resources on social criteria and not just leave these decisions to private individuals in the market place.

At the emerging interface between social policy and development, we see new interest among the latter in different schemes for achieving social security in education and health systems as well as issues particular to rural and urban development. For social policy, the issues are very different. Contained for so long with a discipline that looked only at issues of redistribution and decommodification, the interest now is in questions about the economically productive value of social investments. Clearly each discipline has much to learn from each other as a new consensus is emerging around a post-neo-liberal, integrated approach to social and economic policy.

7
CHANGES AND CHALLENGES
Paul Smyth

INTRODUCTION

For much of the 1980s and 1990s, economic issues dominated political agendas in Australia and similar countries. Social welfare expenditures were constructed as somehow at odds with the sound economic management needed to get economies globally competitive. The welfare state was said to be in 'crisis'. Now we are entering a new social policy period. Economic globalisation proceeds apace but national social policy adaptation is taking a variety of forms, reminding us that social politics still matters. Moreover, in Australia and most other countries we see social expenditures rising not falling. Social spending is beginning to be constructed less as a cost on the economy and more as an economic and social investment. In this chapter, I look first at the new global context of social policy making before exploring those aspects of the emerging social policy agenda that we surmise will shape social research and action over this first decade of the twenty-first century. I will emphasise key economic, social, and demographic contexts, new profiles of socio-economic risk, new measures of disadvantage, as well as identifying the people and places likely to be of central concern.

GLOBAL CONTEXT

At the beginning of the 1990s, the social policy context in Australia was completely overshadowed by the conflict between economic rationalism and the traditional nation-building values of the 'Australian way'. Across the 1990s, this conflict was reinterpreted. Economic rationalism gave way to 'globalisation' as the rationale for less government involvement in economy and society. Former British Prime Minster Margaret Thatcher's slogan, 'There is no alternative', added rhetorical colour to demands for less social welfare. Many people genuinely believed that tax reductions and welfare cuts, wage reductions, and the end of full employment ('social dumping') were all necessary for economic survival (Held & McGrew 2000). While this now appears more a myth than a reality it remains the case that the global context for social policy making has altered and has to be taken into account in thinking through current and future policy scenarios (Castles 2004).

It is not as though the global context only became important in the 1990s. It was always important. The whole history of Australian social policy is incomprehensible without an understanding of Australia's place in the British Empire and then the Commonwealth before the United Kingdom joined what is now the European Union in the 1960s, leaving Australia to find its way into new favoured relationships with the United States of America and also within the Asian region. The global economy at the time of Federation was in fact more 'open' than it is today. The key period for understanding our current global social policy position is the breakdown in the 1970s of the rules for regulating the international economy, which were established at the end of the Second World War (Finer & Smyth 2004).

The postwar world economy was managed through institutions set up at the end of the war (for example, at Bretton Woods in 1944; the General Agreement for Tariffs and Trade, the GATT, in 1947). These institutions, the International Monetary Fund (IMF), the World Bank, and World Trade Organization (WTO) facilitated a significant degree of national autonomy relative to the global economy. Here we should note that this was indeed a relative autonomy and national states were certainly not autarchies independent of international economic exchange. While free trade was set as a long-term goal, it was recognised that in the period of postwar reconstruction, it made good sense for the war-torn countries of Europe, for example, to use tariffs to protect their economies until they were strong enough to engage in free trading; and likewise with the developing economies of post-colonial Africa and Asia. Similarly governments were able to manage their currencies and investment flows. Much of this order was sustained by the strength of the United States economy in the 1950s and 1960s. By the 1980s, the US currency had weakened considerably and this postwar international order had given way to the multinational-led global deregulation we have come to term 'globalisation' (Bell 1997). Governments found it increasingly difficult to manage national economies with increasingly porous borders; while the IMF, World Bank, and WTO reformed themselves around what became known as the free-market-inspired 'Washington consensus', aggressively promoting free trade, small government, and economic deregulation.

Against this background, it began to appear that the Australian government's deregulation of the financial system in 1983, the progressive removal of tariffs, and labour market deregulation, might have been less an issue of domestic politics and more a symptom of a worldwide 'hollowing out of the nation state' (Jessop 2003). Influential commentators foresaw a world without national economic boundaries (Ohmae 1991). According to Reich (1992), citizens would less and less see themselves as occupants of the 'same (national) economic boat' such was the apparent diffusion of economic ownership and control in the new 'global web of enterprise'. Such visions had a basis in the everyday life experience of the so-called advanced economies as manufacturing moved off shore, work opportunities for the unskilled shrank, and the rise of the knowledge economy placed a premium on what Reich called 'symbolic-analytic services'. Once the economic bonds between citizens had dissolved, what would be left of their social and political ties? One of the few meaningful social policy roles that could be ascribed to nation states in this scenario was investment in training and education in order to at least give individuals a chance to make it on the 'global race track' (Latham 1998; Wiseman 1998).

Others were less convinced. Hirst and Thompson (1999), for example, argued that what was happening was less globalisation and more internationalisation. They pointed out that the international economy of the 1990s was less open than in the period from 1870 to1914; genuine transnational companies were rare and most remained nation-based; foreign direct investment remained concentrated in the industrialised countries; and investment generally remained concentrated in three blocs based on the European Union, Japan, and North America. They agreed that while internationalisation could, in theory, become globalisation, there was nothing in the history of these arrangements to suggest that this was inevitable.

Certainly in terms of levels of social expenditure there has been no 'race to the bottom'. In his review of social expenditures in twenty-one OECD countries in the period from 1980 to 1998, Castles (2004) found a picture of dramatic growth. 'In this period when the welfare state was supposedly in continuous crisis and under continuous attack from its political enemies, per capita real social expenditure … increased by no less than 83 per cent or by around 4.5 per cent per annum'. Expressed in US dollars, the figure in Australia in 1980 was $9144 and by 1998 it was $15 538. However, this was also a period of restraint and reduction in non-social expenditures in what were generally times of restrained economic growth. This has given social welfare a heightened profile in terms of political debates over levels of public expenditure. Clearly globalisation is not leading to the death of welfare states. However, there has been significant restructuring as the contests over social expenditure levels play out differently in different countries in ways that reflect the historical 'path dependency' of their social policy development. We are left with a global panorama not of convergence at the bottom but of ongoing social policy diversity (Weiss 2003).

This persistence of national social policy diversity ought not lead to the conclusion that globalisation does not matter. As noted above, the global institutional context of social policy always matters. In this regard, a key development in recent decades has been the emergence of regional blocs such as the European Union (EU) and the North American Free Trade Agreement (NAFTA). Close interdependence within the EU, for example, has had a varied impact on participating countries, with some tendency for big welfare states to tighten spending in some areas and for poorer welfare performers such as Ireland to achieve significant development (Castles 2004). A further factor in the way states adapt to globalisation are the international policy institutions. These include not only the Bretton Woods agencies mentioned above, but also numerous other players including the Organisation for Economic Cooperation and Development (OECD) and the social agencies of the United Nations. Here, as noted in Chapter 6, the form taken by the 'post-Washington consensus' regarding the role of social policy in development will be a significant factor in the way nation states choose to respond to globalisation. Because the thinking and roles of such organisations are in such a flux, they will warrant more than usual attention if we are to fully grasp their impacts on policy making within the nation state (Deacon et al. 1997).

AUSTRALIAN SOCIAL POLICY TODAY

Where does Australia fit in this panorama of social policy adaptation to this period of globalisation? In this regard, other chapters in this book offer richly detailed perspectives on particular policy domains. Here we consider the overall trend in the pattern of social policy and the challenges this trend will present for future policy makers. As we saw in Chapter 5, the 'Australian way' can be best arranged under three themes: employment, wages, and social welfare. For most of the twentieth century, the first two were given priority and a targeted 'safety net' approach sufficed for much of our social welfare. What has happened in the period of globalisation or internationalisation has been a cumulative reversal of these priorities. Not government but the market now determines employment levels and the same increasingly holds for wages. This explains the paradox of increasing reliance on the social welfare system to achieve social goals at a time when the Howard government—rhetorically at least—has been committed to reducing the burden of 'welfare dependency'. Resolving this paradox is the central challenge facing Australian social policy.

Chapter 8 shows the rise and fall of full employment as a policy objective. It also shows how with the rise of non-standard employment the official unemployment figures only give half the picture of Australians without paid work. Importantly, the authors also emphasise the critical role of employment in promoting social well-being; with the links between unemployment, health, housing, education, and poverty outcomes being intimate. There is no reason why paid work could not be reaffirmed as the foundation of an employment-based approach to social security. While much of the early literature on globalisation proposed that full employment was no longer an option, this is fallacious (Mishra 1995). Indeed the projected declines in labour force growth and labour force participation associated with the ageing of the population now appear to bring full employment within reach. In fact, some might argue that the current market rather than a government-driven approach to employment creation will do the job. At the same time, it is abundantly clear that full employment under the current system of labour market deregulation would not be the form of 'welfare by other means' that characterised past Australian social policy.

The numbers of people who work but are poor in the United States of America makes this perfectly clear. The key challenge here is to reverse the decline in full-time jobs. As Gregory (2002) has highlighted, only a quarter of the jobs created in the 1990s were full time. And as Saunders (2005) makes clear, part-time jobs are no protection against poverty. His analysis of the poverty and employment status in Australia in 1998–99 showed that a national poverty rate of 13.6 per cent rose to 35.7 per cent for those households where no one was employed. While this dropped dramatically to 1.8 per cent where there was at least one full-time employed person, for households with someone employed but not in a full-time job, the rate dropped only slightly to 30.4 per cent. With the vast majority of new jobs being non-standard, with entrenched long-term unemployment, and with rising wage disparities, a different approach to job creation and wage regulation will be needed if paid work is to resume its place as the bedrock of social security in the Australian system. As Chapter 8 indicates, major investments in education and training as well as regional development and some measure of public job creation would be essential. Here the critical issue is whether Australia continues down the United States of America's low wage path to job creation or turns more to the high wage-value added path more characteristic of Europe—and increasingly, the United Kingdom.

An inevitable result of Australian governments' giving up on the social regulation of employment and wage policies has been the rising welfare bill. Castles' (2004) survey of OECD countries shows Australian social expenditures have increased significantly with globalisation—a growth trend common to most countries, but especially to those who began with below average social funding. However, we should not think that this means that Australia has embraced the Scandinavian approach to generous, universally provided welfare as compensation for an open market approach to the world economy (Katzenstein 1985). On the contrary, as our chapters on the key social service areas of health, education, and housing show there has been, under the Howard government especially, an increasing trend to 'marketise' services that will increasingly residualise public provision. A continuation of this trend must result not only in the 'poor services for poor people', characteristic of the liberal welfare regime but also, as Kenway vividly shows in Chapter 12 of this book in relation to education, a commercialisation of service. Not only are goods like education removed from citizens as of right, but what is produced becomes less related to human needs and more to what money can buy.

Nevertheless, the traditional safety net continues to play an important role in moderating the increasing poverty and inequality deriving from the labour market (Keating 2004a). But Australian social policy faces an uncertain future. The 1980s and 1990s were very much about unpicking the old social policy frameworks in the name of market freedom and economic growth. Continuation on this path is a possibility, especially with Australia's greater integration with the United States of America. On the other hand, Australia has always tended towards a hybrid welfare form crossing the USA not only with the United Kingdom, but also European influences (and now possibly Asian). It is here we see significant departures from the kinds of extreme neo-liberalism that characterised the 1980s and 1990s especially in the United Kingdom under Margaret Thatcher. If Australia is to begin to reconstruct a social policy framework for the twenty-first century, it is more than likely these departures will follow.

NEW STARTING POINTS

From an international perspective, it could be argued that social policy has entered a more upbeat phase than it has seen for over two decades. This may be less pronounced in Australia where much public debate seems gripped in an ideological deadlock between neo-liberal attackers of our 'welfare habit' (Saunders 2005) and a kind of 'old left' defence of the redistributive gains of earlier times. Internationally speaking, finding a 'Third Way' beyond that deadlock has shaped a new agenda of social policy thinking and practice for over a decade. The term 'Third Way', of course, is no longer in vogue. Early critics, like Hamilton (2003) and Jayasuria (2000), observed the social policy rhetoric of the third way was new but the reality was difficult to distinguish from economic rationalism. Now, however, as we move beyond the 'enabling state' to the 'ensuring state' and from the 'free' to the 'embedded' market, and with a new emphasis on the importance of the public sphere, that critique would seem passé (Giddens 1999, 2003). Here, it appears, are new ways of thinking about the ends and means of welfare that can free us from the deadlock of the 1990s. Here we pick up several strands of social policy thought that may offer starting points for a new social policy agenda in Australia.

Reintegrating social and economic policy

Of critical importance is the way we conceptualise the links between social and economic policy. As we have seen in Chapter 5, the role of social policy in relation to the economy has been differently constructed at various times: the social investment state at Federation; the Keynesian economic state after the Second World War; and, from the late 1980s, what might be called the 'anti-state' of the economic rationalists that left scarce room for pursuing social ends through economic policy. Today there are signs of new alignments between social policy and an economic thought that leaves behind the radical neo-liberalism of the 1990s without returning to the Keynesianism practised in the 1950s and 1960s. A particularly original thinker in this regard is British political economist, Bob Jessop (2003), who wrote of the transition from the Keynesian Welfare National State (KWNS) to the Schumpeterian Workfare Post-national Regime (SWPR). The former was about evening out the booms and busts of unregulated markets through a policy of sustaining full employment, which in turn underwrote spending on income support and services. According to Jessop, this form of state intervention was eroded by a number of factors but especially the 'hollowing out of the state' associated with globalisation. With a transfer of power both upwards to supra-national organisations and downwards to more local jurisdictions, he writes, we no longer have a welfare state so much as a national policy agency embedded in a multilevel system of governance.

More fundamentally, the goals of social policy have changed from the Keynesian preoccupation with security to a focus on innovation as a way of promoting growth. Here Schumpeter's vision of entrepreneurs sparking waves of 'creative destruction' appears to fit the times more than Keynes. While Keynesian policy had emphasised the need for state economic management and redistribution to offer citizens economic security, a Schumpeterian approach, according to Jessop, is about creating 'subjects to serve as partners in the innovative, knowledge-driven, entrepreneurial, flexible economy'. If Keynesianism encouraged a social rights approach to welfare, Schumpeter's political economy leads in the direction of a 'self-reliant, autonomous, empowered workfare regime' (Schumpeterian Workfare Post-national Regime). In terms of social policy, it will lead to a supply-side emphasis on welfare to work, with more or less attention to social justice depending on the government of the day. More generally, Jessop's work is important because it allows us to start thinking about roles for social policy in supporting enterprise, innovation, and growth, and not remaining stuck with a KWNS framework in which, rightly or wrongly, the role of welfare had been quarantined to redistribution and consumption.

An alternative way to think afresh about social policy and the economy is in terms of a 'social investment state'. This approach received early expression in the report of the British Commission on Social Justice (1994) where it was counterposed as an 'Investors' United Kingdom to the United Kingdom of the 'deregulators' and of the 'levellers'. Here the emphasis was to be on economic opportunity in the name of social justice. Economic prosperity and the achievement of social security was to be linked through investment in and the redistribution of opportunities rather than just income. This approach has been taken up in the 'third way's' successor, the 'new progressivism' expounded by the British sociologist Anthony Giddens (2003) and his colleagues; and has similarities with work on the social investment state by Midgley (1999) and Sherraden (2003) in the United States of America.

The 'social investment' approach does not have a single name school of economic theory to which it attaches. We could think in terms of the more radical emphases in Keynes's system emphasising the need for a certain 'socialisation of investment'. In writing about 'embedded markets', Giddens (2003) refers to the work of the economic sociologist, Granovetter, who emphasised the way the market is embedded in culture, law, and the mechanisms of trust. Within economic theory, it can also be linked to the Schumpeter tradition currently expressed in the 'new growth theory', or endogenous growth theory, which emerged over the last decade or so in the work of economists (Sandler 2001). In policy terms, the social investment approach highlights the role of social and human capital in the growth process (and not without controversy as Kenway points out in Chapter 12 of this book). It points to potential government action to develop social and human capital through education, research, and the promotion of technological development. As Nobel Prize-winning economist Stiglitz (2002) observed, there are no cases of successful national economic development where the state has not played a significant role.

The strength of this framework is that it re-entitles people to a range of social rights for sound economic as well as social reasons. Investing in the early childhood years and in life-long learning is paradigmatic of this new reconciliation between economic and social policy. While some criticise the 'social investment state' approach for being more concerned with equality of opportunities rather than with equality of outcomes, it cannot be denied that it goes beyond the 'third way', which tried to marry social democratic social policy with neo-liberal economic policy. New growth theory underwrites positive government action to develop both social and economic capacities. It is more fairly criticised for being too focused on an economic justification for social spending (on the 'worker-citizen') to the neglect of other equally important social domains such as caring and old age (Lister 2004).

Poverty, social inclusion, and capacity building

If the first strand of the new social policy agenda concerns reinventing the productivist elements of the 'social investment state' and the 'Keynesian economic state' for the twenty-first century, the second strand makes us ask in what should we be investing? This was a question that we ceased to ask in the welfare state period, so much so that by the 1990s social welfare had become not a matter of investment but rather a matter of consumption. Welfare was about maintaining income levels sufficient to support a socially agreed minimum standard of living. Key debates concerned the number of people receiving pensions and benefits: were they all really poor? Neo-liberals charged that the official poverty line was too high; while welfare state defenders rallied to defend rights to a minimum of decent living. For both, social expenditure (welfare) was considered in terms of maintaining consumption, not investing in production. Latterly these debates are being transformed as our understandings of disadvantage have been reframed in terms of promoting social inclusion and capacity building. Here the notion of social expenditures as a productive investment re-enters the frame.

The resounding silence that greeted the Senate Poverty Inquiry of 2004 in Australia sheeted home the fact that policy makers were no longer listening to the 'p' word. Ever since the Commission of Inquiry into Poverty reported in the mid 1970s, the annually released 'poverty line'—devised by Commission head, R.F. Henderson—had operated as a kind of social barometer to alert people

CHANGES AND CHALLENGES **137**

when poverty levels had moved beyond the accepted social norms. Following the controversies that surrounded then Prime Minister Bob Hawke's pledge to 'end child poverty' in 1987, disquiet grew around the policy utility of the poverty line. This developed into a notable public controversy involving the Smith Family, the National Centre for Social and Economic Modelling, and the Centre for Independent Studies; as well as the Social Policy Research Centre in 2002 (see Saunders 2005).

The main issue highlighted by critics of the poverty line arose from the fact that it was a measure of relative poverty. In 1973, the Commission estimated that one in eight Australians were in poverty. The same measure in 1998–99 found just over one in five. While this is a substantial increase in the numbers in relative poverty, critics argued that because the economic cake was now larger, those at the bottom were actually now better off than before. The poverty line—even allowing for price increases—had risen by over a third in that time, meaning that the poor at the end of the 1990s were in fact much better off than the poor twenty-odd years before. Fierce disputes over the technicalities of poverty measurement have only served to highlight the fact that poverty is an irreducibly relative concept, requiring a new moral consensus before our measures of disadvantage, which will regain political purchase (Bessant et al. 2005).

The fact that this particular debate had already been played out in the United Kingdom a decade before is indicative of the extent to which Australian social policy had entered something of a time warp (Alcock 1997). If we look at what is happening in the United Kingdom today, at Ireland, New Zealand, and indeed, the European Union as a whole, it is not hard to believe that there is a revival of effort against poverty occurring, which must eventually embrace Australian social policy. Of particular importance are the new languages of disadvantage that are proving capable of enlisting a wider group of supportive policy constituencies than the old discourse of poverty. Here we focus on two. The first emerged among social policy researchers in the British and European welfare states and is expressed in terms of promoting social inclusion; while the second is largely the work of one person, Amartya Sen (2001), whose ideas about 'development as freedom' have been very influential in helping to forge the post-Washington consensus on development policy.

A major difficulty with the old poverty measure was its near exclusive focus on income as a proxy for all aspects of disadvantage and the consequence that the policy response tended to be seen in terms of raising pensions and benefits. It was this need for a wider understanding and measure of disadvantage that led to the social exclusion concept. It emerged in France in the 1980s and by 1989, the European Union had established an 'Observatory' to monitor social exclusion policies. The British Prime Minister, Tony Blair, established a Social Exclusion Unit (SEU) in 1998. In 2000, at the European Council of Lisbon, promoting social inclusion was officially accepted as a policy goal by the EU, with member nations required to report on a biannual basis on their progress (Room 2004).

The SEU famously defined social exclusion as 'a shorthand label for what can happen when individuals or areas suffer from a combination of linked problems such as unemployment, poor skills, low incomes, poor housing, high crime environments, bad health and family breakdown'. The approach emphasises first the multi-dimensional nature of poverty. As Lewis writes in Chapter 11 of this book, this is well recognised in the literature on the social determinants of health; and as we look through each of the individual policy windows, we soon see how housing, transport, employment, income, and educational disadvantages are all connected. Second, the approach focuses on the particular dynamic processes affecting particular population groups. The dynamics of exclusion for the young, homeless, and unemployed person will differ from the poverty of the student. It also highlights the spatial dimension of disadvantage: the challenges to inclusion of a small remote Aboriginal community will be very different to those homeless in the inner city. Finally, as the term 'social' implies, this approach emphasises the importance of relationships and to this extent has some parallel with the concept of 'social capital' associated with Robert Putnam. It can imply strong networks and civic engagement (Jones & Smyth 1999). Although the EU has established a set of social exclusion indicators known as the Laaken indicators, researchers in different countries are still working on ways of making the term more precise and there are different measures in use (Saunders 2005).

The social exclusion approach put issues of poverty and disadvantage back on the political agenda in the United Kingdom. Of course, successful policy language usually has a capacity to load up a variety of moral messages. Levitas (2005) analysed these in relation to social exclusion as the Redistributionist Discourse (RED), which has a fairly traditional emphasis on redistribution to end poverty; the Moral Underclass Discourse (MUD), which is preoccupied with the moral and behavioural failings of the poor; and the Social Integrationist Discourse (SID), which has a characteristic emphasis on welfare to work. But in this regard the language of social inclusion is not unique. Talk about poverty cannot avoid an ethical dimension (Bessant et al. 2005). Its take up has been slower in Australia than in the United Kingdom. The experience in the UK shows that it need not be seen as replacing income poverty measures but both can complement.

Within the literature on development, there has been a parallel transition. The World Bank, for example, has typically calculated the global incidence of poverty with a line set at one US dollar a day. For example, in 1998, 24 per cent of the world's population were poor by this measure. In a critique that has been very influential on both the United Nations and the World Bank, the Nobel Prize-winning economist Amartya Sen has argued for a more complex measure. Sen argues that poverty has less to do with the absence of income than with people's lack of capacity to be who they want to be. He does not prescribe what these chosen 'functionings' might be and they are said to be relative to different contexts. To achieve them, however, people require certain 'capabilities' that depend in turn on a range of opportunities and entitlements. This emphasis on the need for positive investment by governments in people's 'capabilities' clearly aligns Sen with the social liberal tradition (Hall & Midgley 2004). His work has been taken up by Nussbaum (2000) who has begun the task of articulating more precisely the prerequisites required for the 'flourishing' of human capability.

There are differences between the way Sen and the social inclusion writers frame the problem of poverty. With its European origins, the latter has a stronger emphasis on the value of social relations, while Sen's emphasis is more on the individual. At the same time, they have a similar stress on the need for more complex indices of disadvantage than simply income. Both approaches would likely include such indicators as health, housing, education, employment, income and assets, social/civic engagement, recreation, personal safety, and transport. Research based on these frameworks may well provide the much needed set of common understandings about what constitutes poverty in today's world. With an end to the war over income poverty lines, a new debate becomes possible about the real barriers to social inclusion, or human flourishing, and about how these might be overcome. Our growing social expenditures would be recognised less as passive consumption (as necessary as that can be) and more as sound economic, as much as social, investment. Moreover, these research trends are common to countries in both developed and developing economies, and suggest a more global approach to poverty research in the twenty-first century.

Risks, transitions, and social policy

In Chapters 5 and 6, I observed that national social policy histories are typically punctuated by a series of historic compromises. Some writers have said that Australia is currently in search of a new social contract (Howe & Howe 2005). Certainly the worlds of work and family, as well as the demography of Australia, are very different to that which faced the makers of the welfare state in the 1970s. As to the content of any new social contract, it must be said that it is still early days. Nevertheless, as with the work on poverty indicators, some potentially seminal ideas are already in play. Some of this flows from a welcome re-engagement with social policy by sociologists, but more generally it flows from a slowly emerging consensus about what some of the terms of a new social contract might be.

Some sociologists, such as Beck (1992) and Giddens (1999), believe that we have entered a new kind of society, the 'Risk Society' that requires a different form of social policy response to that devised for the industrial age. The latter was associated with a rather simple set of common and predicable risks associated with the industrial economy such as sickness, unemployment, and old age, which over time, after significant class struggle, were met by a collectively provided, standardised form of 'cradle to the grave' social security. These writers, and others such as Baumann (2001), see today as a postmodern world beset with new risks such as environmental hazards that affect all classes, although unequally. It is a world characterised by a new phase of 'individualisation'. Accordingly, social policy needs new design principles; away from the idea of a common standard protection against the old familiar social dangers, to a concept of investment in individuals so that they can negotiate, by themselves, the new more complex and fragmented social and work environments that have evolved in the last quarter of a century. Some attack these views as no more than a third way gloss on economic neo-liberalism. Their resonance with the notions of the 'social investment state' and 'capacity building' discussed above will also be clear. Either way, they signal an ongoing and probably growing engagement of sociology with the development of the new social policy.

As various contributors to this book indicate, the sorts of factors contributing to the new profiles of social risk are: the growth of non-standard employment; the mass entry of women into the paid work force without the creation of policies to enable a balance of work and family; the growth of jobless households alongside those with excessive work; the growth of social expenditures needed to compensate for declines in 'wage earners' welfare'; and the demand from the increasingly knowledge-based economy for a more highly skilled workforce (often requiring retraining across their working careers, or 'life-long learning').

As Ziguras writes in Chapter 9, all of this suggests the need for an approach to welfare that is different to the old model, which rested on a labour market of lifetime full employment—at least for males. The new model needs to reflect the greater incidence of transitions in and out of paid work across the life cycle. A new agreement needs to be struck about the transitions that need to be encouraged by social policy arrangements and those that need not. Clearly some periods of apparent 'unemployment' are for good economic reasons (reskilling, for example) and some for social purposes (such as caring for the family) we ought to value through policy. Here Schmid's (2002) notion of 'Transitional Labour Markets' has done much to show that welfare reform needs to be about more than simply moving people from 'welfare to work'. That may be one valuable transition, but it is not the only one; and it might not always be a good one if the work is of poor quality or if it is at the expense of caring. New social policy arrangements might also recognise other transitions as equally valid: between education and work; between caring and employment; between retirement and employment; and between 'precarious' and permanent employment.

Of course, a new contract around these terms is not inevitable. Social policy is always a site of contest and such a scenario clearly runs counter to that neo-liberal aspiration, still strong in Australia, of a world with minimal government regulation. It is indeed possible that Australian social policy may continue to simply bump along the bottom, with little aim other than getting people from welfare to work. On the other hand, the larger international trend does seem to point towards greater emphases on social investment and capacity building. As the new social indicators make the contours of risk in the new economy ever clearer, it is not unlikely that frameworks such as Schmid's will increasingly guide thinking about a new social policy framework that will enable citizens to negotiate the new mixes of work and welfare required by the 'risk society'.

SUMMARY AND CONCLUSION

In this chapter, it has been proposed that words like investment, inclusion, capacities, risk, and transitions point us to an emerging new conceptual architecture for twenty-first century social policy makers. This is not the language of restoration—as though we might retreat to the world of the 1970s welfare state. Equally it is not the language of neo-liberalism, which has dominated social policy in Anglo-American countries until recent times. And as we saw with recent analyses of globalisation, there is no reason to believe that the new architecture will be shaped the same way in every country. Social politics still matters!

Because of its quite different historical legacy, the social policy challenge presents itself differently in Australia. Here a traditional reliance on making work pay through wage-based welfare and intervention to promote full employment has indeed been hollowed out. A nation that was more reluctant than most to embrace the welfare state now finds itself reliant on welfare rather than paid work to achieve its social policy goals. This might well be reversed through the adoption of a social investment approach designed to both boost employment and make work pay. Either way, Australians will need to make a choice about their welfare safety net. They can follow through with the neo-liberal rhetoric of the 1990s and further marketise services and cut all but the most needy from the welfare rolls. Or, they can reverse the targeting and consider how the safety net might be transformed into a more inclusive system of social services to enable all Australians to negotiate the 'risk society'.

Part Three

AREAS OF SOCIAL POLICY ACTION

This third part of the book contains an analysis of the individual areas of social policy, covering problems and issues, the current policy response, different policy options, and future directions. Rather than adopting a demographic approach that focuses on different groups (such as children and families or Indigenous Australians) we have chosen the key policy areas that contribute to the welfare of all groups. We cover employment and wages, income support, housing, health, education, community services, and financing and taxation. Policies in these areas are central to the level and distribution of material well-being in Australia and impact, either directly or indirectly, on people's relationships and capacity to participate.

Paid work is the important source of income for most Australians and its distribution is a critical influence on inequality and poverty in Australia and well-being in a range of areas including health, personal relationships, and housing. However, as Stephen Bell and John Quiggin indicate, the well-being of many Australians is compromised because Australia's labour market has 'too much unemployment and underemployment, and associated forms of labour market insecurity or disadvantage'. The authors show how the labour market has changed over the past 30 or so years, and examine the effectiveness of a range of policy approaches, concluding that a better approach would be to combine a more substantial effort to improve education and training with targeting public sector job creation.

But for those unable to obtain sufficient, well-paid work, or for whom full-time work is inappropriate due to age, disability, or caring responsibilities, the payments by government through Australia's income support arrangements provide an alternative to poverty or the dependency on the good-will and charity of others. Stephen Ziguras provides a history of the development of Australia's income support system, before identifying the key goals of poverty alleviation, income replacement, and promoting re-entry into paid work. He shows how the latter goal has become more dominant over the past decade, which is also reflected in changed institutional arrangements and the development of the mutual obligation regime.

Next to employment, the cost, quality, and accessibility of housing is the most important determinant of living standards, while the availability of health care and participation in education can contribute to future living standards (through their development of human capital) as well as impacting on current well-being (both material and quality of life). Community services can provide social support, relieve suffering, and develop capacity in a range of ways. In his chapter on housing, Tony Dalton shows how the affordability of housing has become a key issue in Australia for many low-income people, but that the capacity for decisive policy responses is limited by current institutional arrangements. In their chapters on health, education, and community services, Jenny Lewis, Jane Kenway, and Deborah Brennan all deal with very complex and different policy areas but also all point to the increasing use of the private sector and market approaches to service delivery. These changes pose the danger of the development of a two-tiered approach as we are unwilling to pay for social policies that promote universalism and social solidarity. The final chapter by Alison McClelland examines the history of Australia's low tax status and the options and prospects for policy reform.

8

EMPLOYMENT POLICY: UNEMPLOYMENT AND LABOUR MARKET INSECURITY

Stephen Bell and John Quiggin

A capitalist economy turns almost everything into a commodity. Certainly, it forces people to try and sell their labour in a 'labour market' in order to earn a living. Hence the labour market is of central importance to the life chances of the vast bulk of the population. Only the very young, the old, and incapacitated are spared the usually gruelling challenge of 'competing' in the labour market. Obviously, the most humane way of running such a system is to give those who need or want to work a good job on reasonable wages. The labour market quickly becomes inhumane for those who cannot find a good job or any or enough work.

In this chapter, we argue that Australia's labour market—indeed most capitalist labour markets—feature too much unemployment and underemployment, and associated forms of labour market insecurity or disadvantage. The latter term implies a weak or tenuous connection to the labour force through underemployment, involuntary casual or part-time work, and/or low wages or other manifestations of weakness vis-à-vis employers. The direct and indirect costs of such malfunctions in the labour market are reflected in all sorts of economic, social, and health costs (Saunders & Taylor 2002; Watts 2000). A good deal of social policy is directed to problems emanating from the labour market and its various malfunctions—especially unemployment, underemployment, and inequality. Accordingly, a good way to minimise the need for expensive and often difficult social policy interventions is to organise the labour market so that it provides reasonable jobs and wages for those that seek them.

Unfortunately, creating such a labour market is not easy. There are inevitable tensions and conflicts between employers and employees over shares of wages and profits. Also, capitalist economies have rarely created full employment. The so-called 'Golden Age' of capitalism in the post-Second World War era was a rare period of managed capitalism, full employment, and rising living standards for most. But employers are wary of full employment because it strengthens the bargaining hand of labour, leads to upward pressure on wages, and can generate high levels of (wage push) inflation. It was this scenario that saw the collapse of the Golden Age in the 1970s in Australia and many other capitalist economies. The aftermath, in the 1970s and 1980s, was marked by relatively high levels of unemployment and inflation. It is only since the deep recession of the early 1990s that Western economies have been broadly stabilised on a path of low inflation, economic expansion (especially in Australia), and falling unemployment.

According to the official estimates, after over a decade of reasonably strong economic growth, Australia now has an unemployment rate of 5.2 per cent. That sounds reasonably low. However, we argue that a more accurate measure of unemployment would see this number almost double. Also, structural change in the economy is producing a labour market that tends to create causal, insecure, and low-paid jobs. It is this combination of unemployment and labour market insecurity that has played an important role in moderating (wage push) inflation in the 1990s.

This chapter begins by looking at the dynamics of the Australian labour market. We also look at how the economy is producing increasing levels of labour market insecurity and how this and unemployment are increasing economic inequality in Australia.

Based on the assumption that more work and better pay would reduce the need for expensive social policy interventions, we examine the various positions in the employment policy debate. We then examine employment policy in Australia and briefly examine the costs and dilemmas of returning to a full employment economy. We argue that Australia has a half-baked 'full employability' policy aimed at getting people ready for employment, but not a 'full employment' policy that—at least in a direct sense—actually helps create jobs.

CHANGING POLICY CONTEXT: AUSTRALIA'S LABOUR MARKET DYNAMICS

Typical of wider trends in the advanced economies, the Australian labour market has undergone dramatic changes in recent decades. The structure of employment has changed with a higher premium placed on skills and knowledge. At the lower end of the market, traditional unskilled 'blue collar' jobs have been rapidly disappearing, though simultaneously there has been a proliferation of part-time and/or casual jobs in the low-end services sector. For these and other reasons unemployment, underemployment, insecure forms of work, low wages, and rising levels of inequality have all become major problems in Australia's labour market.

The increase and subsequent decline in the official unemployment rate in recent decades is shown graphically in Figure 8.1. A major driver of unemployment has been the size of the gap between labour force growth and employment levels, especially the large gaps opened up in each of the major recessions during the 1970s, the early 1980s, and early 1990s. The main story of the last three decades is that major recessions, as periods of intense job destruction, have a devastating impact on employment growth and are a major factor in driving up unemployment and embedding high levels of structural and long-term unemployment.

Figure 8.1 Unemployment in Australia 1960–2004

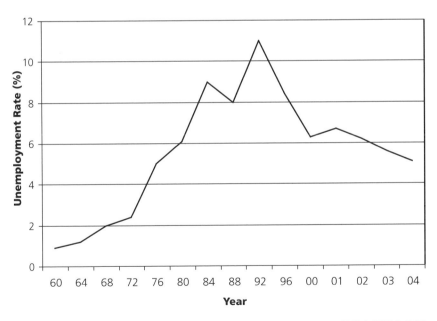

Source ABS Cat. Nos. 6202.0; 6203.0, 6204.

Although the official measure of unemployment currently stands at just over 5 per cent of the labour force, it is important to remember that the method of measuring unemployment used by the Australian Bureau of Statistics (ABS) is highly selective and grossly understates the true level of the problem. One hour of paid employment in the relevant survey reference week (or an hour of unpaid employment in a family business) can remove one from the unemployment statistics. There are also large numbers of people who (for various reasons) are classified as 'not in the labour force'. Argy (2005) estimates that 800 000 people suffer such 'hidden unemployment'. The implication, as Lee and Miller (2000, p. 76) suggest, is that 'the official unemployment rate is not reflective of the true state of the labour market'.

Langmore and Quiggin (1994) consider a range of forms of unemployment not included in the official measure. First, there are persons who have given up trying to find work and who were officially counted as 'discouraged job seekers'. These are part of a larger group who would like work if it were available, but are not looking for a job at present. Mitchell and Watts (1997) estimate that if the hidden unemployment and underemployment of those with a designated marginal attachment to the labour force were properly taken into account, about five percentage points could be added to the official rate of unemployment. Similarly, Wooden (1996) estimates that the official category of 'unemployment' captures only about half of the true level of labour underutilisation (see also Mitchell 2001a; Mitchell & Carlson 2001).

Second, there are underemployed workers—those working part time who would like to work full time (note: during the 1990s, a new and opposite category emerged—those working more than a standard full-time work week who would like to work less).

Third, there are people of working age who have left the labour force and gone on to disability benefits, or taken early access to the old age pension. Some recipients of disability benefits are completely incapacitated for work. However, many people with minor disabilities who would be employable in a properly functioning labour market have ended up on disability benefits. Given that the health status of the population has generally been improving, the large increase in the number of people receiving disability benefits can only be regarded as a form of disguised unemployment.

Similarly, it is often difficult to distinguish between voluntary and involuntary early retirement. Nevertheless, a reduction in workforce participation for workers aged over 50 does not make economic sense in a context where the proportion of the population in this age group can be expected to increase steadily.

Figure 8.2 presents the numbers of persons in the various relevant categories as of September 2003. As can be seen, there are large numbers of people who were not working, who wanted to work, but who were not counted as unemployed. Note also, the large number of persons who have given up trying to find work and who were officially counted as 'discouraged job seekers'.

Figure 8.2 Persons in and not in the labour force

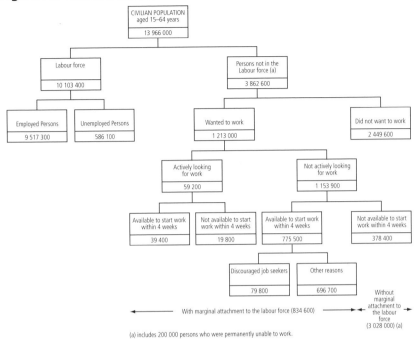

(a) includes 200 000 persons who were permanently unable to work.

Besides underestimating the true level of unemployment, it is also the case, as per a recent survey by Bell (2002) and other sources, that:

■ There has been a steep rise in the level of long-term unemployment, with the duration of unemployment roughly doubling since the late 1970s. This is one of the key and apparently enduring 'scarring' effects of major recessions and periods of high unemployment. At present, almost a third of the unemployed have been unemployed for more than a year and are officially classified as long-term unemployed.

■ Although declining somewhat in the 1990s, the employment/GDP ratios across the advanced economies (including Australia) have been relatively strong since the 1970s. Although there has been 'jobless growth' in a number of sectors (mining, agriculture, and manufacturing), this has not been the case in aggregate terms. Nevertheless, the growth of employment and the relatively strong jobs intensity of output growth since the 1970s has not kept pace with the demand for jobs. Persistent unemployment reflects the failure of the labour market to create enough jobs to satisfy demand. Indeed, the unemployed persons/job vacancy ratio has averaged approximately 11:1 since the early 1970s (Mitchell 2001b, p. 17). While unemployment was once relatively evenly distributed, there is now a strong trend towards jobs-rich and jobs-poor households, neighbourhoods, and regions (Gregory & Hunter 1996). One in six children now grow up in jobless households.

- In the long 1990s expansion, many labour market 'insiders' did well in terms of growth in skilled employment and higher wages. However, there were also many labour market fringe dwellers in low paid and insecure forms of work, while many labour market 'outsiders' languished in unemployment or severe underemployment.

- The employment rate for women has increased substantially in recent decades, and the labour market status of women has improved relative to that of men. In the 1970s, males had about half the unemployment rate of females. Now males have higher unemployment rates than females. Indeed, male full-time employment in the age range 45–54 has fallen by 16 per cent since 1970 and by 32 per cent over the same period in the 55–64 age range (Keating 2004a, p. 115). Youth and the less skilled also suffer relatively high levels of unemployment.

- The most systematic observation across the various trends is that unemployment is overwhelmingly a problem for *low-skilled male workers* facing the effects of structural change in industries or regions that are shedding labour. A particular hotspot in this regard has been labour shedding in the manufacturing sector (Gregory & Hunter 1996). Unemployment levels for such male workers would have been even more acute had there not been a substantial decline in male full-time labour market participation rates.

- Much of the employment created in the current recovery (starting in the early 1990s) has consisted of part-time and/or casual jobs. It is also the case that a significant proportion of new jobs are relatively insecure and poorly paid, while only a smaller number of high-income, high-status jobs have been created. This partly reflects structural change in the economy. Full-time employment losses in the manufacturing and public sectors have in many cases been replaced by employment in the low-end market services sector. Other contributors include rapid changes in the structure of demand, changing product cycles, and heightened competitive pressures, with a greater emphasis on bottom line returns leading employers to abandon assumptions about durable employment patterns in favour of downsizing and greater 'flexibility'. The net effect is far higher levels of labour 'churning' and an associated rise in frictional unemployment, in some cases blending into long-term unemployment (Hancock 1999).

- There has been a major expansion of 'non-standard' forms of work in Australia, particularly casual and part-time work, typically with reduced levels of job security. Sheehan (1998, p. 241) argues that since 1973, one in five full-time jobs have been lost in the economy. Put another way, 'if the 1973 ratio of full-time employment to the population of working age had been maintained through to 1996, the number of full-time jobs available in the Australian economy would have been about 2.8 million higher than was actually the case.' Campbell (2000) shows that between 1990 and 1999, 71 per cent of the growth of employment was accounted for by the growth of casual employment. Over the same decade, the proportion of full-time, permanent employees in the labour force declined from 73.5 per cent to 63.4 per cent. As Campbell (2000, p. 70) argues, 'At the level of the workforce as a whole, casual employment appears to be slowly replacing full-time permanent employment.' Male full-time employment increased by only 5 per cent in the 13 years between 1989 and 2002 (Keating 2004a, p. 115).
- Earnings inequality is increasing (Borland 1999). Significant areas of jobs growth in the services sector (including accommodation and cafes, retail and wholesale trade, and personal and other services) pay at or below average weekly wages. This expansion of low-wage services employment in Australia, combined with unemployment and less equal access to work, has produced a marked shift towards a more inegalitarian distribution of incomes from work. For example, the earnings of male full-time workers in the lowest income decile fell from 76 per cent of median earnings in 1975 to 65 per cent in 2000, while the corresponding fall for females was from 80 to 71 per cent (Keating 2004a, p. 114).

POLICY ISSUES AND RESPONSE

A number of major public policy issues are raised by the labour market dynamics outlined above. One issue is what to do about unemployment and underemployment. A second issue is how to address the problem of increasing inequality born of unemployment, underemployment, and structural change in the labour market. A third, related issue pertains to the role of social policy and the welfare state.

In terms of unemployment and underemployment, these stem from the failure of the economy to create sufficient jobs (or perhaps the right kinds of jobs) to meet the demands for work. The policy debate on how best to create more jobs has traditionally been polarised between neo-liberal 'supply-side' arguments and Keynesian-inspired 'demand-side' arguments.

That there are such different views on how to 'construct' the problem of unemployment points to the fact that social reality is always wide open to differing interpretations. In this case, the differences hinge on competing paradigms (Keynesian versus neoclassical) within the discipline of economics. The debate between these paradigms has been waged for decades. In the postwar Golden Age era, Keynesian interpretations were dominant. Since the 1970s, for a range of reasons (including shifts in the dominant political coalition), neoclassical cum neo-liberal views have been ascendant. The technical debate on these issues is typically waged by labour market economists and other experts, but, as always in politics, the arguments and messages are massaged and propagated by various players including interest groups, think tanks, political parties, trade unions, employers, bureaucrats, central bankers, and governments. In the final analysis, the way in which ideas shape policy debates and politics is a complex affair, but in the case at hand it is governments and their advisers who have the most say in shaping the agenda and formulating labour market and employment policy responses. We will return to the dilemmas facing governments in a moment, but first we need to unpack the policy debate.

Supply-siders tend to draw inspiration from the neoclassical economics paradigm and see unemployment is mainly as an individualised problem of *labour supply*. In other words, those who are unemployed are (market) deficient in some way: including laziness, education or skill deficiencies, an unwillingness to move to where jobs are on offer, asking for 'excessive' wages, etc. The cure for such problems, according to supply-siders, is a dose of 'microeconomic reform' of the labour market, designed to reduce structural rigidities and increase labour skills and 'flexibility'. This might include efforts to force people off the dole to search harder for work, education and skills enhancement, labour market programs (e.g. relocation subsidies, job placement services etc), and/or efforts to reduce wages.

Education and skills enhancement is a good idea, especially since (as above) most of the unemployed are in low-skilled areas of the labour market. However, there is no guarantee that more education and training will create jobs (Webster 2000). Such an approach could end up with better trained queues of unemployed. The critical issue is how to create more jobs, especially in the short to medium term. The view that reducing wages will help price workers into jobs and thus help 'clear' the market is based on a rather simple demand and supply view of the world: if something is cheaper (in this case labour) more will be demanded. Because unemployment is currently most pronounced among low-skilled workers, the advocates of a supply-side program argue for wages cuts for low-skilled jobs. This view has been endorsed by the Governor of the Reserve Bank, Ian Macfarlane. In a speech in 1997, he cited the situation in the larger continental European economies, where labour markets have an institutional framework that promotes 'jobs security, imposes relatively strict minimum wages and conditions, provides easily accessible sickness benefits and unemployment benefits, and increases trade union involvement'. These, Macfarlane argued, 'work against the interests of job creation' (Macfarlane 1997, p. 6). The solution Macfarlane advocates is further movement towards USA, UK, and New Zealand-style labour market deregulation. This, Macfarlane concedes, will reduce wages and conditions for workers and lead to growing wage dispersion and inequality, but it is a price we must pay, he argues. On the question of fairness, he states that 'while income inequality may not seem very fair, unemployment is not very fair either' (Macfarlane 1997, p. 6). Some economists call this the 'diabolical trade-off'.

The problem with this approach is that it is not at all clear that wage cuts actually create much employment (Junankar 2000). If anything, labour markets have become more flexible in the last two decades, yet unemployment and underemployment continue to be major problems (Standing 1997). Also, a wage-moderation or wage-cutting approach to unemployment is not likely to prove to be electorally popular, so governments have not been keen to openly advocate such a policy stance. Instead, governments have tended to adopt various kinds of labour market 'flexibility' approaches, including strengthening the hand of employers in wage bargaining under moves towards 'enterprise bargaining'. The Howard government's new industrial relations legislation is a further push in this direction. Such moves have not led to a substantial widening of wage relativities to date (Keating 2004a, pp. 67–8), although flexibility has increased in terms of working hours and how work is organised. Governments have also worked to make the dole less attractive and various schemes involving skills training and other labour market programs have also been adopted. In Australia, however, these latter programs have tended to be rather poorly funded and ad hoc. The constant churning of people through such programs, often with limited results in terms of employment, has lead to much frustration on the part of those forced through such programs. The basic problem of course is that there are too few appropriate jobs on offer. As a former senior public servant has recently written, unless there are more jobs and better training and skills enhancement 'the present government's policy of requiring unemployed persons to pursue non-existent jobs will continue to be both impractical and morally bankrupt' (Keating 2004a, p. 120).

Demand-siders, by contrast, recognise structural unemployment and supply-side problems, but place much more emphasis in explaining unemployment on economic growth and the *demand* side of the economy. Demand-side analysts tend to draw on the Keynesian paradigm and are more sceptical than supply-siders regarding the ability of unfettered markets to generate full employment. As Mitchell (2000) argues, the main factors that have driven unemployment in the last two decades are weak aggregate demand and inadequate levels of growth, particularly during major recessions. Consequently, demand-side analysts argue that the avoidance of recessions and faster economic growth are central to dealing with unemployment and underemployment. Demand-siders often have a more positive view of government than supply-siders (cum neo-liberals) and they argue that government can play a role in stimulating economic growth—for example, through the careful use of fiscal policy (i.e. taxing and spending powers) to help stimulate the economy (Nevile 2000).

However, such aggregate economic growth may run into limits in terms of current account problems or via higher growth leading to higher inflation. An alternative is a more precise and targeted approach to job creation, mainly through publicly funded public and community sector jobs creation (Bell 2000; Langmore & Quiggin 1994; Quiggin 2000). This approach has the advantage of not being likely to exacerbate current account pressures and is better placed to manage wage pressures and inflation more directly. To the extent that unemployment is mainly a problem for the unskilled, such a program is also likely to be more easily blended with specific skills training. And to the extent that skills upgrading is too onerous or difficult for some, direct jobs creation might also aim to supply low-skilled jobs for those that require them. The biggest problem with such direct jobs creation programs is that they cost money and will confront opposition from those who resist any increase in taxation and government spending.

The practical difficulties of pursuing a strong dose of either a supply- or demand-side approach to unemployment and underemployment has meant that governments have adopted limited versions of each approach and have tended to muddle along on a middle path. Reasonably strong economic growth over the last decade or more has helped reduce unemployment and such a trend has been accompanied by the kinds of supply-side and labour market 'flexibility' policies noted above. However, even after over a decade of economic growth, unemployment has been agonisingly slow in coming down and a range of other adverse labour market trends noted above are apparent. A significant slow down or recession would again bring labour market issues and unemployment into stark relief. Ultimately, a much more substantial policy response in terms of education and training (in order to better match skills to available jobs) and the promotion of targeted public sector job creation are required. Yet, over the last decade or more, reasonable rates of economic growth and the realisation by governments that unemployment and other adverse labour market trends do not seem to be biting politically, has seen the unemployment issue more or less shelved for now.

By contrast, Australian governments have taken the issue of rising market inequality more seriously. Traditional tax and spend social policy and welfare state interventions have had a major effect in treating at least the symptoms of many of the labour market trends outlined above, especially in ameliorating inequality. Indeed, thus far, the effects of the labour market dynamics outlined above in driving inequality have largely been offset by governments using taxation, cash payments, and the provision of services. In other words, although private market income inequality has increased, the total disposable and final incomes available to households have not shown a marked trend towards greater inequality, largely because of various measures taken by government. For example, 25 years ago low-income households in Australia received little in the way of direct income transfers. Today, low-income families with dependent children, living in rental accommodation, might receive almost half of their disposable income from government transfers (Keating 2004a, p. 116). These days almost one-third of all Australian adult residents now receive some form of government income support.

OPTIONS AND FUTURE DIRECTIONS?

Beyond the problems and responses outlined above, another large medium-term labour market issue confronting Australia stems from demographic dynamics. Between 1978–98, annual labour force growth averaged 1.9 per cent, but from 1998–2016, the ABS estimates that this growth rate will average only half the former rate, with labour force growth of only 0.8 per cent annually. Indeed, both labour force growth and the labour force participation rate are expected to decline substantially, due to a slower rate of population growth and an ageing population. Independent of any other shift, these changes should help bring down unemployment and could well lead to future widespread labour shortages. No doubt, targeted immigration programs will continue to play a role in partly dealing with Australia's labour requirements, but labour shortages across many of the advanced economies (or at least those with slow labour force growth) will intensify international competition for skilled mobile labour. In a context in which many of the best paid and most rewarding jobs require high skills, and where economic growth is increasingly related to the skills and talents of the workforce, Australia will need to try and lift the education and skills of the labour force.

In the short to medium term, the labour market divisions and disadvantages outlined above, and that are increasingly played out on a spatial and regional basis, will also need to be addressed. Both supply-side and demand-side policies need to blend in new innovative ways. People need to be educated and up-skilled for the top-end jobs, and over time more of such jobs and areas of employment need to be created through higher levels of education, training, innovation, and investment in the economy. This will hopefully offer more, better, and different opportunities than those that were mainly created in the Australian economy in the last decade—low-end, casual, and part-time service sector jobs featuring low wages.

However, education, retraining, and skills upgrading programs need to be seen in perspective. While useful, particularly in the longer term as part of a national economic upgrading process, in the short to medium term the training route can only be a partial answer to unemployment and labour market disadvantage because it focuses mainly on the supply of labour and not on the supply of jobs. In a recent study of the relationship between skills upgrading and unemployment, Chapman's (1999) 'major conclusion is that the answer to Australian job creation, at least in the short to medium term, does not lie in increasing the skills of the unemployed'. Serious consideration also needs to be given to the little debated possibility that the level of commitment, intellect, and knowledge required to *successfully* participate in the labour market may be increasingly beyond the capacity of many. As the American writer, Larry Letich (1995) has argued: 'It is possible that over the last 100 years, and especially the last 40, we may have created a society that demands more brain power than most people are able to give'. If so, even an advanced 'training augmented' labour market will fail the key distributional tasks of providing jobs and adequate incomes for many of those at the bottom. In this situation, the only solution is to explicitly supply jobs with reasonable wages that match feasible capabilities and talents. This is an explicitly distributional issue that, in an increasingly knowledge-based economy, the market is not solving.

SUMMARY AND CONCLUSION

Despite an exceptionally long period of economic expansion since the recession of the early 1990s, official unemployment rates have only recently returned to the rates prevailing in the late 1970s, and are still well above those of the postwar 'Golden Age'. In part, this reflects the fact that unemployment is an inherently intractable problem, but the slow progress also reflects the fact that reducing unemployment has not, in general, been a high policy priority. If the current expansion continues, it may be argued that the government's strategy of focusing on economic fundamentals, and waiting for unemployment to decline as a result, has been vindicated. If, however, there is another recession any time in the next few years, it is likely that the expansion beginning in 1990 will be viewed as a missed opportunity to achieve a large and durable reduction in unemployment.

If we agree that good jobs and reasonable pay are absolutely central to people's life chances in a capitalist economy, then the labour market challenges outlined above pose some serious problems. At present, labour market disadvantage, unemployment, underemployment, and market inequality loom large. In 20 years' time, if not before, serious labour shortages could emerge in many areas. This will obviously have implications for unemployment and underemployment, although the issue of matching available skills and job vacancies will continue. In the meantime, and probably in the longer term, many Australians (particularly those without skills or those suffering other forms of labour market disadvantage) will remain unemployed, underemployed, or on low incomes. Hence, the problem of helping those who cannot easily up-skill or compete in the labour market should be a priority.

These challenges will confront employment, labour market, and social policy makers with major conceptual and administrative problems. In recent years there have been calls that older forms of statist and top down policy making in these areas should be partly dissolved down into more participatory forms of decision making in neighbourhoods, communities, and regions, and that the state should 'enable' rather than direct (Botsman & Latham 2001; Smyth & Wearing 2002). Similar calls from various quarters have argued that the welfare state was never originally designed for long-term support for the unemployed or disadvantaged and that older welfare state models now foster passive welfare dependency. The new emphasis is now on welfare to work programs and 'mutual obligation' (Considine 2000). While laudable in some respects, many of the agendas and programs say too little about the actual creation of jobs. At their worst, they descend into born-again forms of communitarianism, or mercilessly prod the unemployed and disadvantaged through workfare programs with few jobs in sight at the end.

A further issue that needs to be confronted is that effectively dealing with unemployment, underemployment, inequality, and education and skills upgrading will be expensive. The net costs of the required programs and initiatives (given the various returns and spin offs) are likely to be much lower than the gross costs. However, the next several decades contain a fiscal time bomb stemming from the likely costs of an ageing population, more expensive health care, education and skill enhancement, public infrastructure investment, protection of the environment, and other non-insignificant new expenditures. Keating (2004a, p.148) estimates that new public expenditure requirements will amount to an additional 10 per cent of GDP. If we add new and continuing costs of dealing with labour market disadvantage and social and economic inequality, this amounts to a huge increase in public expenditure and raises serious questions about the fiscal capacity of the state in an era in which public cynicism of governments is rising and taxation increases are regarded by governments as electoral suicide.

9

AUSTRALIAN SOCIAL SECURITY POLICY: DOING MORE WITH LESS?

Stephen Ziguras

INTRODUCTION

Like its wildlife and its football, Australia has an unusual social security system compared with many other countries. It is highly targeted, funded by general revenue, and has flat rate rather than earnings-related payments. The strength of targeting has been to ensure that the poorest benefit most from the funding made available, but it has led to ambivalent public support for some types of payment and high effective marginal tax rates (EMTRs) as people take up work. The low levels of payments also mean that many reliant on social security are forced to live in significant financial stress (ACOSS 2004b; Senate Community Affairs References Committee 2004).

HISTORICAL OVERVIEW

Table 9.1 summarises the main social security changes since the early 1900s. Over this time, there were three main periods of substantial policy change in social security—the early 1900s, the period following the Second World War, and the late 1980s onwards.

Old age pensions were first introduced by the New South Wales and Victorian state governments in 1901. The Commonwealth established a means-tested (on current income and assets) age pension and an invalid pension in 1909.

A one-off maternity payment was introduced in 1912, but the next significant reform was not until the Menzies government introduced a widow's pension in 1942 and a universal child endowment scheme, funded by the introduction of a pay-roll tax. (Kewley 1973, p. 196).

Table 9.1 Main social security changes 1901–2005

Year	Initiative
1901	NSW and Victoria introduce the Age Pension.
1909	Commonwealth Age Pension comes into operation with both income and assets tests.
1910	Invalid Pension commences.
1912	Maternity Allowance introduced—one-off universal payment to mothers.
1928	Contributory national insurance scheme proposed but rejected.
1928	NSW pays child endowment to families as addition to 'living wage'.
1929	Great Depression, 'dole' administered by states, relief works require unemployed to work part-time at minimum wages to receive equivalent to the dole.
1931	Age and Invalid Pensions reduced as an economy measure, Maternity Allowance means-tested.
1938–41	Contributory pensions bill passed and then rescinded due to lack of support.
1941	Universal Child Endowment scheme introduced, funded by state pay-roll taxes.
1942	Widow's Pension introduced.
1944	Unemployment, Sickness and Special Benefit introduced, Commonwealth Employment Service established.
1969	Age Pension withdrawal rates liberalised.
1973	Supporting Mothers Pension introduced.
1976	Assets test on Age Pension abolished, Family Allowance replaces Child Endowment and tax rebates.
1977–80	Supporting Parents Benefit extended to fathers, 6-month waiting period abolished.
1983	Family Income Supplement (FIS) introduced for low-income working families.
1985	Assets test on Age Pension reintroduced.
1986	Family Allowance means-tested, Family Allowance Supplement replaces FIS with higher rate and more generous income test.
1991	Unemployment Benefit activity test introduced—work test amended to include training.
1994	Working Nation labour market programs include training and work experience subsidies, 'reciprocal obligation' introduced.
1995	Maximum withdrawal rate for allowances reduced from 100 to 70 per cent, income test for allowee couples amended so that each partner assessed on own income, with partner's income only assessed if sufficient to reduce their own payment to zero.
1996	Funding for employment services reduced by 30 per cent.

Year	Initiative
1997	Howard government introduces 'mutual obligation' and Work for the Dole, Job Network replaces CES, Centrelink takes over administration of social security payments.
1998–2000	Breaches rise dramatically leading to national campaign.
2000	Introduction of GST accompanied by simplification of twelve family payments into three (Family Tax Benefit (A), Family Tax Benefit (B), and Child Care Benefit). McClure report recommends a single working age social security payment, extension of mutual obligation to parents, more 'in-work benefits'.
2002	Introduction of Australians Working Together package—Parenting Payment recipients activity tested when youngest child turns 13, Working Credit introduced, Introduction of Personal Advisers in Centrelink, Baby Bonus introduced.
2003	Discussion paper released by FACS and DEWR on 'single working age payment'.
2004	Maternity Payment increased and Baby Bonus scrapped, DEWR takes over responsibility for all working age income support payments and employment programs
2005	Disability Support Pension eligibility tightened, Parenting Payment recipients activity tested when youngest reaches school age.

Source: Centrelink 2005; Commonwealth of Australia 2001a; Department of Family and Community Services 2003; Department of Social Security 1990; Kewley 1973; Whiteford & Angenent 2002

During and following the Second World War, the Curtin Labor government planned an extensive series of reforms around the themes of reconstruction and security. Commonwealth powers over taxation were extended during the war, and the there was strong public support for a more interventionist role for government. In 1944, unemployment and sickness benefits were introduced and a special benefit was also enacted to provide an income to those in need but ineligible for any other payment. The Commonwealth Employment Service was established, accompanied by a policy commitment to full employment that was the cornerstone of economic policy for the next 25 years (Smyth 1998).

Little change to social security policy was made during the 1950s and 1960s, but the mid 1970s saw a short-lived flirtation with an idea of a guaranteed minimum income (GMI), a recommendation from the Henderson Poverty Inquiry. The Whitlam government introduced a supporting mothers' pension in 1973, extended to fathers in 1977 by the Fraser government and renamed Supporting Parents Payment. The Whitlam regime also introduced an administrative appeals system, and linked pension increases to average wages. The Fraser government also introduced universal family allowance payments.

From the mid 1980s onwards, continuing high rates of unemployment and an awareness that child poverty had become a significant problem prompted a new round of reforms. The Social Security Review was set up in 1986, chaired by academic Bettina Cass (Cass 1988). A key issue dealt with by the review was how to best assist families with children, and this led to significant increases to payments for low-income families with children, the introduction of the child support scheme, and the Jobs, Education and Training (JET) scheme for sole parents. The Review also examined the structure of disability payments, including how to help people with disabilities retain workforce attachment, leading to the Disability Reform Package in the early 1990s.

Long-term unemployment was another review focus. Many changes were made to unemployment payments in the following decade based on the idea of 'active labour market policy'—that social security should not just provide income for the unemployed, but play a more active role in promoting employment. In 1989, all long-term unemployed people aged between 21 and 54 years were subject to intensive interviews, and the following year this was extended to all long-term unemployed people. The 'work test' was also broadened to become an 'activity test', which could include education and training, or part-time, temporary, or casual work (OECD 2001).

The Howard government, elected in 1996, introduced more changes. In 1997, the Work for the Dole scheme was introduced for 18–24 year olds, and in 1998, the government introduced the notion of 'mutual obligation'. This notion held that receipt of social security created an obligation to 'give something back' to the community (rather than simply doing more to help yourself as was the case under Keating's 'reciprocal obligation'). Mutual obligation requirements could be met by voluntary work, participation in a Work for the Dole program, Green Corps, the Army Reserve, part-time work, or training.

In 1999, the government initiated a further round of reforms and appointed the Reference Group on Welfare Reform. The reference group recommended a greater flexibility in assessment and intervention to assist disadvantaged jobseekers into work, a single working age social security payment, more 'in-work benefits', and an extension of mutual obligation to parents, and possibly those with disabilities (Reference Group on Welfare Reform 2000).

POLICY GOALS

The social security system has several possible aims. The weight given to each of these varies according to individuals or interest groups, the orientation of particular governments, and changes over time. Different aims may be complementary or contradictory, and policy makers often struggle to reconcile these conflicting goals in an attempt 'to support those in need, contain cost, and maintain solidarity structures by mobilising widespread consent for the underlying objectives of social security' (Ditch 1999, p. 3). Overall, there has never been a clear rationale for the level of income support payments, and Kewley (1973) argues that political considerations play a major part with levels being set according to the degree of public support.

The most important aim is the prevention of poverty (ILO 1984), traditionally a key feature of the Australian approach. Systems that primarily aim to prevent poverty tend to emphasise payments going only to those without other means of support, tight eligibility criteria, and strict means tests. The 'means test' itself has long been a feature of Anglo-Saxon systems, dating from Elizabethan poor laws in the 1600s that tried to ensure that only the poor and deserving got assistance (Carney & Hanks 1986).

A system such as Australia's, with poverty alleviation at its heart, raises the key question of what poverty is, how it is measured, and what rate of payment is necessary to prevent it. Arguments about the adequacy of payments have a long history and poverty advocates such as ACOSS and the Brotherhood of St Laurence have pointed to the gap between rates of payment and the Henderson Poverty Line as evidence of inadequacy. Without getting into debates about poverty measurement, it is clear that payments are far less adequate for some groups, particularly young people between 18 and 21years of age, and single adults below age pension age (ACOSS 2004c; Brotherhood of St Laurence 2004).

Payment levels are also influenced by equity considerations. Equity generally refers to notions of fairness with horizontal and vertical equity both being important in income support policy (see discussion about equity in Chapter 14 for definitions). A key horizontal equity goal is to ensure that people with children are not worse off than those without children, while vertical equity has often been used to argue that payments should only be made to those on very low incomes. The tension between these two types of equity can be seen in debates about payments for children. On the one hand, horizontal equity means universal payments that recognise the additional costs of children regardless of income, whereas vertical equity means payments directed at families on low incomes. As a result, family payments in Australia have at times been universal payments, and at others they have been means tested, often driven by economic arguments about the capacity of government to fund these transfers and ensuring that those most in need benefit.

A second potential aim is income replacement and life cycle redistribution. This goal is to compensate people for the risk of reduced income for some period. Many European social insurance schemes are based on this approach, with payments more closely tied to previous earnings rather than a flat-rate received by all. The income replacement goal is associated with redistribution over an individual's life cycle (for example, compulsory saving for retirement through superannuation), and with the contributory principle—that recipients must make payments up to a certain level to qualify.

In Australia, arguments for contributory systems were made from time to time over the last century. These met with little success until the advent of compulsory award-based superannuation payments in 1985 and the introduction of the Superannuation Guarantee Charge (SGC) in the early 1990s. The superannuation system requires employer contributions of at least 9 per cent of gross salary. Benefits are based on the total amount held in a person's account when they retire, itself a function of the amount contributed and hence an income replacement rather than a poverty-alleviation payment. While employees do not technically contribute (unless they pay additional voluntary contributions), the introduction of compulsory superannuation was negotiated with the ACTU accepting a lower real wage increase for workers in return for the scheme.

Since the mid 1980s, an increasingly important goal of the social security system has been to promote re-entry into employment for the unemployed. While a requirement to seek work has always been part of the unemployment payments, requirements were expanded in the early 1990s. The argument was made that the system had to encourage or oblige people to make more effort to get into work. Indeed over the last two decades, this goal has arguably come to outweigh all others for payments to people of working age. Both sides of politics now argue that employment is the best route out of poverty, but, in fact, the low levels of payment mean that employment is often the only route out of poverty. Hence much advocacy and research during the 1990s has been about the effectiveness of the unemployment system in helping people into jobs.

Arguments giving priority to the employment aim drive payment levels in the opposite direction to the aim of poverty alleviation. Economists argue that too high a level of payment of unemployment benefits would reduce the motivation of unemployed people to seek work. The replacement rate is the ratio of unemployment benefits to minimum wages. If replacement rates are too high, there is less benefit gained from moving into work. Despite some arguments to the contrary, Australian replacement rates are not high, being around the OECD average (Martin 1998).

KEY ELEMENTS OF THE CURRENT SYSTEM

All social security payments that currently exist (in Australia and internationally) are 'categorical' in that they are usually available only to people in specific circumstances. The main groups eligible for payment in Australia are families with children, parents under certain circumstances, carers, the unemployed, students, the disabled or temporarily incapacitated, and older people. Table 9.2 provides a summary of the main payments.

Most people with no income from earnings (or from a partner) will now be eligible for some type of payment, but they must be willing to meet certain requirements to qualify (for example, being willing to look for and accept paid employment). One notable exception is newly arrived migrants. Migrants arriving under the family reunion scheme are often required to have an 'assurance of support'. Their relative or sponsor will support them for the first 2 years they are in the country and they are not eligible for any payments unless they can demonstrate that the support is unavailable due to some unforeseen circumstances. Those arriving as asylum seekerson temporary protection visas are in a worse position and may not be eligible for income support under any circumstance (ACOSS 2004c).

Two forms of payment provide an income intended to cover general living expenses. These are, first, allowances (also called benefits) that are short-term payments for people in situations that are expected to be temporary. Some allowances are being phased out including the Mature Age Allowance, Partner Allowance, and Widow's Allowance. The second type, pensions, are paid to people who are expected to rely on social security for an extended period. They are paid at a higher rate than allowances (in 2005 they could be up to $40 per week higher depending on a person's circumstances), and have other more generous conditions. There are also payments in acknowledgment of the extra costs of certain groups. Additional payments, Family Tax Benefit A and B, are made to families with children, and there are a range of other payments or concessions to assist with costs such as housing, medication, travel, and utilities.

All social security payments are targeted and subject to a 'means test', which includes both income and assets, apart from when the Age or Disability Support Pension is paid to a blind person, in which case there is no income or assets testing. Taper rates refer to the rate at which benefits are reduced as income from other sources (mainly paid employment) increases. There is usually a 'free area', which is not subject to a benefit reduction. Allowances have a lower free area and higher taper rates than pensions. These settings were based on the assumption that pensioners could only work part-time and the lower taper rate would not penalise them, whereas recipients of allowances would move straight into full-time work, so the higher taper rates would not matter. The allowance taper rates are still designed so that an individual working at the minimum wage in Australia will not be eligible for any payment.

Table 9.2 Main social security payments (at April 2005)

Payment	Eligibility	Free Area (for singles unless indicated)	Withdrawal Rate
Allowances			
Newstart Allowance	Aged 21 and over, unemployed	$62 p.f.[1], if not used, can be banked up to $1000 p.a.[1]	50% for income between $62–142 p.f. and 70% for income over $142 p.f.
Youth Allowance (YA) (Unemployed)	Aged 16–20 and unemployed, parental income test applies unless considered 'independent'	As per Newstart	As per Newstart
Youth Allowance (Student)	Aged 16–24 and full-time student, other as for YA above	$236 p.f., if not used, can be banked up to $6000 p.a.	50% for income $236–316 and 70% for income over $316
Austudy	Aged 25 or over and full-time student	As per YA (student)	As per YA (student)
Parenting Payment (Partnered)	Responsibility for a dependent child, married or in a de facto relationship	As per Newstart but varies according to partner's circumstances	As per Newstart but these figures vary
Special Benefit	In hardship and with no other sources of income	None	100% for any income
Pensions			
Age Pension	Males aged 65 or over, females qualifying age gradually increasing to 65	$122 p.f.	40% for any income over $122
Disability Support Pension	Assessed as having a disability and unable to work more than 30 hours per week	As per Age Pension	As per Age Pension
Parenting Payment (Single)	Responsibility for a dependent child, single	As per Age Pension	As per Age Pension
Carer Payment	Providing full-time care for a person with a disability	As per Age Pension	As per Age Pension

Payment	Eligibility	Free Area (for singles unless indicated)	Withdrawal Rate
Family			
Family Tax Benefit (A)	Dependent child under 21 or a full-time dependent student between 21 and 24	$32 485 p.a.	Over $32 485 p.a. 20% for differing ranges, then 30%
Family Tax Benefit (B)	Families with one main wage-earner with a dependent child under 16 or a full-time dependent student between 21 and 24	Income of first earner ignored, $4000 p.a. for second earner (or sole parent)	20% for any income over $4000 p.a.

Source: Centrelink 2004, 2005

Notes: 1 p.f. per fortnight, p.a. per annum

The combination of overlapping benefit withdrawal rates and personal income taxes is referred to as the 'effective marginal tax rate' (EMTR). EMTRs over some ranges are very high, so that people lose a very high proportion of any additional income they earn. This is less of a problem if someone moves straight into full-time work but is significant over certain hours of employment. For example, somebody increasing part-time work from two days to three days per week may only receive about 13 per cent additional net income because they face a 70 per cent withdrawal rate and a 17 per cent income tax rate. These high effective marginal tax rates are often described as 'poverty traps'.

High EMTRS are most commonly faced by those with dependent children because of the added effect of the withdrawal of family payments. Beer estimated that in 2002, for example, about a quarter of all sole parents faced EMTRs higher than 60 per cent (Beer 2003). High EMTRs are argued to be a major work disincentive, since they dramatically reduce the returns from working. Countries such as the UK and the USA have introduced tax credits to lower the EMTRs faced by people moving from welfare to work, although they also have the effect of shifting responsibility away from employers, increasing the division between the employed and unemployed, and moving high EMTRs further up the income scale rather than eliminating them altogether (McClelland 1999).

Eligibility for benefits and pensions is based on an individual's circumstances, but the income test takes into account family as well as individual income. This has consequences for two groups; married or de facto couples, and young people. Couples are assessed jointly, which means that if one member of a couple has no income of their own, payment levels vary according to the income of their partners. The Family Tax Benefit (B) is unusual in that the income of the main earner of a couple is disregarded, which means families with millionaire husbands and non-working wives are still eligible. This payment has been criticised as unfairly supporting and reinforcing a traditional family type over others (Apps 2004).

While some young people can qualify as being independent of their parents, most unemployed young people between 16 and 21 years of age, and students up to 25 years, are means tested on their parents' income and assets. These ages are arbitrary and contradict other policy areas that specify the age at which someone is considered to be independent of their parents—for example, the age at which people are eligible to vote is 18.

In Australia and New Zealand, payments are financed from general revenue, by all tax payers, in contrast with the social insurance systems of Europe where financing is from employer and employee contributions, and benefits are related to previous contributions. However, in such countries, those who are not eligible for social insurance benefits (due to lack of contributions or because their entitlements have run out) receive lower rates of payment, usually referred to as 'social assistance', and these social assistance payments are funded from general revenue. With the large pool of unemployed people over the last two decades, these payments have become more important in European countries. In most countries, including Australia, child benefits are paid out of government revenue.

The levels of so-called short-term payments, such as unemployment and sickness benefits, are indexed to inflation measured by the Consumer Price Index (CPI), in order to maintain the real value of the payment as costs go up and to keep replacement rates low. On the other hand, pensions such as the Age Pension and Disability Support pension are indexed to male total average weekly earnings, which reflects the overall income of the bulk of the population. This difference in indexing reflects the difference in policy aims between the two types of payments. Benefits are argued to be for short-term poverty alleviation, so they need to maintain their real value but not reflect incomes more generally. Pensions have a more implicit (albeit limited) income replacement aim so that the value should not lose touch with the rest of the population.

One consequence of this disparity in approaches to indexing is that the gap between pensions and allowances is increasing since earnings generally rise more than CPI. The base level of payment for a single adult receiving the Age Pension in 2005 was $482 per fortnight (including a pharmaceutical allowance paid automatically), $83 higher than someone on Newstart who received $399 per fortnight (Centrelink 2005).

INSTITUTIONAL CONTEXT AND IMPLEMENTATION

Social security institutions and administration have changed significantly in recent times. Up to the mid 1990s, social security policy development and administration were both carried out by the one department—the Department of Social Security. In 1997, a new benefits agency, Centrelink, was established to deliver social security and other payments. It had a separate Board of Management and was contracted to deliver services on behalf of several Commonwealth departments, notably the Department of Family and Community Services (FACS) and the Department of Employment and Workplace Relations (DEWR).

At around the same time as the creation of Centrelink, the Commonwealth Employment Service was replaced with the Job Network of private and not-for-profit employment services, which were responsible for assisting unemployed and jobless people to find work. This made the referral and coordination tasks more complex and also had other consequences. Job Network services had a maximum number of clients they were allocated. If someone did not attend, seemed unmotivated to work, or unable to work, they would stay on the agencies' books but not bring in any money (Considine 2001). Part of the reason for a substantial rise in breach penalties during the late 1990s was at least partly due to Job Network agencies trying to find ways to get non-attending clients off their books (ACOSS 2001; Pearce et al. 2002).

In 2004, responsibility for working age income support payments and employment programs was transferred from FACS to DEWR, and for students to the Department of Education, Science and Technology. In addition, Centrelink was to report to a new Department of Human Services (Howard 2004). These changes bring together responsibility for income support payments and services for people seeing work into the one department (DEWR), which could lead to more coherent linkages between them. However, there are now three different departments with responsibility for social security policy and a separate delivery agency reporting to yet another department. The potential for policy contradictions and confusion appears substantial.

Another relatively recent development has been the rise of administrative law. As in other areas of government service delivery, mechanisms have been set up over time to allow appeal rights against decisions. Within social security, these can be both administrative review (i.e. by Centrelink staff of its own decisions, or by the Social Security Appeals Tribunal (SSAT)) and legal challenge (to the Administrative Appeal Tribunal, the Federal and ultimately the High Court). The sheer complexity of the *Social Security Act* and its administration means that it is inevitable that mistakes will be made. Since the 1980s, Welfare Rights

Centres have been established around Australia to provide advice to social security recipients on processes for challenging decisions. In cases taken to the SSAT, approximately a third are found in favour of the recipient, but in spite of this, few people challenge decisions—perhaps because the appeal system itself is quite complex, and because they think they have no hope of winning.

Despite government taking over much of the responsibility for income support during the twentieth century, charities continued to provide material aid and administer emergency funds. Over the second half of the century, organisations like the Brotherhood of St Laurence and others developed a stronger advocacy and research focus. Charities continued to be seen as, and to claim themselves to be, the voice of the poor. Peak community agencies, such as the Victorian Council of Social Service (VCOSS) and the Australian Council of Social Service (ACOSS), gradually became the most important actors on behalf of the community sector and those living on low incomes, although large charities retained some influence. Many of these charities and ACOSS played a significant role in the campaign on breaching during 2001.

Consumer groups also organised themselves from the 1970s onwards. Groups such as the Women's Electoral Lobby during the 1970s, disability groups, the Council for the Single Mother and her Child, and the Council on the Ageing became more vocal. Welfare rights centres aimed to include and represent consumers' views, with varying success. The Sydney Welfare Rights Centre was particularly influential, supplying two Presidents of ACOSS (Julian Disney and Michael Raper) and ensuring that ACOSS maintained a strong focus on social security.

During the late 1980s, the Social Security review, headed by Bettina Cass, heralded greater involvement in policy making by academics. This intensified during the 1990s, although with academic economists playing a much more significant role. The Melbourne Institute, seen by some as an orthodox economic research unit, received increasing research and evaluation funding from the Federal government, and its head, Peter Dawkins, was a key participant in the welfare reform process.

Compared to their more active roles in Europe, unions and employer groups have played relatively little part in social security policy, being more concerned with industrial relations. This reflects Australia's labourist tradition of enshrining protection within employment systems and treating social security as a residual safety net. An important new interest group can be seen in the rise of right-wing 'think tanks' such as the Centre for Independent Studies. The CIS has been prominent in the media and has played a major role in promoting welfare and tax cuts, and movement towards an American-style system.

POLICY ASSESSMENT

The social security system has been under great pressure since the 1980s. At the heart of the challenge for policy makers is the breakdown of the 'Australian way' (Smyth 1998), in which the major protections were premised on full-time male employment and female household production, tariff protection, centralised wage fixing, and full employment as a central policy goal. In this paradigm, the social security system acted as a second order temporary safety net for those in retirement, or without work or family support. More recently though, it has had to deal with mass unemployment, continued long-term unemployment, and high rates of separation, all of which increased the number of people on benefits and the length of time for which they received them.

One consequence of sustained unemployment and the growth of both two-job and jobless households has been a shift in the means of income redistribution. Intra-family private redistribution of income from working husbands to non-working wives is being replaced by public transfers from working to non-working households, leading to growing expenditure on social security payments. This is turn has led to Treasury concerns to limit or reduce expenditure.

The growth in income support payments due to the breakdown of the 'Australian way' has implications for the political support of social security. For some payments, such as the Family Tax benefit and the Age Pension, public support is high, partly because the Age Pension goes to most people who reach pension age, and there is a sense of having contributed to it by paying taxes over the working life.

Other payments, particularly Newstart Allowance, Parenting Payment (and sole parents in particular), and Disability Support Pension have lower public support and greater concern about the legitimacy of claimants, reflected and occasionally fuelled by political rhetoric. The legitimacy of the social security program is threatened, leading to a downward spiral of more restrictions and requirements. European programs, in contrast, are less tightly means tested, and because they are based on individual contributions, appear to receive much greater public support.

Active labour market policy is still the basic premise for social security policy and is being extended to new groups. It has a diverse range of drivers, ranging from social democratic philosophies to neo-liberal economics. Australia's foray into active labour market policy began with the Social Security Review (Cass 1988), which argued that the social security system should more actively assist the unemployed to adapt to the dramatic restructuring of the Australian economy.

Other influences included paternalist accounts of welfare dependence (e.g. Mead 1997), which prescribed the role of the state as a wise but firm father figure, deciding how poor people should go about meeting their own ambitions since they are incapable of achieving them themselves. Neo-liberal economic accounts argued that in order to minimise unemployment, the moral hazard posed by unemployment payments had to be counteracted by greater conditionality to ensure that unemployed people search more actively for work (eg. Layard et al. 1991).

More recently, communitarian positions have emphasised the importance of community networks of support and obligation in promoting social inclusion. These have been posed as a necessary counterweight against, on the one hand, the overbearing and impersonal nature of state intervention, and, on the other, the individualism and social disengagement promoted by the market (Deacon 2002). In Australia, these have been promoted strongly by Noel Pearson (e.g. Pearson 2000b) in relation to Aboriginal communities.

The 'mutual obligation regime' is the Australian current expression of active labour market policy. It can be summarised as imposing vigorous job search requirements, the threat of large sanctions, a 'work-first' employment philosophy (in contrast to training or skills development), and the idea that the unemployed owe something in return for income support payments. Mutual obligation has been widely criticised by the community sector and policy analysts for imposing unreasonable and counter-productive requirements on the unemployed (Ziguras et al. 2003) and for its lack of mutuality (Moss 2000). It does, however, command popular support (Eardley & Matheson 2000; Roy Morgan Research 2000). This may be because most people believe that requirements help unemployed people maintain contact with the labour market and, as Pusey (2003) has argued, a strong ethic in Australian culture is that people should work for a living if they can.

Mutual obligation has also been backed up by a rhetorical war on 'welfare dependence'. The term welfare dependence, consistently utilised by Howard-government Ministers, is now part of the mainstream discourse. It has been used to stigmatise social security further, denoting a kind of psychological weakness, a moral or character failing on the part of the recipient, which requires not support or opportunities, but discipline. This discourse feeds into tabloid media preoccupation with individual responsibility and failings. It also provides the rhetorical background for a reform agenda mainly focused on changing the behaviour of individuals rather than tackling structural barriers to employment, such as the over-supply of labour, the casualised labour market, or employer unwillingness to employ people with disabilities or the long-term unemployed.

FUTURE OPTIONS

As in many other areas of government activity, the social security system seems to be in a state of permanent remodelling. The most immediate changes are a continuation of the mutual obligation approach based on the McClure report (an option of incremental adjustment). The government announced sweeping changes to social security entitlements in the 2005 Budget. In future, parents with a youngest child over 8 years will no longer be eligible for Parenting Payment (PP) and will instead be required to seek part-time work and receive an enhanced Newstart allowance. Similar changes apply to people with a disability able to work more than 15 hours per week, who will no longer qualify for the Disability Support Pension (DSP). While the government insists that the primary aim is to improve the employment prospects of those out of work, it is also clear that some initiatives will reduce social security expenditure since Newstart has a lower base rate, higher withdrawal rates, and lower tax rebates than the PP and DSP. This means a much lower weekly payment for those totally reliant on income support and also that those taking up work will get less money in their pockets. It seems unlikely to have much impact on moving people into employment.

A more ambitious proposal suggested in the McClure report, was to create a new single workforce age payment, to reduce the anomalies between different types of benefits. The government published a discussion paper on this idea (Commonwealth of Australia 2002) but then shelved it in the lead-up to a Federal election in 2004. A single payment may do little to address the basic problems of inadequate payments, but it may overcome some anomalies. Interestingly, the New Zealand government has signalled that it intends to introduce a new system along these lines (NZ Minister for Social Development and Employment 2005). There is a long tradition of shared initiatives across the Tasman, so the single payment concept may well be pursued again, although the Howard government seems disinterested in pursuing this avenue.

A more dramatic but unlikely change would be the introduction of a guaranteed minimum income (GMI) paid to all adults regardless of their circumstances. There are various ways in which this could be paid, but a common variant is the 'negative income tax', which would replace the entire income tax and transfer system with a new system that would provide a minimum income for all adults, and then withdraw it at a uniform rate as other income increased (Dawkins et al. 1998). GMIs are attractive to some economists as they have the potential to overcome poverty traps associated with targeting and high marginal tax rates. However, no country has ever introduced a GMI, partly due to its high cost, the fact that it is more complex than is sometimes assumed (Saunders 1988), and lack of political support for obligation-free payments.

A final possible reform direction lies in Schmid's (1998, 2002) notion of transitional labour markets (TLMs). Schmid argues that changing employment and life-course transitions require new policies that will allow people greater flexibility in moving between full-time work and other activities such as caring, education, and retirement. In effect, he proposes that active labour market policies be expanded to allow people to move both in and out of paid employment more easily. This will have social benefits in promoting socially useful activities (e.g. caring) and economic benefits by ensuring the people maintain a connection with the labour force, and by fostering a more highly skilled workforce.

Transitional labour markets require an 'active approach' in that they should both provide not only financial support but other assistance (such as for training and caring for others) for people to make transitions between employment roles. They embody the principle of increased capacity building central to active labour market policy, but are also directed to people who wish to move out of work, as well as those who are unemployed. Discussions of TLMs in Australia have been linked to contributory mechanisms (e.g. Ziguras et al. 2004). A stronger income-replacement emphasis in the social security system would allow for a more politically sustainable method of funding though tripartite financing models (such as for superannuation but with more progressive government subsidies). It may also reduce the stigma inherent with tightly targeted programs because more people would be eligible for payments.

Finally, two other trends will impact on the future of social security. We can assume a continuation of at least moderate economic growth over the immediate future (admittedly a risky prediction) and we can also assume that population ageing leads to a diminishing labour force. In these circumstances, the number of people who are able to move from welfare to work will increase as job opportunities become available. Indeed this trend has already started; the proportion of people of working age on income support has declined since the mid 1990s as a result of strong growth in full-time jobs (ACOSS 2005).

The future may be one of even greater restrictions and targeting, and more obligations aimed at further reducing numbers on benefits and social spending. This would see Australia becoming closer to the US model of workfare and stigmatisation. However, an alterative future may see the political rhetoric describing social security as the 'welfare burden' becoming less tenable. As conversations about the need to support caring and education continue, the space may open up for social security payments to be seen as having useful social and economic benefits in addition to the alleviation of poverty. We may be able to understand income support payments, not as a burden to be reduced by moving people off benefit as soon as possible but as a means for expanding choices. The income support system would be more than simply protection from risk from poverty, it would become a system of social opportunity.

10

HOUSING POLICY IN AUSTRALIA: BIG PROBLEMS BUT OFF THE AGENDA

Tony Dalton

INTRODUCTION—THE NEGLECT OF HOUSING AND THE POLICY PROCESS

The vast majority of Australians are well housed, have secure tenure, and can afford their housing. Outright owners, who make up about 38 per cent of households, are the best-off. Purchasers constitute approximately 32 per cent and, although they have to make a big effort early in the life of their mortgage, they typically find their housing becomes more affordable over time, as they pay off the loan and their incomes rise. Among private tenants the picture is a little more mixed. For most households, say those in the top 60 per cent of the income distribution, private rental housing suits those who want the flexibility to make decisions about where they live, their relationships, and their housing type. Those in the lower 40 per cent of the income distribution are likely to face high housing costs relative to income, and to have few choices about their housing type and location. Overall, approximately 95 per cent of households obtain their housing in the private market. Only 5 per cent live in public housing and overwhelmingly they are very low-income households who pay no more than 25 per cent of their income in rent.

In general, the cost of housing, tenure, and location choice influence the opportunities that household members have to participate in social and economic life. Housing therefore has great bearing on the distribution of material well-being of households. The problem is that for an increasing number of households, housing costs, tenure arrangements, and location choice are unacceptably lowering the material well-being of a significant proportion of low-income households. The outcome is poverty and reduced access to jobs and services, and, for some, there is the appalling outcome of homelessness. This problem is closely associated with another problem: the limited prospect of reform leading to improved security and affordability. There are at least three important features of current housing policy and housing policy processes that support this claim.

First, housing policy is not a prominent policy area in the affairs of government. For example, apart from interest rates, there is little housing policy debate at election time, and party commitments are not subject to the policy competition that occurs in other policy areas where political parties seek to outdo each other. This contrasts with other areas of policy discussed in this book, such as health, income security, and labour market policy, where debate and competition is greater. Second, housing is not prominent in public administration. A scan of the titles of Commonwealth government inner and outer ministries and parliamentary secretaries reveals an absence of housing over the past decade. Within state governments there are ministers for housing. However, housing ministers have little responsibility for monitoring and regulating the broader housing market. They are primarily responsible for public housing provided through mega community and human service ministries. These ministerial arrangements are further complicated by continuing disputes about whether housing is a Commonwealth or a state government responsibility.

Third, there are no civil society constituencies able to insist on the development of a well-supported future-oriented housing policy. Organisations such as the Housing Industry Association, representing industry interests, are sometimes successful in persuading governments to stimulate demand for housing through grants to home purchasers. Non-government organisations such as the councils of social service, tenant unions, community housing organisations, and homeless persons advocacy groups have similarly influenced budget measures and program development. However, policy development and advocacy on housing issues by organisations and groups outside of government has been episodic and fragmented, and has not required political parties and government agencies to develop the capabilities necessary for forward-looking and 'joined-up' housing policy.

However, this absence of a coherent public policy approach to housing should not be taken to mean that the housing market (which is a shorthand term used to refer to the totality of individual transactions involving housing property and services) is not strongly influenced by policy—far from it. This market is shaped in many ways by government policy, as are all markets. Indeed, long-term stable markets cannot exist without rules that guide buyers, sellers, and other actor interactions, and the housing market, made up of sellers, landlords, purchasers, tenants, land developers, builders, real estate agents, and so on, is no exception. Therefore, housing policy includes not just the obvious, like public housing provision, support for homeless persons, and first home buyer grants, but the many things that governments do at Commonwealth, state, and local levels that influence the way in which the housing market works. These actions and instruments include income support and bond assistance for low-income private tenants, the exemption of owner-occupied housing from capital gains tax provisions, tenant advice services, grants and stamp duty concessions for first home owners, negative gearing provisions for landlords, landlord–tenant legislation, prudential regulation of mortgage-lending finance institutions, levies on developers used to pay for infrastructure, and planning rules that shape the layout and built form of dwellings. It also includes support for research, such as through the Australian Housing and Urban Research Institute (AHURI), which can increase the level of knowledge about the way in which the housing market works and the effects of government measures.

It could be thought that because housing policy is largely uncontested and governments already shape the housing market in a multitude of ways, that there is little need for change. This is not the case. There is overwhelming evidence of growing and deepening levels of disadvantage in housing markets. This chapter begins with a brief introduction to the history of urban housing provision. From the late nineteenth century and throughout the twentieth century a model of housing provision developed that by and large worked well for most, including lower income working people. Its legacy is both high quality affordable housing for most households and expectations that a market system can deliver. However, during the last two decades of the twentieth century it became clear that this model now cannot provide good quality affordable housing to households in the lowest 40 per cent of the income distribution in the way that it did once. The key changes creating this decline in affordability are covered in the chapter through an explanation of the changes in housing demand and supply arrangements. The problem is that housing policy debate and processes do not recognise these major changes. Instead housing is discussed through issues that remain disconnected. The chapter concludes by identifying the need for a 'joined-up' approach to the consideration of housing policy issues.

AUSTRALIAN HOUSING IN RETROSPECT—HISTORICAL CONTEXT

Australia became an urban home-ownership society in distinct stages. Figure 10.1 shows that early in the twentieth century the proportion of households in home ownership and private rental were roughly equal. Then through the early decades of the last century the rate of home ownership grew to nearly 53 per cent. Australia was being developed as a home-ownership society during the early part of the twentieth century. It became one of the rapidly urbanising settler societies, which included Canada, the USA, and New Zealand, where home ownership coupled with a ready supply of new housing was becoming the norm (Frost 1991, ch. 6). In the post-Second World War period, Australia was confirmed as a home-ownership society when the proportion of households who were outright owners or were purchasing increased from 53 per cent to 70 per cent in the period 1947–61, again within the context of a steady supply of new housing. However, for some age cohorts the home-ownership outcome has been considerably greater than 70 per cent. Neutze and Kendig (1991) have calculated that for household heads born between 1925 and 1965, the rate of home ownership has been approximately 90 per cent.

Figure 10.1 Housing tenure of households and total occupied dwellings 1911–2001

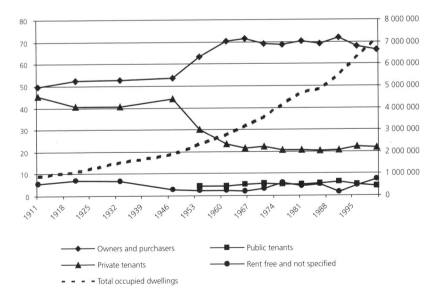

Correspondingly, households in private rental housing declined sharply in period 1947–61 from 44 per cent to 23 per cent. Public housing does not feature until the post-Second World War period. From 1945, public housing began to be provided by state governments using Commonwealth government funds provided through the Commonwealth State Housing Agreement (CSHA). The initial growth in supply was large so that by 1954 4.3 per cent of households were public housing tenants. It is important to note the recent trends indicated in Figure 10.1. It shows that there has been a decline in owner occupation from 71.7 to 66.2 per cent in the decade 1991–2001. This reflects a slowing down in the entry of households into home ownership headed by those born in the 1970s (Wulff & Maher 1998; Yates 1999, 2000). Correspondingly there has been an increase in private renter households from 20.7 to 21.8 per cent in the same period and a decline in public renting from 6.3 to 4.3 per cent of households.

What historically has produced this tenure outcome along with the continuing steady supply of new housing? It is important to ask this question because it should not be assumed that mass owner occupation is an inevitable feature of affluent urban societies or that supply responds in a direct way to unmet demand. There are many societies, some with higher standards of living than Australia, which have lower rates of owner occupation and where long-term renting is the norm among affluent households (Hill 1996, ch. 7). Also there are times when there has been a shortage of houses. An analytical approach that helps to identify the reasons for the sustained steady growth in housing supply and growth in owner occupation is to distinguish between how housing is paid for—demand—and how housing is produced—supply. Further, wrapped around and shaping the demand and supply arrangements are the very many forms of federal, state, and local government laws, regulations, and programs that influence the way in which people behave in the housing market.

For most Australians, housing demand has always been closely associated with the level and distribution of wages. In the second half of the nineteenth century, the level of wages enabled most working households to afford a better standard of housing than working households in the UK, from where most immigrants came (Frost 2000). By the twentieth century, wage levels and arrangements were institutionalised in what Castles (1985) calls the 'wage earners' welfare state' within a broader contested and dynamic set of societal arrangements that Roe (1998) calls the 'Australian Way'. This was an institutional arrangement between employer interests and organised labour overseen by the state. One of the functions of the state was to enforce a 'minimum income' or 'living wage', which was greater than what many employees would have won in direct employer–employee negotiations. More broadly these arrangements were possible for two reasons. First, tariffs on imports, another feature of the settlement, protected local employers from foreign competition. Consequently, they could price their goods at the level that enabled them to pay wages set in this way. Second, the export of agricultural and mineral exports to Europe resulted in a high level of national income (see also Chapter 5).

Coupled with low levels of taxation, this wages system meant that a large proportion of households had sufficient resources to become purchasers (Davison 1981; Frost 1991, ch. 6). As Davison (1981, p. 184) notes, 'although the higher-income occupations did fare better than the lowest, their advantage was only marginal'. It also meant that purchaser households became outright owners at the end of their working lives. They lived in debt-free housing, supported by a modest aged pension paid by government directly from taxation revenue (Castles & Mitchell 1994). For households who rented, their housing was owned by owner occupiers who were also small-scale investors with one or a few dwellings. Again investment in rental housing was not restricted to wealthy households but was spread across the income range. This is the pattern of investment that continues to characterise the private rental market often described as a 'mums and dads' investment market (Berry 2000; Yates 1996).

In response to this high level of demand, a dynamic and distinctive house building industry supplied new suburban housing. The industry was constituted by speculative builders, contract builders, building material suppliers, building workers, and financial intermediaries (principally building societies). The speculative builder was the main supplier of suburban housing and contract builders supplied more expensive, custom-built housing (Butlin 1964; Davison 1981). The speculative builder produced small numbers of houses each year, taking advantage of new easy-to-use materials, such as galvanised iron; new forms of construction; and a ready supply of labour, which resulted from reduced craft union control and a deskilled labour force. In this context, they purchased the land, borrowed working capital, organised sub-contract labour, sometimes undertook some of the work themselves, and acted as a sales person. Consequently, Australian cities were among those where 'the dream of a private, sanitary, and salubrious house was in the nineteenth century most amply and democratically realised' (Frost 1991, p. 102). Although there has been some change, this system of suburban housing production has continued. Although there are now larger volume builders, much of the supply continues to be produced by many builders who organise subcontractors to produce a small number of dwellings each year (Greig 1992). In 2001, the largest four builders in each state were producing less than 40 per cent of new dwellings (HIA 2002).

A PARTICULAR TYPE OF HOUSING POLICY: DISTINCTIVE POLICY ELEMENTS

As this urban housing system developed, it was shaped by governments in many ways. Initially it was colonial (state) governments, then local government, and then, following Federation, the Commonwealth government. The responsibility for housing has never been clear. Like many policy areas in the Australian federal system, responsibility was not formally defined or assigned to one of the three spheres of government. Nevertheless, between these three spheres, governments have developed a vast array of measures that shape housing outcomes. While space does not permit a discussion of all the elements of government activity, it is useful to categorise the extent of involvement in three ways: market-supporting, market-supplementing, and market-replacement measures (Berry 1983).

Market-supporting measures establish the institutional preconditions necessary for private production and market exchange. A housing market depends on government-made and -enforced rules. They include a legal system specifying property rights, landlord–tenant relations, and credit and exchange rules. Government also defines spatial arrangements including measurement, land titles, and land use zoning. Some consumer protection arises from building regulations, specifying minimum construction standards (Marsden 2000). However, the advent of the Torrens title system was historically probably the most important market-supporting measure (Wells 1989, p. 87). Following the initial seizure of Aboriginal lands, its redefinition as 'Crown Land', and its sale to private individuals, the Torrens title system made the subdivision, sale, and transfer of land much easier than the English old title system.

Market-supplementing policies modify the economic relations between different groups in the market. Governments leave people free to interact in markets, while also supporting or restraining them in various ways. In housing, this is done by supporting most households, albeit quite unequally, in the following ways:

- through below-cost residential infrastructure provision, tax subsidies, and expenditures

- by supporting some groups relative to others by regulating the rules of exchange—for example, in the finance system
- by providing substantive support to particular groups—for example, by supplementing renter incomes, making grants to first-time purchasers, and mortgage interest subsidies.

All of these measures have been important. However, the standout feature for home ownership was finance system regulation and borrower assistance in the decades following the Second World War. This directed concessional finance into owner-occupied housing by favouring borrowers over depositors. These measures included a system of state and federal government-owned banks, regulating bank lending rates and assets, government-provided mortgages through war service home loans, and establishing a government-owned insurance company to insure mortgages provided by building societies (Merrett 2000; Wood 1990). For private rental housing, the standout feature has been the tax system that enables landlord investors to offset losses on rental housing against income tax payable on other forms of income, otherwise known as 'negative gearing'. The consequence of both concessional finance for owner occupiers and landlord-investor tax concessions has been that more dwellings were built and more invested in these dwellings than would otherwise have been the case.

Market-replacement happens when governments directly provide goods and services otherwise provided through the market. Administrative criteria replace market relations, as in public or social housing provided by government or non-government-not-for-profit agencies. In Australia, this began with the CSHA and the construction of the public housing from 1945, which was closely aligned to the requirements of new postwar industries so that they had a nearby workforce (Eather 1988; Jones 1972; Peel 1995). A great deal of public housing in the post-Second World War decades was built near new factories, power stations, ship yards, and steel smelters so as to house male workers and their families. To a lesser extent, public housing was used to replace inner city housing—both private rental housing and owner-occupied housing, particularly in Melbourne and Sydney—that was judged by a movement of public health professionals, social workers, clergy, and planners to be slums and unfit for human habitation (Howe 1988; Reiger 1985). From the 1970s, following massive industry restructuring and the sharp reduction in the demand for industrial workers, the role of public housing changed. In the context of increasing numbers of single female-headed households, increased levels of unemployment and underemployment, deinstitutionalisation and homelessness, public housing was redefined as housing for very low income and otherwise disadvantaged households. As a consequence, there has been a concentration of very low-income households that are often disadvantaged in other ways in public housing (Hall & Berry 2004).

THE CHANGING CONTEXT AND THE ISSUE OF HOUSING STRESS

Contemporary demand and supply side arrangements are no longer producing the same outcomes as for much of the postwar period. Not much has changed in terms of numbers of new dwellings. The housing industry continues to add more than 165 000 new dwellings to the housing stock each year. However, there have been significant changes in patterns of household access. One indicator is the small decline in the rate of home ownership and an increase in the level of private renting from the mid 1990s, as shown in Figure 10.1. Further, underneath this aggregate home-ownership rate, there is evidence of an increase in the rate of outright ownership and a decline in the home purchase rate. Over time, this suggests there will be a longer term decline in home-ownership rates (Wood et al. 2005; Wulff & Maher 1998; Yates 2000).

What more can be said about the housing market that is exhibiting this tenure change? In housing studies, this question leads first to the issue of housing needs and the indicators that are used to estimate the number and characteristics of households experiencing housing problems, eligibility for assistance, and the allocation of resources by governments to meet these needs. In Australia, the two measures most commonly used to indicate problems are housing stress and housing affordability.

Housing stress is used to measure housing needs, primarily of low-income renter households. It was a term developed in the early 1990s during the National Housing Strategy, a major Commonwealth government housing policy review. The National Housing Strategy (1991) defined housing stress as occurring when income units (families) paid more than 30 per cent of gross income on housing and were in the lower 40 per cent of the income distribution. The analyses indicate a significant growth in the level of housing stress for such low-income families. In the period 1981–2001, the proportion of private rental tenants in the lowest 40 per cent of the income distribution experiencing housing stress increased from 47 per cent to 65 per cent. The picture is more alarming for private renters in the lowest 20 per cent of the income distribution. For them, the proportion experiencing housing stress increased from 76 per cent to 81 per cent (Wood et al. 2005, pp. 55–9). The types of households most affected are single person households, single-parent households, and couples with children. Another indicator of increased housing stress among private tenants is the increase in the time that renter households rent in the private rental market before moving into owner occupation (Wulff & Maher 1998).

Housing affordability is a measure primarily used to estimate first-home purchaser affordability. There are different ways of measuring affordability, but generally they are a ratio of the cost of a median-priced dwelling in relation to median income. The substantive research examining housing affordability (Berry 2003; Wood et al. 2005; Yates 2000, 2003) indicates a decline in purchaser affordability. Most recently, the report, *First Home Ownership*, prepared by the Productivity Commission (2004), agreed that affordability had 'declined considerably in recent years—generally and for first homebuyers' (Productivity Commission 2004, p. xv). However, it was more cautious than the previous research about the significance of the longer term trend in affordability decline.

SOCIAL, ECONOMIC, AND POLITICAL ASPECTS OF CHANGE

What factors might lie behind this increase in housing stress and decline in housing affordability? The concepts of supply and demand can help us to understand the main development, although the following discussion omits much of the detail and the complex interactions that each of these developments trigger in the housing market. However, one critical outcome of the supply and demand processes, increased house prices, is noted. The price of housing is both an outcome of the demand and the supply of housing. Following are the key developments on the demand side in recent decades:

- *A change in the composition of household types*. In 1971, the average size of households was 3.3 people, whereas by 1996 it was 2.7. Most of this decline in average household size can be attributed to the growth in the number of small households of one or two people and the decline in large households. The growth in one-person households in the period 1971–96, from 14 per cent of all households to 22 per cent, is particularly significant (Australian Bureau of Statistics 1998). Reasons for the growth in single-person households are increases in the marriage breakdown rate, adults not partnering, and single, aged, widowed people. In housing terms, it means an increase in the proportion of households with only one income available to meet housing costs. It is noteworthy that from the mid 1960s, housing affordability depended increasingly on two-income households (National Housing Strategy 1991, p. 13; Yates 1981).

- *Significant changes to the labour market* (see also Chapter 8). This includes increases in casual work, which is subject to termination at short notice, part-time work, and contract work, often described as precarious work (Campbell 1997). This type of work also tends to be low-skilled and low-paid. While for some (such as students), part-time and casual work arrangements are preferred, for others it can mean underemployment (that is not working as much as they would like) and insecurity (and therefore being less able to predict future income). These changes shape the pattern of housing demand, although their impacts will be mediated by household composition (Winter & Stone 1999; Yates 2000). However, low-paid, precarious work reduces the capacity of households to enter into long-term lease or mortgage arrangements. Landlords and lending institutions also have their rules and criteria, and use these to exclude people who have uncertain future income.

- *Increasing earnings inequality and increased income inequality.* These changes (according to some studies) are closely connected with changes to the labour market (see also Chapter 8), with the top-income earners receiving increased income and low-income earners receiving decreased income relative to the mid point in the overall income distribution. This changing income distribution shapes the pattern of housing demand as this changing income distribution of individuals is also reflected in a more unequal income distribution of households (Saunders 2001). It means that low-income earners are increasingly disadvantaged relative to moderate- and high-income earners, and experience less capacity to pay rent, save for a deposit, and repay a mortgage. It also means that higher income earners have greater capacity to pay rent, save, and repay a mortgage. Single low-income households experience the greatest relative disadvantage in a context where house prices and affordability are adjusted to the increase in two-income households and the increased female workforce participation rate from the 1960s onwards (Yates 1981).

- *Two government policies that have reduced the capacity of young households in the housing market in recent decades.* First, there is the impact of the Higher Education Contribution Scheme (HECS), which results in young graduates having to repay a debt. In 2003, the total accumulated HECS debt was $9 billion, with $8500 as the average amount owing by graduates (Australian Bureau of Statistics 2004). This reduces the capacity of young people to take on housing debt as first-time purchasers. Second is compulsory occupational superannuation, with all employees forgoing some part of their wages to provide for retirement. Again, this reduces the capacity to pay for housing

(Senate Select Committee on Superannuation 1994). Identifying these aspects of public policy should not necessarily be seen as an argument against HECS or compulsory occupational superannuation. However, it is important to recognise the effect that these policies have on housing outcomes through their impacts on household income.

There have also been significant changes on the supply side in recent decades.

- *A revolution in the Australian finance system during the 1980s* following the work of the Committee of Inquiry into the Australian Financial System (Committee of Inquiry into the Australian Financial System 1981). This neo-liberal oriented Inquiry supported minimum regulation and competitive finance markets, rejecting the post-Second World War model of policy making that imposed a broader range of economic and social objectives on the flow of finance in the economy (Dalton 2002). The key changes that followed were deregulation of housing interest rates and asset controls, reduction in the number of Australian banks through takeovers and the sale of government-owned banks, and emergence of mortgage originators, such as Aussie Home Loans and Wizard Home Loans. There are now many more mortgage lenders providing housing loans. The earlier era of fixed interest long-term loans has given way to 'high loan to valuation' loans, home equity loans, non-conforming loans, split-loans, redraw loans, and off-set accounts (Productivity Commission 2004, pp. 46–8). Since the mid 1990s, housing interest rates have fallen and have remained low. This has enabled borrowers to borrow more within repayment-to-income ratio constraints and fully utilise these new arrangements. In turn, this has fuelled house price inflation and increased consumer spending ahead of modest real income growth (Berry & Dalton 2004).

- *A steady increase in the volume of capital being lent for housing* through the new flexible lending system, which is considerably more than that required by purchasers of new dwellings. There are a number of drivers in this greater demand for housing investment capital. First, there are owner occupiers who are trading up in the market. Second, there are owner occupiers borrowing in order to extend and upgrade their dwelling. Third, there are the investors in rental housing, many of them borrowing against equity in their owner-occupied dwelling, continuing the pattern of small-scale landlordism noted above. This form of investment has grown steadily in recent decades. In 1985, investors were responsible for investing approximately 13 per cent of housing finance but by early 2005 were responsible for 32 per cent of housing investment. Owner-occupier investment in the same period declined from 83 per cent to 68 per cent (Australian Bureau of Statistics 2005). This has resulted in continuing increase in the supply of rental housing and perhaps underpins the increase in the proportion of private rental housing since 1996, evident in Figure 10.1. However, as noted above, during this period the level of housing stress among low-income renters has increased. The evidence shows that this overall increase in supply has not increased the supply of rental housing that is affordable by low-income households (Berry 2003; Yates et al. 2004).

■ *The cost of supply of new housing is an important supply-side consideration.* However, it is important not to overstate this because new dwellings each year represent an increase in the total stock of approximately 2.3 per cent of all dwellings. There are two factors in the housing development process that potentially increase costs. First, there is the rate at which land is released for new housing development. There is evidence that the time taken to bring new housing land on to the market has increased due to complex and demanding planning processes (Berry & Dalton 2004; Productivity Commission 2004). However, a trend that has moderated land costs in recent decades is a decline in the average size of new lots. Second, the method of infrastructure financing has largely shifted from long-term debt financing by public utilities, paid for by rates based on property values, to up-front developer charges, which are reflected in the price of the dwelling. Exactly what the price effect of developer charges has been depends on estimates of how much the increase has been passed forward to the purchaser and how much has been passed back to the original owner of the land (Neutze 1997, p. 121; Productivity Commission 2004).

■ *The movement of households between dwellings and the exchange of dwellings in the market*, which is a much larger source of housing supply and, in the context of the other factors discussed above, is associated with a sustained increase in house prices. Mobility data for metropolitan Melbourne reminds us of the dynamic nature of housing supply in the existing housing stock. In a 12-month period (2000–01), 7.7 per cent of owner-occupier households moved and 33 per cent of private rental households moved (Australian Bureau of Statistics Victorian Office 2004, p. 28). The rate at which there is movement in the housing system changes. One indicator of this change, presented in Figure 10.2, is the number of dwellings, houses and units, and vacant house blocks intended for house-building sold in Melbourne. Behind these annual totals is the totality of decisions by many households to offer their dwelling for sale, to sell at a particular price, and, for purchasers, to decide what they can afford. It also shows considerable change and volatility in the outcome of these linked decisions.

Figure 10.2 Metropolitan Melbourne: number of annual sales

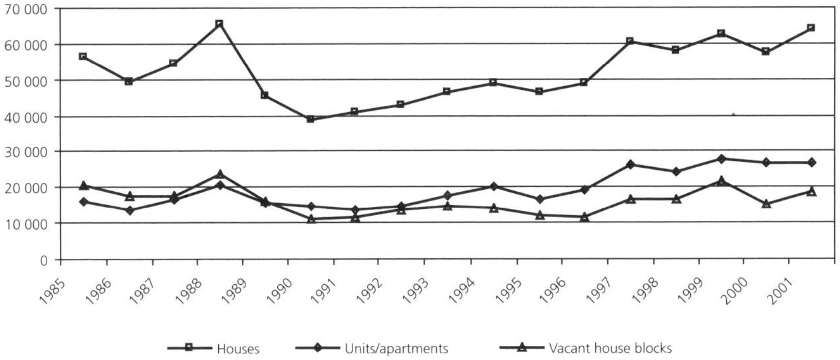

Source: Valuer General—Victoria (2002)

The combined effects of demand and supply factors in the housing market shape housing prices and, in the Australian case, this has resulted in sustained real house price increases over many years.[1] Figure 10.3 presents the trend line for real house prices over the last four decades and shows a long-term increase in real house prices. It also shows that there have been three distinct booms in house price increases, the first in the late 1960s and early 1970s, a second short sharp one in the late 1980s, and a third sustained one from 1997 to 2003, indicating almost a doubling in real house prices. Overall, Australia has experienced a long-term sustained real house price increase. The Productivity Commission (2004, p. 16) states, 'Since 1970, real house prices for (detached) houses in Australia have more than trebled, representing a trend increase of around 2.3 per cent a year. By international standards, this is a high rate of price increase.'

Figure 10.3 House price increase in Australia (real price index)

Source: Productivity Commission 2004, p. 16

This is a national average. The rate of increase in some cities, such as Hobart, Adelaide, and Brisbane, has been lower than the rate of increase for Sydney and Melbourne. Also, within each city the rate of increase varies considerably (Berry & Dalton 2004). However, overall house price increases have both increased the net wealth of owners relative to non-owners and have reduced housing affordability for purchasers. Increasing house prices require households to accumulate more savings required for a deposit and require more income to service the loan. The households that are most disadvantaged are those in the lowest 40 per cent of the income distribution (Berry & Dalton 2000; Yates 2000). The recent house price boom has accelerated the decline in affordability and the Productivity Commission (2004, p. 39) comments that:

> The recent sharp increase in house prices in most parts of Australia has seen affordability for the first and other home buyers decline. Indeed, the duration, geographical spread and cumulative extent of the price increases sets the recent boom apart from previous booms in the past 30 years.

Over time, house price increases also increase the level of housing stress in the private rental market. A number of factors have come into play. House price increases have slowed down the rate at which young households move into home ownership. This has the effect of increasing demand in the private rental market despite increased levels of supply. This new rental housing is not affordable for long-term low-income renters or households saving for home ownership. Indeed the evidence is of an increasing shortage in the supply of affordable private rental housing for low-income families (Wulff & Maher 1998; Yates & Wulff 2000; Yates et al. 2004). This shortage is exacerbated by the static supply of public and social rental housing due to the long-term decline in CSHA funding and the higher cost structures associated with targeting allocations to very low income and otherwise disadvantaged tenants, and underinvestment in the stock. Already the supply of public housing has begun to decline and at current levels of funding this supply will continue to decrease as state housing authorities are forced to raise the capital required to maintain the stock by selling other stock (Hall & Berry 2004).

CONCLUSION

This chapter has argued that Australia developed a housing system during the twentieth century that did well in meeting the housing needs of the vast majority of Australian households. This happened because the provision of housing developed as an integral part of a broader set of social and economic arrangements in metropolitan cities. In the last decades of the twentieth century, the housing system has increasingly failed to meet the housing needs of a growing proportion of low-income households. Associated with this failure, there have been changes in household formation, labour market and income distribution changes, and education and retirement income policy impacts. It is also connected with change in the governance of the finance system, new housing development costs, and the pattern of sales in the housing market.

These factors give rise to complex interactions. However, they also give rise to one very clear outcome, steady house price increases. This is a fundamental problem in a context where there has been increasing housing stress, declining housing affordability, and growth in household income inequality. The problem is compounded because house price increases are consistently celebrated by those who own and others who benefit through their participation in industries such as real estate, media, housing construction, and finance. The broad endorsement of house price increase is evident in the statement by the Prime Minister, John Howard (2003), 'I don't get people stopping me in the street and saying John, you're outrageous, under your government the value of my house has increased'. The only consistently negative response has come from those with responsibility for macro economic policy, principally the Reserve Bank of Australia (2002, 2003). However, Reserve Bank concerns do not include housing stress and affordability issues.

Otherwise housing policy and program debates, as noted in the introduction to this chapter, remain episodic and fragmented. In the area of planning, the focus is largely on the high cost of infrastructure and urban containment. Homelessness policy focuses mainly on service development. Policy and assistance for first home owners is largely a response to housing industry pressure for a demand stimulus, and policy in relation to building standards focuses on energy conservation. For public housing, the policy focus is mainly about service quality and asset management. These policy and program debates remain disjointed and to fail to focus on housing stress and affordability issues. This is unlikely to change much until there is a greater degree of mobilisation of civil society interests sufficient to force political party engagement. This did happen in the post-Second World War decades and resulted in policy innovation. Future mobilisation could therefore result in further policy innovation (Dalton 2002). Recent examples are the National Summit on Housing Affordability (2004) and the National Affordable Housing Conference (Centre for Affordable Housing 2005). The National Summit in its *Call for Action* proposed both *market-supplementing* measures (national housing tax reform, and regional land and infrastructure planning for affordable housing), and perhaps a new *market-replacement* measure in the form of 'substantially increased public and private investment in developing low-cost housing' (National Summit on Housing Affordability 2004, p. 7). This summit also supported increased visibility and status for housing policy by calling for the appointment of a Commonwealth government cabinet minister for Housing, Urban and Community Development. However, government action will depend a great deal on how this and subsequent calls for action are owned and endorsed by civil society groups campaigning in a society that continues to celebrate house price increases, and is unclear about how to apportion responsibility for housing policy within Australia's federation.

NOTE

1.   Real house prices are the prices paid for dwellings measured in a way that makes an allowance for the effects of inflation. Real house prices are calculated by adjusting nominal prices by the rate of inflation at the time.

11

HEALTH POLICY IN AUSTRALIA: MIND THE GROWING GAPS

Jenny M. Lewis

Open a newspaper, turn on the television, or tune in your radio on any given day, and there is a high probability that you will hear a health story. Common topics in the 'crisis' mode are that Medicare is on the brink of collapse, public hospitals cannot cope with demand and have been putting ambulances on by-pass, or doctors are deeply unhappy and are threatening to withdraw their labour under current conditions. The other common mode is the 'heroic medicine' story: that a new miracle cure for a particular disease has been found, or that someone involved in an horrific accident has just had his or her severed hand reconstructed and reattached.

Health policy in Australia has been described perhaps most memorably by Sid Sax as a 'strife of interests' (Sax 1984). Health policy can be seen as the financial arrangements that determine who pays for what, or as the constant arguments between powerful interest groups that leave the less powerful without a say, or as ideas about what health actually means, and therefore, what health policy includes. Each of these (financing, interests, and ideas) indicate something significant about health policy in any country. Who pays, and for what, signifies to what extent health is seen to be a public good. Who has power in health policy debates indicates who has the ability to influence the health policy process. How we define what health and illness means shapes the contours of health policy and its legitimate concerns.

In this chapter, I deal with each of these areas of financing, interests, and ideas within a framework where health policy is defined as a complex network of continuing interactions between actors who use structures and argumentation to articulate their ideas about health (Lewis 2005). I begin by outlining the key structures in the health field, and with a short history of national health insurance in Australia, then important actors and interests of various types are identified. A consideration of the crucial role of different ideas about health follows—from curative and individual to preventive and community-based views. I conclude with some recent developments in health policy in Australia and a discussion of possible futures.

AUSTRALIAN HEALTH POLICY ELEMENTS AND STRUCTURES

Australian colonial governments, subsequently state governments, had initial responsibility for health. Today, there is a mixture of responsibilities for health across the three levels of government—Commonwealth, state/territory, and local. Although relative responsibilities have changed greatly since Federation in 1901, the states still retain the major responsibility for service provision, including hospitals, community and public health, and dental services. The Commonwealth has generally limited itself to issues of financing through partially funding hospitals, medical services, and pharmaceuticals, leaving the states to deliver services either directly or indirectly.

The Commonwealth is the biggest funder of health services, with its share of recurrent health expenditure at 49.6 per cent (see Table 11.1 and AIHW 2004). There are now few areas in health where the Commonwealth has not become involved, as can be seen in Table 11.1. Basic powers over health remain with the states, including the regulation of medical and allied practices and practitioners (with some exceptions in the territories). State and local governments contribute 20 per cent of recurrent health expenditure. The result is an intermeshing of Commonwealth and state activities that causes a considerable confusion of accountability and responsibility, and a significant amount of blame shifting and cost shifting between the different levels of government. Two examples follow that give the flavour of this complicated fragmentation and devolution.

In Australia, public hospitals receive funding from both the federal and state governments according to the 5-yearly Health Care Agreements, but state/territory governments are responsible for hospital functioning, generally through boards. So states/territories have more direct links than the Commonwealth with hospitals and it is a state government responsibility to ensure that there are enough beds available. However, aged care is both funded and directly overseen by the Commonwealth. The source of funds in Table 11.1 demonstrates this split clearly, with a slightly higher contribution from the Commonwealth than the state governments for hospitals, compared with a big difference for aged care. An area of ongoing dispute is the lack of places in aged care facilities (Commonwealth), which means that public hospitals (state/territory) have nowhere to discharge elderly (but not very sick) patients. The result is that not very ill elderly people remain in hospital longer than necessary, waiting for aged care places. This is not the best outcome for these individuals and it reduces the number of places available for those who are acutely ill.

Table 11.1 Selected items of recurrent health expenditure by source of funds for 2000–01 ($million)

	Government			Non-Government				Total
	Commonwealth	State/Local	Total	Health Insurance Funds	Individuals	Other	Total	
Total hospitals	9 147	7 368	16 515	2 225	543	925	3 693	20 208
Aged care	2 877	284	3 161		737		737	3 899
Medical services	8 419		8 419	287	1 078	492	1 857	10 276
Pharmaceuticals	4 397		4 397	36	3 580	73	3 689	8 085
Community and public health	602	2 488	3 090			5	5	3 095
Dental services	322	341	663	520	1 893	8	2 421	3 084
Total recurrent health expenditure	28 408	11 435	39 842	4 160	11 224	2 070	17 454	57 297

Source: AIHW (2004)

The final row is the total recurrent health expenditure but the columns do not add up to the totals, as not all items are included in this table.

Another example is the provision of publicly funded dental services. As dentistry is not included in Medicare, and little of it occurs within hospitals, the Commonwealth has limited involvement in funding dental services—10.4 per cent of dental expenditure is by the Commonwealth, compared with 81.9 per cent for medical services. The Commonwealth's involvement in dentistry has been in the form of special purpose grants to state governments for School Dental Services and the training of dental therapists, and the provision of dental services to armed forces personnel and war veterans, and to Indigenous Australians through Aboriginal Health Services. The Keating (Labor) government established a national dental program in 1994 to provide services to low-income earners. This was funded by the Commonwealth and administered by the states, but was abolished after three years by the new (conservative) government. One reason given for this was that waiting times had been reduced and so the program was no longer required (Lewis 2000), but in defence of its abolition, the Commonwealth's line (oft cited in health policy in Australia) was 'that is a state government responsibility'.

HISTORICAL CONTEXT: THE UPS AND DOWNS OF NATIONAL HEALTH INSURANCE

A key goal of health policy is ensuring that individual citizens are able to access health care. This important goal relies on some form of health insurance— generally a mixture of public and private funding and services. Australia has a national (universal) health insurance scheme—Medicare. The Commonwealth government collects funds for it through taxation (including the Medicare levy) and uses them to finance medical services and public hospital care. There is also a significant private sector, with 30.4 per cent of recurrent health expenditure coming from private health insurance funds, individuals, and other non-government sources (see Table 11.1 and AIHW 2004). Australia has a Pharmaceutical Benefits Scheme (PBS), which provides access to listed prescription medicines. Listed pharmaceuticals are subsidised by the Commonwealth, whose contribution amounts to 54 per cent of expenditure on this. Individuals make co-payments (which are lower for concessional patients) for listed drugs and bear the full cost of those not listed on the PBS, hence the 44 per cent contribution to expenditure by individuals on this item (see Table 11.1).

Compared with other wealthy democratic countries (apart from the United States of America, which still does not have one), Australia was late in establishing a national health insurance scheme. Table 11.2 outlines the key events in national health insurance in Australia. The rising costs of medical care and the inability of governments to control fees led to situations where many people could not afford to pay for care, so successive governments began to intervene. Some unsuccessful attempts were made by the Chifley (Labor) government to introduce a National Health Service, along the lines of the British scheme, in Australia in the 1940s. In response to this, and partly in response to the urgings of the medical profession, the Commonwealth expanded its powers in relation to health in 1946 via a Constitutional Amendment, and a 'civil conscription' clause[1] was added by the opposition.

Table 11.2 Timeline of key health insurance events and changing views of health in Australia

1940s	Chifley (Labor) government attempts to introduce national health service along British lines
1946	Constitutional Amendment
1949	Pharmaceutical Benefits Scheme begins in some states

Preventive and social concerns important post-Second World War—focus on living conditions, nutrition, and housing

1950–72	Page Plan of voluntary insurance under Menzies (conservative) government

Curative and individualistic notions of health predominant

1972–75	Whitlam (Labor) government introduces Medibank
1975–82	Medibank slowly dismantled by Fraser (conservative) government
1983	Medicare and Community Health Program introduced by Hawke (Labor) government

Curative (Medicare) and preventive (Community Health Program) focus, but emphasis squarely on curative care

1996–98	Private health insurance rebate introduced by Howard (conservative) government Medicare levy surcharge for the wealthy introduced
1999	Lifetime health cover introduced
2004	Medicare Plus introduced—safety net payments and incentives to bulk bill concessional patients

Curative and individualistic notions of health predominant

Sources: De Voe (2003); Gillespie (1991); Gray (2004)

The Constitutional Amendment gave the Commonwealth power to legislate for any benefits to provide care in relation to pharmaceutical, sickness, and hospital benefits, and medical and dental services, but no power to compel doctors and dentists to enter salaried employment or provide services for a prescribed fee (Rydon & Mackay 1995). These changes both lessened the barriers impeding the creation of national health policies and ensured that doctors and dentists could not be compelled to enter salaried employment or provide services for a prescribed fee. This remains an important component of the bargain struck between the state and the medical and dental professions in Australia, and gives Australian health policy its own unique logic.

After the failure of attempts to introduce a national health service, a plan of subsidised voluntary health insurance (the Page Plan, named after the then Minister for Health) was progressively introduced from 1950 to 1953. Over this period, the various elements of the eventual scheme—a national pharmaceutical scheme inherited from the previous government, a means-tested medical benefits scheme with heavy involvement from friendly societies (which later became private health insurers), hospital benefits with co-payments from users, and means testing for places in public wards—were fought over and finally resolved. As James Gillespie (1991) records, the Page 'scheme' was actually a pragmatic and unplanned set of programs, which were defined by at least suspicion, and often outright opposition, from the British Medical Association (which became the Australian Medical Association in 1962). By the mid 1950s, an earlier postwar emphasis on prevention and social conditions had been replaced by one that saw health as curative and individualistic.

Australia continued with a residual (or voluntary) health insurance system until the 1970s. When the Whitlam government, elected in 1972, introduced universal insurance (Medibank), they had to do so without breaking the 'civil conscription' clause, by leaving doctors and dentists to set their own fees. However, this new Labor government did not control the Senate, so Medibank legislation was rejected three times and passed into law only a few months before the government was dismissed in 1975 (De Voe 2003). The Community Health Program was introduced alongside Medibank and remains in place today as an early example of a 'new public health' approach (discussed later in this chapter). From 1975, until the government changed in 1983, universal insurance was gradually dismantled by the Fraser government. The Hawke government reintroduced it as Medicare in 1983.

The method used to pay doctors is fee-for-service and this was an important concession made in the forging of Medibank in order to win over general practitioners (GPs) so that they would agree to being paid by the government on behalf of patients, rather than directly by patients (Scotton & MacDonald 1993). Under the original Medicare arrangements, patients pay no out-of-pocket costs for visiting GPs who bulk bill Medicare (charge the national insurance commission directly), but contribute co-payments to those GPs who do not.

Health services are not all funded through the Medicare program, or by any level of government. Only 69.4 per cent of total expenditure on health is public (Table 11.1 and AIHW 2004). Although all Australians are covered for medical and public hospital care by Medicare, many also have private insurance. The proportion of the population with private insurance was at its lowest between 1996 and early 2000, ranging from 30 to 33 per cent. The Howard government regarded this level as problematic and a range of policy changes (discussed later in this chapter) have been introduced since then, which increased insurance uptake to 45.7 per cent at the highest point, recorded in September 2000. At the end of 2004, 43.0 per cent of Australians had private insurance (PHIAC 2005).

One of the main reasons for taking out private health insurance is to be able to receive treatment more quickly, either as a private patient in a public hospital, or in a private hospital. Another is to have a greater choice of doctor (although this 'choice' is often effectively made by hospitals, referring general practitioners, and health insurers). It can also be used to get partial reimbursement for visits to dentists, physiotherapists, and other health professionals not covered by Medicare, as these services are otherwise only available for those who can afford to pay the full cost, and for those who are eligible (and can wait) for publicly funded care. The unstated judgment is that, while access to doctors and hospital services should be available to everyone regardless of their ability to pay, other health services are seen less as public goods.

HEALTH POLICY ACTORS AND INTERESTS

In health policy, there are many powerful actors, and the battles are strongly disputed, protracted, and bitter. The traditional strength of the medical profession, the need for governments and insurers to control the demand for health care, the complexity of health systems, and community expectations in this area, where life and death are involved, are all important contributors to this (Lewis 2005).

Although it is now 30 years since Robert Alford's important book on health politics appeared (Alford 1975), his description of dominant, challenging, and repressed structural interests still provides leverage for understanding interests in health policy. In his classification, professional monopolists are the dominant group whose interests are served by existing social, economic, and political structures. Corporate rationalists are the challenging interest, emphasising rational planning and efficiency ahead of deference to the expertise of medical professionals. Equal health advocates represent repressed structural interests, striving for better access to services against the weight of entrenched structures. This provides a useful starting point for understanding the distribution of power among interest groups in health politics.

Since the 1970s, organised medicine has been increasingly challenged by governments, insurers, and large health service delivery organisations in

Australia, as elsewhere. Yet medicine remains firmly entrenched in health politics. This is the case in relation to both formal structural arrangements and informal networks, and it means that medicine's power is infused throughout the health policy system and embedded in health policy agendas (Lewis 2005).

The elite of organised medicine has an ongoing dialogue with various governments, through a set of formal mechanisms. These mechanisms have changed as a result of reforms over the last 30 years, but have not been accompanied by a generalised loss of power by medicine (Lewis 2002). In relation to informal structures, health policy has a small, homogeneous, and stable group of influential actors. The elite group with influence is comprised of those with medical qualifications working in academia and public teaching hospitals (Lewis & Considine 1999). Those who advocate for improved services for disadvantaged groups still find it difficult to be heard above the din created by the clash of medicine and high-ranking health bureaucrats.

BIOMEDICINE AND THE SOCIAL DETERMINANTS OF HEALTH

Struggles over health policy, such as those described in relation to health insurance, clearly involve conflicts between interest groups and the strains they place on structures and financial arrangements. But they also involve ideas about health that support particular actors and shape the range of possible policy options. The dominant paradigm in health is biomedicine, which sees the human body as a machine that sometimes breaks down and needs to be fixed. Health policy, then, is largely about individualistic, curative interventions within the health sector.

Taking a more preventive view is the field of public, or population, health, which focuses on measures to protect and promote the health of specific communities and whole populations. The 'old public health' functions familiar to us include quarantine, proper sewage disposal and the provision of clean water, food safety regulations, immunisation, and other measures. These remain important, but a number of 'new public health' functions, which focus more on community involvement and the social determinants of health, have been emerging since the 1960s and 1970s. Alternative views cast health as a product of society rather than of individual attributes and behaviours. Prevailing views of health that have underpinned Australian health policy are included in Table 11.2.

In the 1960s and early 1970s, community health programs appeared in a number of countries, including Australia in 1972. By the late 1970s, primary health care was regarded as a means to achieve health for all in the Alma-Ata declaration (WHO 1978). This declaration importantly emphasised the need to address the underlying social, economic, and political causes of ill health. Despite efforts in countries like Canada (Lalonde 1974) and the UK (Black 1980), a long period of inaction on the social determinants of health followed.

Some countries began taking up these ideas again in the late 1990s and early 2000s (WHO 2005). Policy in these nations began to emphasise that the multiple influences on health status from the social and environmental context are crucial, with inequities in society contributing significantly to unequal health outcomes (Marmot 1999). The realm of health policy then expands to encompass a bigger range of causes and areas for intervention that are multi-sectoral (Lewis 2005). Canada, Sweden, and the UK are at the forefront of this new focus on the social determinants, but Australia's national government has not embraced this approach.

PRESSURES ON HEALTH POLICY

As other chapters in this volume indicate, containing public sector expenditure became an increasingly important goal for wealthy nations, from the 1970s onwards. A number of features specific to health policy ensured that this sector embraced this trend. The ever increasing availability and use of new and expensive technologies in treating patients exerts strong pressure on health budgets. The greater and more widespread use of a growing variety of pharmaceuticals[2] is leading many commentators to argue that the Pharmaceutical Benefits Scheme is unsustainable (Harvey 2005). Population ageing means that more people are living longer and sometimes requiring more complicated and expensive treatments as they age. There is more chronic illness and disability, as lives are saved through new interventions.

On top of these economic and demographic changes, citizens' attitudes to health change as expectations of what health care services can provide are upgraded. Consumers of health care are now more informed and articulate, and more assertive in demanding choice and quality in health services. Interest in and the use of alternative therapies has grown rapidly, and more diagnostic tests are ordered as consumer expectations rise and the threat of litigation, in the case of failure to diagnose accurately, increases. At the turn of the twenty-first century, it seems that the demand for health services might be limitless.

Given these pressures, it is not surprising that health care expenditure in Australia increased over the last three decades from approximately 5 per cent of GDP to 9.3 per cent in 2001 (OECD 2004). The extreme case is the USA, where health expenditure accounted for 13.9 per cent of GDP in 2001. The driving factor of cost containment in health policy in Australia is also present in less wealthy countries. Efforts have been made to marketise and privatise the provision of health care in South-East Asian nations, where systems are centralised and publicly funded. As Ramesh and Asher (2000) point out, this is puzzling, given the low cost and relatively equitable systems they have, which compare favourably with countries with predominantly private systems.

Table 11.3 Health expenditure as a percentage of GDP and life expectancy for selected countries

Country	Health expenditure as a percentage of GDP in 1990	Life expectancy (years) in 1995*
Australia	7.8	75
Canada	9.0	75.1
Indonesia	2.01	64
Japan	5.9	76.4
Malaysia	2.96	71
New Zealand	6.9	74.2
Philippines	2.15	66
Singapore	3.0	76
Thailand	4.98	69
United Kingdom	6.0	74
United States of America	11.9	72.5

Sources: OECD (2004), Ramesh & Asher (2000)

*Figures for OECD countries are for males only (female figures are generally about 5 years higher).

Table 11.3 shows the percentage of GDP spent on health and life expectancy for a range of wealthy (OECD) countries, as well as South-East Asian nations. The enormous differences in terms of what is spent on health is clear, ranging from 11.9 per cent for the USA at one end of the scale, to just over 2 per cent for Indonesia and the Philippines, and not a great deal more in relatively wealthy countries like Malaysia and Singapore (both at 3 per cent). Despite the variance in wealthy countries' expenditure on health (from 5.9 to 11.9 per cent), life expectancy varies by just 4 years. Clearly, spending more on health does not guarantee longer life. There is a gap of approximately 10 years in life expectancy between the poorest countries (Indonesia with 64 years) and wealthier countries, such as Australia (75 years) and Japan (76 years).

CHANGING CONTEXT: BACK TO THE PAST?

The last decade has seen a significant political shift in Australian health policy away from universalism and towards a two-tiered approach. Medicare is now under pressure from a range of changes introduced by the Howard government (Gray 2004). Since taking office in 1996, the government has introduced a private health insurance rebate, and a Medicare levy surcharge on those earning more than $50 000 per person or $100 000 per household, who did not take out private health insurance. When this failed to produce much movement into private health insurance, lifetime health cover was introduced in 1999 (Gray 2004). Premiums became age-rated (so that younger people pay lower rates) and there was an incentive to take out insurance at a younger age, or be financially penalised for joining a fund at an older age.

Another significant equity concern is that the rate of bulk billing has declined substantially over the last decade, from 80 per cent of consultations in the mid 1990s to 70.9 per cent in December 2004 (Department of Health and Ageing 2005). Declining rates of bulk billing, which have a disproportionate effect on the poor, and the subsidisation of private health insurance, which amounts to a transfer from the less to the more wealthy (Denniss 2005), indicate that equity of access to care has declined over the last decade.

The Medicare Plus package introduced by the Howard government includes financial incentives to encourage doctors to bulk bill concessional patients (which many generally do in any case), but there is no incentive to bulk bill all patients in order to decrease out-of-pocket costs overall. Access to GPs for the poor will be relatively well protected under Medicare Plus, but others will see a decline in bulk billing.

Australian doctors continue to set their own prices outside public hospitals, but other forms of payment for GPs have been introduced during the 1990s, including allowances and target payments, in recognition that there was a need to move away from a fee-for-service system. However, the bulk of GPs' incomes remains fee-for-service based. Organised medicine continues to claim this is the only proper way of reimbursing doctors. Safety net payments are also part of the Medicare Plus package. These were directed at reducing the amount of out-of-pocket expenditure for those requiring frequent visits to the doctor. But they do not help people on low incomes who often do not reach the safety net threshold. Indeed, figures on safety net payouts show that they are low in poor electorates and high in wealthy electorates (Gray 2004). The safety net is also proving to be inflationary (Swerrisen 2004).[3] Within its first year of operation, the government cut back the scheme, the cost of which had blown out from the expected $440 million over 4 years, to approximately $1 billion (Stafford 2005).

The biggest equity failure in health policy terms in Australia relates to Aboriginal people. The crude but reasonably straightforward measure of life expectancy indicates that Indigenous Australians live an average of 15 to 20 years less than non-Indigenous Australians, and have much lower levels of access to primary health care services (ABS 2003b). This is partly a reflection of the relatively disadvantaged socio-economic position of many Indigenous people, partly a reflection that many live in rural and remote locations, and partly a legacy of colonisation. Australian health policy has failed to close the gap in life expectancy between Indigenous and non-Indigenous people.

In terms of efficiency, there is evidence that publicly funded health systems are less costly to run than private systems. Comparisons of public and private hospital costs have shown that public hospital costs are 91 per cent of the cost of private hospital care (Duckett & Jackson 2000). Medical fees are higher in the private sector, and this causes staff recruitment problems for the public sector by increasing rather than reducing pressure on public hospitals (McAuley 2004). The amount spent on health in Australia is growing as the private sector grows. It is clear from the American situation that it is possible to spend a lot more on health than Australia does, yet have large numbers of people with no insurance at all (about 40 million Americans) and no improved health status.

On the broader stage of ideas about health, there has been little that suggests a national level agenda to move away from traditional, biomedical concerns, towards more inclusive and societal-based approaches to health policy. While some state and local governments are going ahead with partnerships and place-based strategies that should lead to better health and well-being, the Commonwealth has shown little interest beyond providing a small amount of funding for three Health Inequalities Research Collaborations, which finished in 2003, and allocating funds to particular areas. Commonwealth expenditure on population health consists of a series of line items against which amounts of money are allocated (for example, immunisation, cervical screening, and prevention of drug abuse). There is no apparent shift towards a broader conception of health, and no strategies that attempt to address the social determinants.

POLICY OPTIONS AND FUTURE DIRECTIONS

The main objective of national health insurance is to try to ensure equity of access to care. Medicare has provided universal coverage and reduced the out-of-pocket costs for health care, providing a financial benefit for the poor as well as adding to their financial and psychological security (McClelland & Scotton 1998). It is clear that there is a more equal use of services where no out-of-pocket costs are incurred (those things covered by Medicare), compared with those things that are not, such as dental care (National Health Strategy 1992). This indicates the problem for those on lower incomes even accessing medical care as bulk billing rates decline and the gap between the Medicare rebate and the amount charged by doctors increases. Financial barriers to health service use could be removed through policies that re-emphasised the universal nature of Medicare, by encouraging bulk billing for all patients and abolishing the private health insurance rebate.

The percentage of Australians now covered by private health insurance is 43 per cent. With the private sector strong and growing, it is unclear how sustainable Medicare is in terms of the population continuing to support the notion that everyone must contribute to it, even if they opt to 'go private'. The changes made through Medicare Plus only increase the benefits to those who are wealthier, and they do little to increase bulk billing rates or make general practitioner visits affordable for everyone.

Abolishing the private health insurance rebate would lower costs overall, and slow the loss of health professionals from the public to the private sector, which is exacerbating shortages in the public sector. It would also stop the inequitable transfer of funds from the wealthy to the poor. The safety net payments are shifting funds to the wealthiest areas of the country and are proving to be inflationary. The combination of financial incentives to take out private health insurance and the safety net might lead to a situation in which the government moves to regulate so that higher income earners are forced to use the private system and may not want to have to contribute both to this and to Medicare.

Attempts to change to a different paradigm of health, such as a social determinants approach, have occurred elsewhere. The United Kingdom is a good example. A number of policies introduced since 1997 have a stated aim of reducing health inequalities (see Department of Health 1999, 2001, 2002). Health Action Zones and Health Improvement Programmes focus on 'health improvement' rather than 'health care', are directed at the problems of inequality and social exclusion, and join up health and social care within local areas. Alongside these developments were a number of policy actions aimed at promoting opportunity and economic regeneration, reducing social exclusion through tackling poverty and low income, improving educational and employment opportunities, rebuilding local communities, and supporting vulnerable individuals and families (Nutbeam 2003). In the United Kingdom, health care reforms have been linked with the wider set of public sector reforms to address the underlying determinants of health inequalities (Department of Health 2002). It reaches far beyond the current Australian government's view of what health policy includes. While it is not yet apparent whether these changes have brought success, there has clearly been an important change in the government's conception of what health means in the United Kingdom.

In Australia, there have been recent changes in the way that state and local governments are conceiving of health, more in line with social determinant approaches that hark back to the intentions behind the Community Health Program in the 1970s. Two contemporary examples from Victoria highlight these moves. Primary Care Partnerships were established in 2001, with the aim of increasing coordination between primary health care services, and improving the health and well-being of communities (based on local governments, usually two or three per partnership). The policy documents refer to the strategy as being based on a social model of health, which has a focus on health promotion and not just the delivery of curative care (Department of Human Services 2000).

While Primary Care Partnerships are community-based, and founded on a model of health that includes health promotion, their central purpose is the coordination of health services. Neighbourhood Renewal, which is based on improving the places where people live and helping people find employment is probably the closest example of a social determinants approach to improving health and well-being (Department of Human Services 2002). These and similar shifts in policy are the next steps required in getting beyond biomedical policy approaches. The intractable problems of health inequalities that exist in Australia today—such as Aboriginal health—require a radical rethinking about what health means, if things are to change.

NOTES

1. Commonwealth of Australia 1995, *The Constitution as Altered to 31 October 1993*, Section 51, 23A, Australian Government Publishing Service, Canberra.

2. From 1991–92 to 2001–02 there has been an annual growth rate of 9.2 per cent for pharmaceuticals, compared with 4.4 per cent for recurrent expenditure overall (AIHW 2004 figures).

3. For a detailed discussion of the changes to Medicare in 2004, see Gray (2004) and Swerrisen (2004).

12

EDUCATION POLICY: MARKETS AND SOCIETY

Jane Kenway

INTRODUCTION

From the mid 1980s onwards, Australia experienced rapid and extensive changes in education policy at the Commonwealth and state government levels, and under Labor and Liberal governments. Prior to this, Commonwealth and state education policies, particularly schools' policies, broadly sought to ensure equal, universal provision for all Australians. Along with this came high degrees of centralisation and regulation. Economic policies always had a presence but this was often contested, with the result that educational values were, for the most part, kept to the fore. Further, public education was seen to be in the public interest—a public good (Reid 2005). However, the policy changes of the mid 1980s and beyond resulted in neo-liberal economics becoming the main discourse informing most education policy decisions, and corporate management becoming the main discourse informing most administrative processes. Notions of 'the public' lost currency and 'the market' became a pivotal concept providing languages, ideologies, and practices that have impinged upon every sector of education. Although manifest somewhat differently in different sectors, market forms of educational provision are now taken for granted by those who dominate education policy circles; they are foundational. Only quite recently have these master discourses been challenged by policy makers who have sought to correct what some see as 'market failure'.

Such 'corrections' have largely been directed towards the schooling sector and have sought to return social issues to the education policy agenda in the interests of social cohesion and the socially excluded. These initiatives have usually arisen at the state not the Commonwealth level, and from Labor not Liberal governments. By and large, Commonwealth Liberal governments have maintained the neo-liberal marketisation agenda, stressing education's role in servicing the economy through the development and provision of human capital and exploitable knowledge. But certain state governments have adopted a new set of policy discourses that draw from notions of the 'Third Way' and 'new social policy'. Such policies do not involve a return to centre stage of the government and the marginalisation of the market. Rather they seek to find a middle way between the two.

My focus in this chapter is on the marketisation of education and on such contemporary alternatives to it. I begin with some background about the general parameters of the Australian education system, and then explain how market systems of education work, using the example of the university sector. This is followed by a discussion of some of the problems of a market approach to education. The final section considers the rise of 'Third Way' and 'new social policy' approaches to education. I will argue that, overall, education policy is dominated by neo-liberal economic policies but that such policies are profoundly social. In remaking education along market lines, education policy makers seek to shape society according to certain values and certain interests. The extent to which alternative approaches will successfully challenge the hegemony of the market remains to be seen and will depend, in part at least, on whether recent incarnations of notions of social democracy are sufficient to confront the view of society implied in the market discourse.

EDUCATION POLICY IN AUSTRALIA: ELEMENTS, CONTEXT, AND PROCESS ISSUES

Education is a major field of public and social policy (see Marginson 1993). It involves universities, schools, technical and further education colleges (TAFEs), adult and community education, and preschools. Education policies exercise direct control over all public sector educational institutions. Further, in such policies' ambit of influence is the burgeoning private sector of education. This includes private universities, not-for-profit private schools (Catholic, 'Independent', fundamentalist Christian, and non-denominational), and training providers (usually run for profit). Currently 68 per cent of the school-age population is in government schools and 32 per cent in private (non government) schools (DEST 2005).

Education policy is largely developed by state (and territory) and Commonwealth governments separately, and also nationally, involving the states and the Commonwealth together. Complex funding arrangements exist between the states and the Commonwealth. Public funding for education comes from tax-payers via governments, and private funding comes from individuals (fees, donations, bequests), and from business and industry for such things as research, consultancies, and teaching programs in universities, and in the form of sponsorship in different sectors. Government money continues to outstrip the amount provided by other sources, with the balances differing over time and across sectors.

Complex divisions of responsibility exist between these political levels. For example, the states have the responsibility for public schools and provide most of their funding (although parents increasingly pay some fees). But the states also influence the curriculum of private schools, mostly through the public examination system. Private schools are constituted as independent. Some have their own system as is the case of low-fee Catholic schools; others, usually high-fee private schools, are constituted under their own individual governing councils. However, they all receive government funding, much of which comes from the Commonwealth government, particularly for Catholic systemic schools, which also receive some money from state governments. Private schools also benefit from indirect government assistance in the form of various types of tax relief. Despite the states having the main responsibility for government schools, the Commonwealth government also develops policies for the schooling sector, drawing its warrant from Section 51 (xxiiiA) of the Constitution with its 'benefits to students' provision (Smart 1978). This provision allows it to influence state governments' policies through tied and matching grants, funding to private schools, and a national approach that brings the states and the Commonwealth together into partnership arrangements. In contrast, the Commonwealth government has the primary responsibility for the public funding of the university sector and largely drives the direction of the sector, but it also collaborates with state and territory Ministers of Education in a national 'quality' system of university recognition and accreditation. However, increasingly university funding comes from private sources, such as international students, and now also fees from Australian students.

Education policy addresses system- and sector-wide issues such as curriculum, assessment, research, training, institutional management, and the employment of staff and industrial relations. Each of these policy terrains is contested and contestable, and many different lobby groups participate in the politics associated with them. For instance, industrial relations are currently a matter of concern in the university sector as the Commonwealth government seeks to move university staff from enterprise bargaining arrangements to individual contracts. It plans to impose funding penalties upon the universities that do not comply with this arrangement. The National Tertiary Education Industry Union (NTEU) sees this as a direct challenge to the recent pay and conditions arrangements put in place for employees through enterprise bargaining between the union and individual universities. It sees the wider implications as including the potential loss of staff bargaining capacity in relation to university management. As this example suggests, education is a highly politicised field of public policy. This is partly because it involves and invokes many competing sets of interests, interest groups, and values; many different *policy actors*.

Education generally is expected to serve national as well as sectional interests, to be an agent of social selection and of social advancement or mobility, to allocate as well as challenge cultural values, and to produce workers as well as citizens. For example, with regard to schools, over time fierce debates have raged over what have become enduring and recurring policy issues, including public funding for private schools, literacy and numeracy, different approaches to assessment and particularly assessment for university entrance, vocational versus general curriculum, the quality of teachers and principals, approaches to school improvement and effectiveness, student retention and its relationship to employment and education, and equity and social justice. Each issue has its own genealogy. Each is regularly settled and unsettled in policy terms as governments of different political persuasions, state and Commonwealth, take power, denigrate, and dismantle the policies of their opponents, and replace them with their own. The current Commonwealth Liberal government's proposed Australian Technical Colleges (ATCs) are a case in point. These colleges move into the space already occupied by TAFEs and Vocational Education in schools, and will potentially duplicate provision. But, from the Commonwealth government's perspective, ATCs will have this government's stamp on them, not that of its predecessors.

For *policy analysis*, it is important to identify the enduring issues in each education sector and to trace the nuances of their specific policy trajectories over time and place (Taylor et al. 1997). It is also helpful to analyse the relationship between policy systems—for example, the relationships between education and welfare policy as illustrated by the Youth Allowance. This allowance is related to school retention policies and also to income support policy. It requires young people (aged 16–17) to participate in education or training in order to receive income support (Edwards 2004). Further, it is important to try to understand such trajectories within wider policy and power dynamics; not only state and national, but also international. Australian education policies follow many of the policy trends in other OECD countries—for example, key education policies have travelled to Australia from England and New Zealand particularly; the devolution of school management being a prime example (Townsend 1998). It is not possible to understand Australian education policies without some appreciation of the evolution of Commonwealth–state relations and the various manifestations of federalism that have emerged over time. Although, it is the case that many 'national frameworks' or 'national goals' can readily be publicly agreed upon, behind the scenes states' rights are often juxtaposed against Commonwealth intervention or 'interference', or visa versa. Attempts to nationalise such substantive things as the curriculum in schools, or state-based exams and credentialing systems, often meet with state resistance. Equally, there is often rivalry between states about policy outcomes for issues such as achievement in literacy and numeracy tests. A sense of shifting demographics and their implications for policy is also an important factor in understanding policy changes. Such shifts place pressure on particular sectors of education and on the public sector per se. The baby boom bulge is a topical example, but other examples include the movements of populations between schooling systems and the implications this has for the demand for educational provision in certain places and systems.

Wider policy and power dynamics also entail *systems of thought* that inform the directions of policy and are translated into policy discourse. Historically, one categorisation of such systems of thought has been as either left wing or right wing and mapped onto the Labor and Liberal political parties. Such categories are difficult to sustain given the movement of both major parties to the Right and the splintering within parties along Left/Right lines. For example, Keynesian economic theory favoured the idea that public investment should support economic and social development. In turn, this theory underpinned the public policies directed towards the universal public provision of education that guided much education policy for the three decades or so after the Second World War. Economic rationalism, specifically free market liberalism, public choice, and human capital theory (Pusey 1991) superseded Keynesianism and contributed to what some call 'post welfare' society (Tomlinson 2001). This involves pressures to downsize and privatise much of the public sector and to outsource many of its previous functions. Indeed, the current Commonwealth Liberal government's enhanced funding support for private schools can be understood in the context of theories that support the shifting of costs from the public to the private purse. More students in private schools means more parental expenditure. The Commonwealth policy push to promote 'values' in education via its *Values Education Good Practice Schools* project can also be read in this context. The private sector of schooling is constructed as the custodian of worthwhile values, while government schools are seen as lacking moral codes and thus requiring curriculum remediation. Such claims serve to enhance the status and pulling power of private schools and this in turn supports further the marketisation agenda to which I will now turn.

POLICY ISSUE: THE MARKET AS THE DOMINANT POLICY DISCOURSE

So what is the theoretical scaffolding that supports the marketisation imperative I alluded to at the outset? What is 'the market'? To market advocates, it is simply a process of exchange between producers and consumers, sellers and buyers. Its key features are identified as competition and choice, and the interaction between the two is seen both to continually enhance quality and to keep prices contained (see also the discussion of efficiency in Chapter 2). The drive for custom, it is argued, is the incentive for effort on the part of the producer, who, in benefiting the consumer, benefits 'himself'. However, for the market to function effectively as the sum total of purposive (active, informed, and goal-directed) individual choices, it must be free from outside interference. A freely functioning market, it is said, will deliver order and progress. These sorts of ideas are most popularly associated with two historically prominent economists Fredrick Hayek from Austria and Milton Friedman from the USA (Olssen et al. 2004). Their work has had a significant influence on education policy makers, who tend to map education on to the market's circuit of exchange in the manner demonstrated in Figure 12.1 with regard to schools.

When these ideas are applied, in the abstract, to education policy, the following broad premises are developed:

- education is a private economic commodity in which free, rational individuals invest
- the free, competitive market rather than the state will ensure the quality of education
- the social benefits of education arise as a result of the sum of the individual choices and investments of producers and consumers
- the minimal role of the state.

Setting minimum 'standards' only, government should support consumers' choice. Education should be provided privately and the costs should be born by those individuals who most directly benefit from it.

Figure 12.1 The market process in education

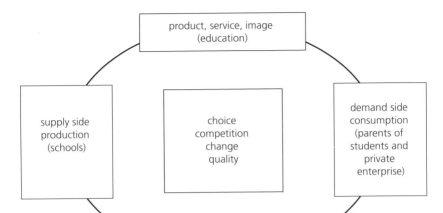

So what is the *policy process* here? How have such ideas been translated into policy? The market metaphor now heads up a policy and administrative lexicon in education policy that includes such terms as *intellectual property, educational services, products, packages, sponsors, commodities and consumers, clients, value-added education, user pays, choice, competition*, and so on. Educational purposes and language have become subsumed by the purposes and language of the market in ways amusingly satirised in Watson's (2004) book on *Weasel Words* and more seriously critiqued in Watson (2003). The actual processes involved are privatisation, commercialisation, commodification, and corporatisation (Marginson 1997). Once highly controversial, now the language and the processes they describe have become naturalised and normalised; contested primarily from the policy margins if at all.

At all levels of policy, education is usually either implicitly or explicitly conceived of as a business that produces a commodity. Students, parents, and other 'users' (business and industry) are understood as its consumers. Education consumers, those who 'shop around' are the 'targets' of market research, which discovers their needs, preferences, and decision-making processes, and of publicity campaigns to create demand and to persuade them to 'buy here'. Users are also 'targeted' as investors (sources of funds). And, in order for institutions to attract consumers/investors they have to be well packaged. Packaging is partly about marketing a product and an image to those outside the school, university, kindergarten, or TAFE college. It involves such things as the recruitment of marketing experts, and the re-orientation of staff (human resources) towards external rather than internal relations. And further, packaging for the market is about being strategic and developing a 'product/market mix' that allows the educational institution to gain a 'differential advantage'. This means making decisions about which aspects of 'the product' to emphasise, resource, and promote, and which to discard because of their lack of marketability. It further means making decisions about which 'segments' of the market to 'target' for research, publicity, and investment. It means keeping a constant weather eye on 'the competition' in order to assess relative strengths and weaknesses, and having an eye to the future and seizing new market opportunities ahead of one's competitors.

Policy makers attempt to, and often do, hold the reigns in the marketisation process. They do so via various financial rewards and penalties and other 'steering' and 'quality control' mechanisms. For instance, the Commonwealth currently has in place certain accountability 'conditionalities' with regard to the funding of schools. These include the publication of schools' performance data and also the expansion of standardised testing. Such technologies of control become a form of surveillance over the market, steering it in approved directions. Education markets do important ideological work *for* policy. Performance data, for example, has the potential to lead to league tables, which then has the potential to hook schools into the competitive arrangements that pit institution against institution in the education market place.

There are many global imperatives that have contributed to the government's market orientation; factors such as the growth of world trading blocks, the internationalisation of the labour market, the rising power of supra-national corporations, international money markets, and the rapid growth, development, and extensive application of information and communications technologies. Within this global context, the power of the nation state, its capacity, for better or worse, to control its subjects and their form of life, is significantly altered (Apple et al. 2005). As governments struggle to transform their national economies and as they direct their resources accordingly, they transfer certain responsibilities and costs away from the state to civil society. We see the opening up of public infrastructures and government services to competition from economic organisations worldwide. As Ziguras (2005) indicates, Australian universities are increasingly being caught up in a global trade in educational services and are subject to the global rules of the game established by the World Trade Organisation (WTO) via the General Agreement on Trade and Services (GATS).

Australian policies with regard to the university sector are influenced by many international agencies and this is having major implications for the knowledge work of the university sector. In a recent paper presented to the OECD on the entrepreneurial university, some of its key tasks are articulated. The entrepreneurial university:

- responds to varying student needs and circumstances
- takes account of labour market requirements and employer needs
- embeds entrepreneurial skills and ethical values in course offerings
- develops application linkages for research
- undertakes collaborative research with industry
- participates in research commercialisation ventures
- establishes diverse sources of income
- provides commercially valuable services
- plans for growth in total income
- competes successfully in its markets
- collaborates with others for full service delivery
- employs flexible staffing strategies
- manages intellectual property strategically (Gallagher 2000, p. 2).

Government policies have encouraged universities to understand themselves as direct economic agencies of government. As such, they are expected to enhance the government's 'capacity building' work and, thus, to gear university activities towards directly supporting productivity gains, enhancing international competitiveness, and creating an ideological climate of support for 'missions' sanctioned and encouraged by government policies. Many argue that the triumph of economics over university education is now complete (James 2000). This triumph is manifest in various intertwined forms of what Foucault calls 'governmentality': the 'conduct of conduct'. These include rationalisation, corporatisation, and marketisation.

Rationalisation is the code word for reductions in government funding and the associated restructuring. These have led to universities cutting costs (rationalising too) and finding non-government sources of funds—'diversifying their funding base' and achieving 'flexibilities'. On this matter it is interesting to note that even though universities have achieved high degrees of 'flexibility', with the Commonwealth government providing roughly only 40 per cent of their funding, they nonetheless still find themselves tightly controlled by the government's policy agendas.

A second form of governmentality is *corporatisation* (Jarvis 2001). Business management principles are applied to and by university management in their quest for 'continuous improvement' (Duncan 2000). For example, academic 'output' is now subject to 'performance management systems' (PMSs), through such things as key performance indicators (KPIs), quality audits, and the like. 'Quality' is a key word in much university policy, although there is considerable dispute about what it actually means. Universities are encouraged regularly to compete with and also 'benchmark' against each other with regard to such things as generating income for research. Indeed, income generation tends to be treated as a product in its own right. Merit for the university is defined accordingly and published in various forms of league tables.

Marketisation proceeds hand-in-glove with *corporatisation* and *rationalisation*. Government policies have encouraged universities to charge increased fees and to offer more and more user-pay schemes; thus providing 'choice' and responding to 'needs'. Selling the university to a wide variety of clients is now a central way to raise money to cross-subsidise the university for the loss of government money. International students feature here. Full-fee-paying overseas students are now a significant and essential part of university income. One in five students comes from overseas and any drop in international student numbers leads to considerable concern in the university sector.

The Organization for Economic Cooperation and Development's (OECD) landmark document on the knowledge economy argues that 'in the long run, knowledge, especially technological knowledge, is the main source of economic growth and improvements in quality of life' (OECD 1996, p. 13). Universities are now understood as 'essential to economic growth through the provision of highly trained specialists, expert knowledge and scientific advances' (Bok 2003, p. 1). Such views are evident in *Backing Australia's Ability*, the Australian government's policy major science and innovation policy ensemble introduced in 2001 and built upon considerably since then (Commonwealth of Australia 2001b, 2004). Within this innovation agenda, technology is understood as the driver of economic growth and commercial application is understood as the primary purpose of research and development. Knowledge must have a practical use and produce tangible outcomes. The most valued research in this context is applied 'end user' research; that conducted in partnership with 'industry'. Research links with industry act to reinforce the commercial orientation of research. This is accorded much higher value than research that provides critical commentary, stimulates public debate, and represents not intellectual property but intellectual freedom. This climate generates a reluctance to engage in the informal and free exchange of ideas. Knowledge and innovation that cannot be measured by standards based on techno-efficiency and geared towards profit are marginalised within this system: as 'knowledge is and will be produced in order to be sold, it is and will be consumed in order to be valorized in a new production: in both cases, the goal is exchange' (Lyotard 1984, p. 4).

POLICY ASSESSMENT OF MARKET APPROACHES

Market approaches to education have been subjected to extensive critique by policy analysts and activists (Bok 2003; Lauder & Hughs 1999). I will distil some of the key points here. Markets are not necessarily the people friendly, life enhancing, neutral processes of exchange that they are portrayed as. Markets are invariably imperfect, complex, and far from neutral. Take a case in point—the 'choice' discourse. This apparently simple concept now has iconic status in the policy rhetoric. But there is no such thing as a totally free choice for all. There are mass markets for the masses, elite markets for the elite. Market capacity determines market location. Further, the noun, 'market' is invariably accompanied by the verb 'market', which involves advertising and ideology, and the power invested in them (Meadmore & Meadmore 2004). These construct and constrain choices. Markets then are not just economic, but social and political. They require a shift in focus from the collective and the community to the individual, from public service to privatised service, and from other people to the self. Civil and welfare rights and civic responsibility give way to market rights in consumer democracy. Markets cannot be premised on the assumption of fairness or equality. And so, by definition, they run counter to the various policies for social justice.

There are many reasons why market models and methods are not appropriate to education policy. The techniques suggested for marketing and packaging educational institutions drastically over-simplify the complexities involved in the educational process. Such techniques suppress beneath their apparently neutral concepts of choice, quality, needs, and satisfaction, matters associated with difference, inequality, power, and conflict. It is only by suppressing such matters that they can both assume an automatic compatibility between markets and education and ignore the ever-present potential for the loss and diminishment of certain knowledge and students (Lucey & Reay 2002). The overall advice about the educational marketing enterprise given to educational managers by marketing and management experts is contradictory. On the one hand and according to one set of ideas, they are to undertake market research in order to identify the needs of various clients (parents, students, and the wider community). They are then to satisfy these needs. On the other hand and according to other edicts, they are to market themselves in order to gain a 'competitive edge'. This suggests that they will be involved in constructing needs, but will only be able to satisfy some.

Defining 'needs' is an elusive process. How, in the market economy of education, are a parent's views of the child's needs weighed up against a teacher's professional judgment about the child's educational needs and against a manager/ marketer's judgments about the institution's 'differential advantage' or 'unique selling position'? How are needs identified and on what grounds are decisions made about their satisfaction? Whose choices, whose needs, and whose judgments matter? For example, in Australia's universities, internal and public dissent are discouraged. They are bad for the image and may draw unfavourable government attention. This has implications for the knowledge work of the university (Coady 2000), which at its best has conventionally been underpinned by the principles of open and critical intellectual inquiry and free speech, or as Duncan (2000, p. 62) calls it 'independence, diversity and disputatiousness'. When policies ensure that budgets follow bodies in education, management values follow market values. Image and hype, an obsession with reputation, emulation, and rivalry, and the substitution of financial management for educational management come to dominate the scene. Further, the payment of increasingly high fees intensifies the notion of education as a commodity and of the customer rights of its student 'consumers'. This shifts the weight of responsibility for learning from a student–teacher partnership to the teacher alone. As educators know, this is not a good recipe for learning.

To conclude, the quality of education, a matter central to current education policy, can actually be placed in jeopardy under marketisation because in the educational market place, yield, output, quantity, and turnover and ensuring the buyer a credential may overshadow educational purposes. Or, to be more specific, educational purposes and the notion of quality are redefined in accordance with the market context. This narrows the purposes and focus of education. Under the influence of market logics, knowledge at all levels of the system becomes redefined as property to be selected and promoted according to its exchange value rather than its use value in a wide variety of circumstances. Institutional offerings are thus skewed towards the market. Less and less is education seen as a means towards self-expression and fulfilment, or towards the development of cultural and social understanding and responsibility, and aesthetic, critical, and creative sensibilities (Bullen et al. 2004). Its purposes become simply utilitarian. Educational democracy is redefined as consumer democracy in the educational supermarket. *Buying* an education becomes a substitute for *getting* an education. Further, as Krimsky (2004) observes, when science serves the private interests, the 'lure of profits' has the potential to corrupt research. This risk is little recognised in the science and innovation policies I noted earlier, as we explain in Kenway et al. (2004a).

FUTURE DIRECTIONS AND OPTIONS

As I mentioned at the outset, market approaches to education, particularly in the schooling sector, are now seen in some policy circles as problematic, particularly for social cohesion, the socially marginalised, and for future education policies and practices that might seek to build social cohesion and redress social inequalities (Gerwitz 2002; Thomson 2002). Such concerns have been accompanied by a search for alternative systems of thought to inform new policy directions. As is further explored in Chapter 7, approaches informed by free market liberalism, public choice, and human capital theory and so forth have been challenged by what has become known as the 'Third Way' (Giddens 1999). This approach to policy seeks to move past distinctions between Left and Right, and to reassemble the relationship between the market and the state. As Hamilton (2003, p. 122) points out, it seeks to graft 'traditional social democratic concerns for equality and social justice onto an economic system based on free markets'. It also seeks to challenge the competitive individualism of neo-liberal policies with alternative policies aimed towards rebuilding the social fabric. As the subtitle of the Giddens' book indicates, it seeks 'the renewal of social democracy'. The policy concepts that have arisen have come to be associated with 'new social policy'. The key word here is 'social'. The policy lexicon includes such concepts as the *social investment state* (it distances itself from the Keynesian welfare state), the aim of which is to develop *social investment strategies* to address the problems of *social exclusion/inclusion* and to bring about the 'redistribution of possibilities'. This involves the development of *social capital*, the facilitation of *social partnerships* involving governments, business, and third sector groups who will be involved in *community capacity building,* and the support of *social entrepreneurs* who will link diverse groups and assist those people who were formerly on welfare payments to be more socially 'empowered'. Policies are 'joined up' across departmental divides. They involve 'mutual obligations' between the various parties. The notion of the 'Third Way' is most closely aligned to New Labour under Tony Blair in the UK. However, a number of its guiding premises have travelled to education and other policies in Australia and been taken up by governments of various political hues, but most particularly by parties with a long-term interests in social justice. Recent policy developments in South Australia illustrate the point.

In March 2002, the Labor Premier of South Australia established the government's *Social Inclusion Initiative.* The Social Inclusion Initiative focuses on Aboriginal health, drugs, homelessness, young people taking the lead in social change, youth employment, young offenders, and school retention. Staying at school or undertaking alternate forms of education are seen to boost young people's chances of gaining employment and thus of enhancing their life choices and chances. *Futures Connect* (Department of Education and Children's Services 2002) was South Australia's first school retention and transition strategy to arise from the *Social Inclusion Initiative*. It aims to provide 13–19 year old students with access to the services and mentorship of various partners, and with a set of tools for planning their future. These tools include a 'learning pathways plan', a 'transition portfolio', and a 'transition pathways plan'. Other policy initiatives focus on school attendance and on programs to ensure 'at-risk' young people's 'attachment to school' (the option of part-time schooling when they feel unable to cope with full-time study), and the Innovative Community Action Networks Program wherein communities advise on what local youth need to assist them to stay at school. As part of the *Social Inclusion* agenda, the South Australian government launched the *Making the Connections* in October 2003.

> The well-being and success of young people is vital to South Australia's success now and in the future. Leaving education before completing year 12 or its equivalent will not serve our young people well in a dynamic and changing environment. The speed and scale of change and the global context call for new skills and adaptability. Ongoing training and development will be required if our young people are to meet those challenges and develop personal skills for a positive future (Social Inclusion Unit 2005).

The quote from the South Australian *Social Inclusion* web site is illuminating, for it appears to involve a shift in register from access and inclusion to a focus on human capital. But it could also be argued that even the 2002 policies are informed by human capital theory, given that they focus on education as an individual investment and place much of the responsibility for change on the individual student and fail to challenge existing education and economic systems. It is this sort of policy 'back story' that leads critics of Third Way policies (Hamilton 2003) to argue that the grafting of a social democratic discourse onto a market discourse is problematic. It fails to challenge the structural arrangements that underpin the contemporary neo-liberal policy settlement and that lead to a lack of social cohesion and inclusion in the first place.

This raises wider questions for those who seek to effect social change through education policy. Are policy challenges inevitably only ever ameliorative and cosmetic; 'correcting' for market failure? How might the neo-liberal approach to education be challenged (Olssen et al. 2004)? How can the knowledges that are currently marginalised reassert themselves (Kenway et al. 2004b)? Are any other systems of thought available that are not only post-welfare but post-market (Gerwitz 2002; Reid 2005)? And finally, as with many areas of social policy, how might education better address questions of justice in a globalising Australia (Apple et al. 2005; Thomson 2002)?

13

COMMUNITY SERVICES: CHALLENGES FOR THE TWENTY-FIRST CENTURY

Deborah Brennan

Community services are central to the functioning of modern societies and to the electoral fortunes of modern governments. While pensions, benefits, and other forms of income support tend to dominate discussion about social policy, community services such as child care, aged care, family support, and disability services are the everyday face of the welfare state for many Australians. *Who* should provide such services (the family, the market, the state, or non-profit community organisations), *how* they should be funded, and in *what ways* they should be delivered are all highly contentious issues. Services will play an increasingly important role in the twenty-first century as governments come to grips with challenges such as population ageing, increased women's labour force participation, and growing numbers of people with disabilities. In addition, community expectations concerning the quality and accessibility of services are likely to rise as the population becomes more educated and 'consumer savvy'. In short, governments face major challenges in managing the provision of services, particularly as many issues cross traditional boundaries (whether these are government departments, funding programs, problem definitions, or federal jurisdictions). Social workers and other welfare practitioners can expect to be centrally involved in practical issues such as gaining access to services for clients, and should seek opportunities to participate in the policy debates surrounding them.

Community services have been at the centre of trends in public sector reform in Australia and similar societies. These trends have been variously labelled as 'new public management', 'reinventing government', and establishing 'market bureaucracy' (Brennan 1998a; Considine 1996). These new forms of governance reflect a distrust of public (but not private) bureaucracies and a desire to place markets and competition at the centre of government. Both Labor and Coalition administrations have demonstrated their desire to 'reform' public administration and to develop new relationships between the market, the state, and the non-government welfare sector. Exposure to competition, marketisation, and the growth of the contract state have thus had a powerful impact on the delivery of Australian community services. This chapter explains the importance of community services within the Australian welfare state and examines some of the major trends in the funding, delivery, and administration of such services, focusing upon child care, aged care, and disability services. It builds on Considine's assessment that many contemporary public sector reforms 'have been devised as a direct challenge to the role of the postwar Keynesian welfare state, and therefore to the role of social work and welfare practice' (Considine 2000, p. 74). The conclusion of the chapter suggests some ways that community service providers and policy practitioners with a commitment to a just and cohesive society, might respond to these challenges.

HISTORICAL CONTEXT

While the services under discussion in this chapter have independent and complex histories, there are common themes. Australian governments have a long tradition of funding and supporting private and community-based service provision; indeed, charities and other non-government welfare organisations were central to early government attempts to create a private welfare sector. Child care services, residential care for the elderly, and support services for people with disabilities developed in a mixed economy of private, community, and government provision. Informal care provided by family, friends, and neighbours remained the major source of support for many individuals and households, but in recent decades there has been an 'increasing formalisation and public support of care' (Fine 1999, p. 274).

Since the 1970s, a radical transformation occurred in the way that many decision-makers—senior public servants, ministers, and service providers—think about and practise government. Not all of the changes ushered in as part of this project have been negative for community services. Many of the precepts of the new governance strategies—such as the importance of having a more responsive bureaucracy and the value of devolving decision-making and resource-distribution to local communities—have resonances with the public administration ideals expressed by public service reformers of the 1970s, as well as with the goals of contemporary community organisations, peak bodies, and democratic socialists. Issues of shared concern for both groups include: what services should be provided by government and why? What should be the role of the private for-profit sector and the private not-for-profit sector? Through what mechanisms should funds be allocated to service delivery organisations and on what basis? The advocates of 'reinventing government' criticise what they call the one-size-fits-all approach of government agencies that deliver services. This critique echoes the frustrations expressed by citizen and consumer groups concerning bureaucracies that are insensitive to local needs, engage in decision-making from afar, and apply formula-based responses to complex human problems. It would be inaccurate to assume that these ideas are driven exclusively by the 'neo-liberals' or 'economic rationalists'. Nevertheless, the implementation of these ideas holds considerable dangers for those who are committed to the notion of the public sector as a set of institutions and services that are owned by the whole community and that remain, through the political process, at least indirectly accountable to all citizens, rather than simply to individual 'consumers' (Brennan 1998b).

The introduction of a national competition policy (following the Hilmer Report), the drawn-out activities of the Council of Australian Governments (COAG) in reviewing health and community services, the Audit Commission report into the general functioning of the Commonwealth government, and changes to the structure of the Commonwealth public service introduced by the Howard government have all been informed, in different ways, by the desire to fundamentally rethink what the public sector does and how it relates to other parts of the economy and society. Labor and Coalition governments appear to have shared a desire to fundamentally reform public administration and to develop new relationships between the market, the state (or public sector), and the non-government welfare sector. In the decade since the mid 1990s, governments have placed greater emphasis on getting value for money in service provision and on measuring outputs and outcomes, rather than inputs and processes. At the same time there has been an intensified focus on 'clients' and 'customers', and the introduction (or intensification) of measurement and evaluation of individual and corporate performance. Some of these changes have the potential to improve service provision; others have led to unproductive competition between service providers, the closure of small, community-based agencies, and reduced access to services, particularly, though not exclusively, in rural and remote areas (McDonald 2002).

SIZE AND SCOPE OF THE SECTOR

There are various ways of defining and classifying community services, but by any measure, they account for a large proportion of social and economic resources. The Productivity Commission defines community services as including those activities 'which assist or support members of the community in personal functioning as individuals or as members of the wider community'. According to the Commission's *Report on Government Services 2005*, more than $13 billion was spent on community services in the last financial year. This was equivalent to 9 per cent of total government outlays (AIHW 1997, p. 3; SCRGSP 2005, p. F3). According to the Commission, a little less than half of this expenditure related to aged care services, about 25 per cent to disability services, 18 per cent to children's services, and 11 per cent to protection and support services. Another way to think about the magnitude of social provision is to consider the fact that in 2004–05 the Department of Family and Community Services (FaCS) spent more than $68 billion—over one-third of total Commonwealth outlays (FaCS 2005, p. 17).

In addition to looking at the value of direct financial transactions relating to welfare services, the Australian Institute of Health and Welfare (AIHW) has put a dollar value on the extensive *unpaid* services provided by community service organisations and informal care providers (family, neighbours, and friends) and has estimated the value of tax forgone (sometimes called 'taxation expenditure') by governments in relation to welfare services. Using this comprehensive approach, the AIHW estimates the total value of welfare services in 2000–01 at $43.2 billion (AIHW 2003, p. 123).

Another source of information about the scale of community service provision in Australia is the ABS survey, *Community Services Australia*. This provides information about many dimensions of community service activity including expenditure, employment, volunteering, and government involvement. *Community Services Australia* adopts a wider definition of community services than the one used in this chapter—it also includes employment placement services and interest groups involved in community service advocacy. Nevertheless, much of the information in the survey is highly relevant for the analysis presented here.

The ABS *Community Services Australia* survey shows that in 1999–00 there were 9287 employing businesses and organisations involved in the provision of community services. These included 2800 'for profit' businesses, 5398 'not for profit' organisations, and 548 government organisations. According to the ABS, expenditure on community services by these organisations has increased by 28 per cent since 1995–96. The biggest increase was by 'not-for-profit' organisations, whose expenditure rose 47 per cent to $7.1 million; expenditure by 'for profit' businesses increased by 16 per cent to $2.1 million, and government organisation expenditure rose by 6 per cent to $3.4 million (ABS 2001).

Community services are a major source of employment in Australia, especially for women. In 2001, more than 237 000 people were directly employed in community service occupations—an increase of 27 per cent since 1996. We can get a glimpse of how significant this is by noting that, in the same period, the number of people employed in all occupations in Australia grew by only 8.7 per cent (AIHW 2003, p. 145). The community services workforce is highly feminised, as Table 13.1 shows, and most employees work on a casual or part-time basis. The extent of part-time work varies within community services but is particularly high in aged care, disability services, and child care. Workers in community services, not unexpectedly, tend to have low incomes in comparison with the rest of the workforce. Table 13.1 also shows that the largest group of community service workers was child and youth service workers, and the second biggest was those working in aged or disabled care.

Although changes to community services are often debated in terms of their impacts upon clients, it is important to bear in mind the impacts on community service workers. The two dimensions are inter-related, since the difficulty in attracting and retaining skilled workers is a major issue for all services under consideration in this chapter.

CHILD CARE

Child care provides a fascinating instance of the transformation of Australian community services and of the growing significance of markets. According to the ABS, just under half (49 per cent) of all children aged under 12 in Australia used some form of child care in 2002, and the trajectory is for sustained growth (ABS 2003c). The 2002 figure included 34 per cent of children aged less than 1 year and 88 per cent of 4 year olds. Once children start school, use of child care declines; thus, while 50 per cent of 5 year olds use some form of care (mainly out of school hours services), only 33 per cent of 9–11 year olds do so. Child care is clearly a service of fundamental importance to Australian families. Enabling parents to participate in the labour force is one important reason for the provision of child care, but it is not the only one. Ensuring that young children have educational and developmental opportunities—regardless of parental labour force status—and providing respite for 'at home' parents are other important reasons for providing this service.

Child care is a significant item of government expenditure. Commonwealth expenditure alone grew from $525 million in 1991–92 to $1.6 billion in 1998–99, and services have expanded accordingly. The total number of services supported by the Commonwealth increased two and a half times (from 3972 to 10 050 services) between 1991 and 2001, while the total number of Commonwealth supported places grew almost threefold (from 168 276 to 500 034) in the same period. Different types of services grew at different rates. The biggest growth was in outside school hours care, which grew fivefold in the decade from 1991 to 2001 (AIHW 2003, p. 242).

Table 13.1 Persons employed in community service occupations: selected characteristics, 2001

Occupation	Aged 45+ (%)	Part-time (%)	Female (%)	Indigenous (%)	Number
Child and youth services	26.2	49.7	93.4	2.2	101 701
Family services	42.9	40.1	76.9	5.8	11 678
Disability services	43.7	53.7	84.8	1.2	30 895
Aged or disabled care	50.1	70.0	84.8	2.0	51 792
Other	38.7	29.1	86.5	4.8	40 990
Total	36.7	50.6	83.8	2.7	237 056

Source: AIHW 2003, p. 144

Child care provision in Australia emerged from the efforts of philanthropists and educators. Although some state governments regulated the provision of child care, it was not until the early 1970s that government became involved in a major way. In 1972, the Commonwealth government introduced the *Child Care Act*, making subsidies available to non-profit child care centres. Over the ensuing decades, the rationale and mode of supporting child care varied somewhat depending upon the party in power, but it remained a bedrock principle that public money went to support non-profit child care only. Community-based services received modest operational grants, and parents had access to income-tested subsidies to reduce fees. Australia's community child care model was internationally admired. It was not a 'one size fits all' model of government delivery, such as those that prevailed in eastern Europe, nor one were families dependent upon the vagaries of markets, as in the USA. Instead, governments provided funds for which non-profit organisations competed through a submission process, and services were diverse, accountable to users as well as governments, and embedded in their local communities. As the demand for child care grew, and governments came under increasing pressure to expand provision, the idea of having the private sector pick up the tab for capital costs became increasingly attractive to governments. In addition, the inequity of having one group of parents—those using private, for-profit services—denied fee subsidies became difficult to defend. In 1991, operational subsidies for non-profit child care services were brought to an end, and replaced by income-related subsidies that could be claimed by the users of either for-profit or non-profit, community-based care.

Private, for-profit providers dominate the provision of centre-based day care for children below school age. As of June 2001, 67 per cent of long day care services were owned by private-for-profit businesses (AIHW 2003, pp. 234-5). Other forms of Commonwealth-funded care, which are not likely to be profitable, remain overwhelmingly in the hands of non-profit community organisations. Thus, as Table 13.2 shows, approximately 96 per cent of outside school hours care, 97 per cent of family day care, and 99 per cent of occasional care is under the auspices of such groups.

As a result of Federal government largesse, and the promotion of market alternatives to community-based provision, Australian child care has become 'big business', with huge private profits being underwritten by the Commonwealth government. Major child care corporations are now listed on the stock exchange and their owners feature in *Business Review Weekly's* list of Australia's richest individuals. ABC Learning Centres, the largest corporate child care player, owns more than 200 centres around the country and each week more than 20 000 children under school age are cared for in centres owned by this one company. This concentration of ownership has reduced the diversity that used to prevail in child care, and parent management (a feature of Australian child care for decades) is a thing of the past. In the half year to December 2004, ABC Learning Centres made an after tax profit of nearly $15.5 million, an increase of 59 per cent over the previous corresponding period; owner Eddy Groves is now one of Australia's richest men. ABC Learning has adopted an 'aggressive acquisition strategy', which is likely to involve taking over even more centres owned by private individuals. It has also been successful in absorbing its competitors. Three rival groups, Child Care Centres Australia, the Peppercorn Management Group, and FutureOne have all been taken over by ABC Learning.

Many large child care corporations have strong connections with Liberal Party figures, including high-profile former MP Larry Anthony, the former Minister for Children and Youth Affairs, who joined ABC Learning as a non-executive director just a few months after losing his seat in the 2004 federal election (this would not be permitted in many other democracies where former ministers are required to wait, sometimes for several years, before joining companies or consultancy firms that relate to their previous political responsibilities or where their connections might be seen to offer a business advantage). ABC Learning is chaired by Sally-Anne Atkinson, former Liberal mayor of Brisbane. Child Care Centres Australia (now absorbed by ABC) was developed by Liberal powerbroker, Michael Kroger, in association with his father-in-law, former Liberal Party leader, Andrew Peacock. FutureOne was chaired by a former Victorian Liberal minister, Vin Heffernan (Horin 2003; Jackson 2003).

Table 13.2 Commonwealth-funded children's services and type of ownership, 2001

Type of ownership	Long day care centres	Family day care	Outside school hours care	Occasional/ other care
Private-for-profit	66.9	3.2	3.6	0.7
Community-based	33.1	96.8	96.4	99.3
Total	**100.0**	**100.0**	**100.0**	**100.0**
Total number of agencies	4,073	408	5,407	162

Source: AIHW 2003, p. 235

What has been the impact of this shift towards private, for-profit child care? Undoubtedly, at least in the short term, access to services has increased. The opportunity to make a profit from child care has attracted funds into the industry and relieved the pressure on governments to build new services (though it has greatly intensified pressure on fee subsidies). But there are indications of downward pressure on standards and quality. As community child care has declined as a percentage of all Commonwealth services, pressures to reduce licensing standards and to abandon the existing system of accreditation in favour of industry self-regulation have intensified. When state regulations have been under review, interventions by private child-care lobby groups have, almost without exception, been directed towards driving standards down. In 2003, Eddy Groves (owner of ABC Learning Centres) challenged the Queensland regulations concerning staffing during lunchtime and during breaks (Horin 2003). From a business point of view, regulations governing staff qualifications, group sizes, adult/child ratios, and basic health, nutrition, and safety requirements are barriers to profit. From this perspective, it is of course quite rational to try to reduce such 'costs' (Teghtsoonian 1993).

Another concern is that policies geared towards gender equality and intended to have beneficial effects for mothers and babies—paid maternity leave, for example—could be seen as antithetical to the business interests of private child care providers. In the midst of an intense public debate about the possibility of introducing such a scheme in Australia, the 'Money' section of the *Weekend Australian* reported, 'The main area which could affect private childcare companies is the proposal to introduce some form of paid maternity leave, which would affect demand for childcare services as more women stayed at home longer after giving birth' (Fraser, 2002).

Despite the explosion in the number of services and the considerable expenditure on child care, unmet demand, a looming shortage of labour, and the cost of care remain major concerns. Although there has been a significant improvement in meeting previously unmet demand, private for-profit companies are unwilling to set up in areas that are unlikely to be profitable (e.g. where there are large numbers of low-income families) despite expressed needs for care. The ABS Child Care Survey, conducted in 2002, showed that, despite considerable progress in meeting demand, parents require additional places for 47 800 children in outside school hours care; 46 300 places in long day care, 37 600 in occasional care, and 29 100 in family day care (AIHW 2003, p. 244).

AGEING AND AGED CARE

Like child care, aged care involves complex and highly political questions about the role of governments, markets, and families. The anticipated growth in the proportion of the Australian population aged over 65—and especially in the proportion of those over 80 years—undoubtedly presents challenges for Australian governments and service providers. Yet given its relatively youthful population and low-cost, targeted social security system, Australia is well placed to deal with these demographic changes. On current trends, spending on income support will increase from approximately 6.8 per cent of Gross Domestic Product to 7.4 per cent by 2041–42 (Department of FaCS 2002, p. 5). The provision of appropriate services, including respite and residential care, and community support to maintain elderly people in the own homes and communities will nevertheless present substantial challenges.

While income support for the elderly has been a Commonwealth government responsibility since the establishment of the Age Pension in 1908, a combination of private for-profit, charitable, community, and government organisations has provided services for the elderly. With the expansion of social provision that occurred in Australia after the Second World War, aged care became a policy arena of Commonwealth government concern. During the

1960s, the Commonwealth introduced subsidies for private nursing homes and this led to rapid growth in this form of provision. Hostel care, for residents with higher levels of independence, developed separately. Since the early 1980s, there has been an attempt to reorient aged care away from nursing homes (which, in addition to being expensive, are also quite isolating) and towards forms of support and care that enable elderly people to remain within their communities. The implementation of the Home and Community Care program (HACC) in 1985 signified a decreased emphasis on residential care, and a desire to give greater priority to community care. HACC provides services to older people as well as to people of all ages with disabilities, and their carers. The program is jointly funded by the Commonwealth and the state/territory governments, and its purpose if to 'avoid premature or inappropriate admission to long-term residential care' (AIHW 2003, p. 300).

A major restructuring of the residential aged care system took place with the introduction of the *Aged Care Act 1997*. Under this legislation, the previous two-tier system of nursing homes and hostels was replaced with a single system and the contributions of residents were substantially increased. The Howard government's *Strategy for an Ageing Australia*, released in 2001, and updated in 2002, provides a framework for addressing the challenges of an ageing population. It emphasises participation and access to services across the lifecourse, not just in old age.

Although Australia, like similar Western countries, has experienced a growth of government funding and support for aged care services, the vast majority of older people live in households in the community (only 5 per cent of those aged over 65 live permanently in residential care) and, where assistance is needed, families remain the main providers of practical, everyday support (AIHW 2003, p. 283). Most older Australians are independent, active members of the community, and it would be a mistake to think of them as primarily the *recipients* of care; the over 65s provide a great deal of care and support to others—especially spouses, children, and grandchildren—and make significant contributions through volunteer work.

Nevertheless, there remain serious gaps and inadequacies in Australia's system of aged care services. The National Aged Care Alliance (NACA), which represents twenty-four peak organisations, including providers, unions, and consumers of aged care, has urged the Commonwealth government to develop benchmarks for aged and community care service provision, specifying quality standards and adopting realistic funding levels. The Alliance argues that current funding for community care is inadequate. It raises concerns about inadequate coordination between the Commonwealth and the state/territory governments in relation to Home and Community Care, and draws attention to the problems of attracting and retaining high quality staff (a major concern in child care as well). The Alliance argues that, since 1997, the government has used an indexation formula that does not reflect the actual costs of the industry, thus driving many providers into a precarious financial position. Although additional funds were made available in the 2004 budget, the Alliance argues that the pay rates of staff in residential aged care are unacceptably low in comparison with other sectors and that this will result in critical staff shortages. The increasing dependency levels of people accessing aged care facilities requires staff who are adequately trained to deal with complex needs and challenging behaviours. Benchmarks for staffing levels and skills mix are urgently needed (NACA 2005, p. 3).

Another issue for the aged care sector is dealing with the increasing number of aged persons who suffer dementia. Currently there are approximately 180 000 dementia sufferers in Australia; this is projected to grow to approximately half a million by 2040 (NACA 2005, p. 4). Evidence suggests that appropriate care in the community can delay admission to residential are, but this depends upon adequate funding, planning, and coordination.

DISABILITY SERVICES

The philosophical underpinnings and policy rhetoric of contemporary disability services in Australia and similar countries are deeply influenced by human rights principles. Although, arguably, all three types of service provision under consideration in this chapter have been shaped by 'rights talk', there is no doubt that disability advocates have been most deeply influenced by these ideals. Policy ideas emanating from the USA, Canada, and the European Union, as well as Australia, use a rights model to argue for income support and services that encourage personal autonomy and dignity through flexible, individually planned services (Tilly 1999). The United Nations is working towards a convention to promote and protect the rights of people with disabilities and, within the Asia-Pacific region, it has encouraged the establishment of a framework that would deliver 'an inclusive, barrier-free and rights-based society' for people with disabilities (AIHW 2003, p. 331). The belief that people with disabilities should have the same opportunities as others to participate in society seems to be widely shared.

In theory, a number of the policy directions of the new public management are consistent with measures to increase the independence and autonomy of people with disabilities and their carers. Ideas such as individualised funding and consumer-directed care, for example, are underpinned by the principle of encouraging individualisation and consumer control—allowing the person to purchase services and assistance from beyond the established disability service sector if they so choose (Belli 2000; Laragy & Frawley 2004).

But, in their day-to-day lives, people with disabilities do not experience many elements of this rights-based approach. Often they lack access to the basic services and amenities that are necessary for a dignified life. In its 2005 Federal Budget Submission, ACROD—the National Industry Association for Disability Services, which represents over 550 non-government, non-profit organisations in the disability area—advised the Commonwealth government that, 'In every State and Territory in Australia there are long queues for accommodation support, respite, therapy and community access services, with only the most desperate of applicants receiving a service' (ACROD 2005, p. 12).

In relation to the labour market, the most basic means of enhancing independence and autonomy for many people, discrimination and exclusion are common. People with disabilities have an unemployment rate far higher than the rest of the community; the labour force participation rate of men with disabilities is 52 per cent, compared with 86 per cent for non-disabled men of working age, and for women the figures are 42 per cent and 67 per cent respectively. People with disabilities are far more likely than others to work part-time, and thus receive substantially lower earnings. Further, the additional costs and time required for transport, the lack of suitable facilities and arrangements within many workplaces, and the prejudices of employers and the public, exacerbate the problems encountered (Wilkins 2003).

Despite these acknowledged barriers, the Commonwealth government has expressed concern at the growth in the number of Disability Support Pension recipients and has increased the pressure on people with disabilities to seek employment, labelling then as 'welfare dependent' and introducing legislation that will make it more difficult for them to obtain and remain on income support. Yet, at the same time as it is urging Disability Support pensioners to seek work, the Commonwealth government limits the number of job seekers that disability employment services can assist. As a result, aspiring job seekers are turned away and have to wait many months for assistance.

Key organisations representing people with disabilities have called for additional services and supports, especially disability employment packages, to help those seeking to re-enter the labour force. It is clear that there is substantial evidence of unmet demand. In 2002, the AIHW concluded that, across Australia, there were 12 500 people in need of accommodation and respite places, and an additional 8200 places for community access services were needed (AIHW 2002). Further evidence comes from the Australian Bureau of Statistics, which reported in 2003, that of the 957 000 people with disabilities needing assistance, 35 per cent reported that their needs were only being partly met and 5 per cent reported that their needs were not met at all (ABS 2003d).

According to the Disability Council of NSW, many people with disabilities face highly restricted housing and accommodation possibilities. In NSW alone, approximately 2400 people with disabilities (including 250 children) live in large residential centres—with a further estimated 2000 living in Commonwealth-funded aged care facilities. For the vast majority of adults with disabilities, there is no option but to live with ageing carers. Approximately 2500 people live in state government-provided or -funded supported accommodation, usually within the 'group home' model of support. For many people, housing options are limited, often due to the limitations of care funding and services.

Although this chapter has considered ageing and disability services separately, it should be noted that there are close links between disability and ageing, as well as between disability and health services. Inevitably, as the population ages, we will experience an increase in the incidence of disability. Yet 'policies, funding models, service designs and service provision have not kept pace with this expanding interface' (ACROD 2005, p. 2).

CONCLUSION

The trends in community service provision discussed in this chapter present a picture of uneven development and mixed outcomes. In each of the areas under consideration, there have been some gains in terms of expanded provision and funding, but many of the initiatives have been founded upon a philosophical approach that constitutes individuals as consumers whose primary interests are personal and private, rather than as citizens with a *collective* interest in services of a decent standard—services that will serve the common interests of children, the elderly, and the disabled members of our society. Notions such as community, solidarity, justice, social capital, and equity have been marginalised in recent policy debates about child care, aged care, and disability services. Such notions are seen either as irrelevant or as a smokescreen for other motives. The philosophies that underpinned the provision of publicly funded and provided services that bind citizens together in a common cause have been replaced by a focus on markets, individuals, and personal gain. Where does all this leave welfare workers and policy practitioners? The current wave of interest in new public management techniques needs to be scrutinised and monitored carefully—especially in relation to community services and welfare policies. To the extent that its approaches resonate with the needs of individuals and community organisations for more flexible, responsive, and decentralised decision-making, it can provide a basis for constructive action. But community and welfare workers need to be alert to the moments when 'reinventing government' becomes a justification for cost-cutting, privatisation, and blocking out the voices of citizens. A strong, strategic role for government in planning and funding community services need not in any way diminish civil society; rather, it can enhance and strengthen the non-government sector and deepen its capacity for promoting the interests of all members of the community, particularly the most vulnerable.

14

TAXATION: PAYING FOR POLICY

Alison McClelland

> The oldest, more important and most controversial power of government has been its power to raise taxation. The taxation power of the monarch was the centrepiece of the Magna Carta and it was again the principal issue in the dispute that led to the American Revolution. To this day, taxation continues to be a vital underpinning of government power. Indeed, the advance of government since World War II and especially the welfare state, has depended upon the power of government to tax and spend (Keating 2004b, p. 145).

INTRODUCTION

We can pay for our social policy proposals through philanthropy, some kind of user pays arrangement, or through taxation. For most of the last century, we increasingly relied on taxation as the method of financing our expanding welfare state and our growing expectations of citizenship rights. But taxation, as one of the most coercive areas of government activities (Eccleston 2004) is also one of the most contested, with differences of ideology and values affecting how taxation levels and different types of taxes are seen, and with differences in power influencing the tax polices that are adopted. Taxation is seen by some as the price we pay for living in a civilised community, as one of the responsibilities of citizenship, and as how we respond to the 'needs of strangers'; thus reflecting reciprocity in a complex and diverse society. At the other extreme, taxation is seen as confiscation and theft, as a threat to individual freedom that must be minimised at all costs. For many, tax is a burden that has to be endured, a necessary evil, with the relationship between the taxes people pay and the services they expect from government frequently opaque and unclear, and the expectation of tax cuts regularly revisited.

The dominance of the last two views about taxation in the public discussion about tax policy raises the question of how improvements to social policy can be financed if the priority is given to tax cuts over improvements to public investment and government payments and services. These questions are particularly pertinent in light of Australia's tradition as a low tax country when compared with most other welfare states, especially the countries of Europe and Scandinavia. Through the 'wage-earners' welfare state' or the 'Australian way', in the past our egalitarian aspirations were more reflected in the pursuit of secure employment (for male breadwinners) and high minimum wages, than through the universal citizenship-based expenditure programs developed in Europe (see Chapter 5 for more detail). However, as we shall see later, the changing nature of the wage-earners' welfare state poses particular challenges for Australia's capacity to respond to the policy requirements in a number of areas that are documented in the other chapters in this book. Tax policy change can also be hard to achieve, partly due to Australia's weak institutional capacity for policy change (Eccleston 2004), and also because of the technical nature of much of the analysis, making it difficult for many citizens to contribute to some of the debates in an informed way.

In this chapter I expand on these issues. I first cover the goals, elements, and context of Australia's tax system, then move to examine the issues and options for reform, concluding with a discussion of how the tax policy process operates.

AUSTRALIA'S TAX SYSTEM—GOALS, ELEMENTS, HISTORY, AND INTERNATIONAL COMPARISONS

The three main goals of taxation policy are adequacy, equity, and efficiency. Simplicity is a fourth goal, although perhaps not of the same order and priority. The goal of adequacy refers to the principal function of taxation, which is to raise sufficient revenue to fund necessary government expenditure. However, the level of taxation regarded as adequate depends on views about the extent of government's responsibility for the well-being of its citizens. Proponents of neo-liberalism support less government involvement and lower levels of taxation, whereas social democrats are more likely to be concerned if inadequate taxation hinders government action, and to support higher levels. The more 'liberal' regime of the United States of America had tax revenue at 29.8 per cent of Gross Domestic Product (GDP) in 2002, in contrast with the 'social democratic' regime of Sweden, with tax revenue of almost 55 per cent (see Figure 14.1 later in this chapter).

The goal of equity refers to the need to levy taxation according to some notion of fairness. Its importance also arises from government's redistributive role in correcting unacceptable inequalities in ownership and access to economic resources, goods, and services, and in the capacity to participate in different aspects of community life. Again, the extent and type of government action required to achieve a more equitable society varies with different ideologies and values, as explained in some detail in Chapter 2. In tax policy, the equity goal has two aspects. One is vertical equity, commonly understood to mean that individuals with greater economic resources should pay more tax than individuals with fewer resources. To assess this we judge where taxes are progressive, proportional, or regressive (see glossary in Table 14.1). Income taxes are generally regarded as progressive, as marginal tax rates increase as income increases, whereas the GST and many expenditure taxes are regressive. However, while the income tax system is nominally progressive, effectively its progressive nature is undermined by the limitations in the income tax base, which allow for loopholes and opportunities for tax minimisation, more often to the benefit of higher income earners. The other aspect of equity, horizontal equity, is commonly interpreted to mean not only treating people in equal economic circumstances in the same way, but also acknowledging differences in needs, in particular the presence of dependent children, in assessing their capacity to pay through the tax system.

The increase in the taxation and expenditure of governments in Australia and elsewhere for much of the twentieth century has changed the emphasis on the redistributive function of taxation. When government activity was limited, there was a much greater emphasis on how the tax system alone acted as an agent of redistribution. However, with the increase in government activity and in levels of taxation generally, the focus is now more on the combined impact of government spending and taxation on inequality. There is also an interest in lifecycle redistribution, how the combined impact of taxes and benefits helps people deal with their changing circumstances over their lives. Analysis of the incidence of government taxes and spending indicates that the average household pays more taxes than it receives in benefits at certain stages in the life cycle (for example, younger couples without children), but also that it receives a net benefit at other vulnerable stages, such as the presence of children and old age (Harding 1995).

Table 14.1 Glossary of tax/social security terms

Direct taxes	Taxes levied on entity who is expected to eventually pay—personal income taxes, company taxes, some levies, charges, and contributions.
Indirect taxes	Taxes on expenditure and activities—the GST, excise taxes. Taxes that are passed on from the liable entity to another entity (usually to the consumer).
Incidence	Where the cost of paying the tax eventuates—this can be hard to determine and the incidence of some taxes, payroll taxes for example, is unclear.
Progressive	A tax is progressive if it takes a higher proportion of a wealthy person's income than someone who is less wealthy.
Proportional	A tax is proportional if it takes the same proportion of income from people with different levels of income or wealth.
Regressive	A tax is regressive if it takes a lower proportion of the income of a wealthy person than someone who is less wealthy.
Tax level	Total amount of tax, usually calculated in dollar terms or as a proportion of GDP or Gross Domestic Product (the total amount produced in a country or the national income).
Marginal tax rate	The percentage of the last dollar taken in tax—seen to influence incentives to work.
Average tax rate	The percentage of total income taken in tax.
Effective marginal tax rates (EMTR)	The percentage of the last dollar taken when the combined impact of tax rates and withdrawal of government payments is taken into account—can be much higher for low-income earners than the top personal tax rate.
Tax expenditure	Assistance to individuals or companies delivered through the tax system rather than through direct government payments—can be in the form of a tax exemption, deduction, offset (rebate or credit), lower tax rate, or deferral of tax payment.
Tax credit	A reduction in tax liability, usually by effectively raising the tax-free threshold for certain groups including families with children, low-income earners, people on pensions and benefits, and self-funded retirees. Can be refundable (paid to people with insufficient tax liability so they can benefit from the full amount) or non-refundable (meaning that it is restricted to reduction of tax for the specific purpose).
Tax base	The range of income, expenditure, and wealth included for purposes of calculating tax liability.
Bracket creep	The extent to which a person's income becomes liable to a higher tax rate because of the failure to index income tax thresholds in line with inflation.

Sources Costello 2005; The Commission On Taxation and Citizenship 2000; Warren 2004

Figure 14.1 General government revenue as a proportion of GDP 2002

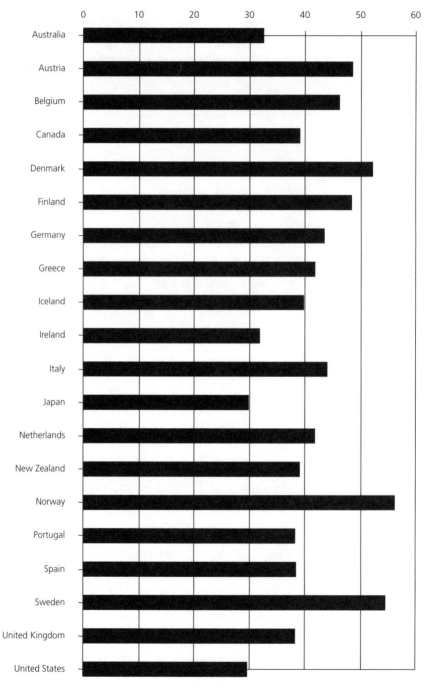

Source: Keating 2004a

The third goal of efficiency is most commonly interpreted to mean that taxes should not reduce productive economic activity and the level of economic and employment growth. A common concern is that higher taxes will reduce economic growth as they will reduce incentives to work harder, save, and produce goods and services. There is little conclusive evidence that the levels of taxation applying in Australia and most other countries do compromise economic efficiency. Keating (2004a, pp. 29) assesses the evidence, concluding that there is no 'strong economic case against present levels of taxation' and that, 'the net effect of taxation on economic performance depends on the level and structure of taxation, how productively the revenue is spent, and where the incidence of taxation lies, which in turn depends on the nature of competition in the goods and factor markets'. The goal of simplicity is frequently called upon with the increase in the complexity of tax legislation in Australia. However, there can be a conflict between the goals of equity and simplicity, as calls for simplicity (for example, no exemptions on the GST or a single income tax rate) are often at the expense of arrangements put in place to recognise special needs and differing capacity to pay.

Table 14.2 shows the main forms of taxation in Australia in 2002. It illustrates the contribution of income tax, representing 55 per cent of all tax revenue in 2002–03 and over two-thirds of Commonwealth revenue. Most personal income tax revenue comes from the regular collection of income tax from wage and salary earners through their employers in the form of PAYE (pay as you earn) taxes. Company income taxes are also important, contributing approximately one-third of all income tax revenue. The next main source of revenue is from consumption—from goods and services—with the Commonwealth taxes, GST (the Goods and Services Tax) and excise taxes (from alcohol, cigarettes, and petrol), providing most revenue. When all Commonwealth and state government consumption taxes (including gambling taxes) are aggregated, consumption taxes make up approximately 30 per cent of revenue. Property taxes are the third area of taxation, with the main taxes on fixed property being local government rates and state government land taxes. There are also taxes on property transactions, most of which are also state taxes and include stamp duties on the buying and selling of property and on financial transactions. Finally, payroll taxes are an important source of revenue for state governments, representing almost one-quarter of state and local government taxation.

Prior to Federation, the early taxes levied by state governments were customs duties and taxes on alcohol and tobacco, followed by the introduction of death and land taxes. Income taxes were initially state taxes, introduced by different state governments during the latter part of the nineteenth century and the early part of the twentieth century. With Federation, the Commonwealth government gained the sole constitutional authority to levy excise taxes. Times of war and economic upheaval saw the Commonwealth expand its taxing power.

Table 14.2 Structure of taxation in Australia 2002–03

Main Tax Type	Commonwealth		State and Local		All Taxes	
	$m	%	$m	%	$m	%
Taxes on income						
Personal	91 477	47				38
Company	35 079	18				14.7
Total (1)	131 278	67				55
Taxes on goods and services						
GST	31 257	16				13.1
Excise	20 787	10.7				8.7
Gambling			3 843	8.8		1.6
Motor vehicle			4 691	10.8		2
Total (2)	59 194	30.5	11 997	27.6	71 191	30
Payroll	3 085	1.6	10 147	23		5.6
Property			10 371	23.8		4.4
Financial transactions	13		10 989	25.2	11 002	4.6
Total (3)	194 313	81.7	43 503	18.3	237 816	100

Source: Costello 2005 (tables 10 & 11)

1. Also includes prescribed payments, income tax paid by super funds, and income taxes levied on non-residents in addition to taxes identified above.

2. Also includes taxes on international trade, insurance, levies, and franchise taxes in addition to taxes identified above.

3. Also includes Commonwealth payroll taxes (FBT and Super Guarantee), Commonwealth property taxes, and other minor taxes in addition to major taxes identified above.

The Commonwealth first took over income taxes from the states in 1915, and then again on a permanent basis during the Second World War. While the Fraser government returned the power to tax income to state governments during the 1970s, no state government introduced an income tax and their authority was subsequently withdrawn. The Wholesale Sales Tax (WST) was introduced by the Commonwealth in the 1930s and remained until the introduction of the Goods and Services Tax (GST) in July 2000.

The 1950s and 1960s were a time of relative stability (Eccleston 2004) before the changing economic context of the 1970s, during which time tax policy became the subject of renewed debate, although there was little reform introduced. One change concerned the progressive elimination of death taxes, once an important component of state government revenue, accounting at times 'for up to 30 per cent of state tax revenues' (Saunders 1983 cited in Smith 2004, p. 85). The poor design of death taxes left them open to abuse and exploitation by wealthy people, and therefore disliked by the public. Consequently, when they fell victim to interstate competition following their abolition by the Queensland state government of Bjelke-Petersen, other states followed suit. Another more recent change was the negative impact of High Court judgments on state governments' taxing powers, which rendered many state government taxes on goods and services (the other main tax base in Australia apart from income tax) unconstitutional, labelling them as excises. Competitive pressure has accompanied other state taxes, including payroll taxes and taxes on business and financial transactions, and while many still remain, state governments tend to keep a careful eye on how other states levy such taxes.

The growing dominance of the Commonwealth government over Australia's taxation system is an important feature of Australia's history. The Commonwealth government collects over 80 per cent of all tax revenue, with state governments collecting approximately 15 per cent despite their responsibility for approximately 40 per cent of government expenditure (Warren 2004). Another feature has been the steady increase in the level of taxation, until the latter part of the last century, in order to finance our expanding welfare state. The growth was particularly strong during the 1960s and 1970s, when tax increased from just over 20 per cent of GDP to approximately 33 per cent in 1986, where it now stands (Keating 2004a). However, as Keating (2004a, p. 145) comments, the last two decades have seen an 'arbitrary tax ceiling' limit government's capacity to respond to important expenditure needs. Yet this ceiling also represents an historic continuity, in that it has maintained Australia's position as a low tax country, a reputation that successive governments, including Labor governments, have tended to celebrate. In 2002, Australia was the fourth-lowest taxed country of comparable developed countries (countries belonging to the OECD—the Organisation for Economic Cooperation and Development), with only Ireland, Japan, and the United States of America having less tax (Keating 2004a). Figure 14.1 illustrates the different levels of a number of comparable countries.

Many Australians regard themselves as highly taxed, with several factors probably contributing to this perception. The first is the dominance of the global personal income tax collected by the Commonwealth. In contrast, many other countries have income tax in different forms—for example, as a general income tax, and as specific taxes and levies including employer and employee social security contributions. Income taxes in other countries are also sometimes levied by more than one level of government—by national and state governments especially. This varied way of taxing income makes it less visible than in Australia where the Commonwealth's income tax dominates. While Australia's Superannuation Guarantee Charge (SGC), levied on employers towards their employee's superannuation, is sometimes regarded as a tax, its tax status is not clear-cut. The Medicare Levy is certainly a specific income tax but even by taking this into account, in comparison with other countries, Australia has very few hypothecated taxes (taxes that are earmarked for specific purposes). The second reason that Australians may regard themselves as highly taxed is because debates about income tax tend to focus on marginal tax rates and not average tax rates, with regular crises about average wage earners facing record level marginal tax rates recurring every 5 years or so in Australia. However, average tax rates provide a more accurate reflection on what people have to pay overall as a proportion of their income. They are much lower than marginal income taxes, and over the past 20 years for people on average earnings, average tax rates have not increased but have remained at about 23 per cent of income (Keating 2004b). Analysis also shows that after taking into account government payments, average tax rates for average workers in Australia are lower than in the low-taxed USA—at 23 per cent in 2001 in Australia, compared with 24.65 per cent in the USA (ACOSS 2003).

The changing economic and social environment has limited the increase in tax revenue in Australia and worldwide. The end of the long boom of the 1950s and 1960s promoted a concern that government spending and taxing— the welfare state—was contributing to the economic difficulties experienced in Australia and elsewhere. The welfare state was considered by some to be in crisis and with its growth needing to be severely restricted. In English-speaking countries, especially Australia, the USA and the UK, there was a decided shift in favour of neo-liberal economic policies that advocated cuts to government spending and taxation. But worldwide, it was also recognised that economic change towards global and service-based economies had implications for tax systems. In Australia, four tax problems were identified. The first was problems with income tax rates and the effective incidence of income tax, with large-scale avoidance and evasion becoming apparent in the 1970s. The second was the narrow base of the Wholesale Sales Tax (WST) and its negative economic impacts. Third was the Commonwealth/state tax imbalance in taxing powers, and fourth, problems with the double taxation of company income (Eccleston 2004). Two inquiries into Australia's tax system (the Asprey Committee and the Matthews Committee) recommended significant changes, including the introduction of a GST, a capital gains tax (CGT), taxes on the transfer of wealth, changes to company tax, and indexation of the income tax thresholds. However, little tax reform occurred until the mid 1980s, with the Hawke government's changes to the income tax base, followed by the Howard government's ANTS (A New Tax System) changes in 2000 to the consumption tax base (with the introduction of the GST). Despite some useful changes from both packages of tax reform, a number of problems and issues remain.

PROBLEMS, ISSUES, AND THE CHANGING CONTEXT

Early in the twenty-first century, Australia's tax policy still needs to adjust and respond to a number of perennial problems and to a different economic and social climate. The first and most significant issue, according to some (ACOSS 2003; Castles 2002; Keating 2004a, b), is that Australia does not have sufficient tax revenue to respond to this new economic and social context. Australia's old welfare state had distinctive features that enabled it to achieve reasonable egalitarian outcomes with much lower levels of taxation and expenditure than many other countries. Castles comments that:

> The Australian paradox of state activism without state expenditure can only be properly addressed through an understanding of the unusual development of Australia's economic institutions in the early days of the century that made the living standards of ordinary Australians a function of the systems of industry protection and wage regulation rather than of the generosity of state spending programs (2002, p. 41).

But, as Chapter 5 describes in more detail, the conditions for these egalitarian outcomes (which did not cover a large number of women or Indigenous Australians) have broken down as a result of the interactive impacts of the following:

- the end of full-employment, especially full-year, full-time employment, alongside the growth in non-standard employment
- increasing rates of marital separation and divorce

- declining home ownership and increased housing insecurity
- increased long-term reliance on income support
- the dismantling of protection and deregulation of industrial relations, with increased earnings inequality and pressures on low wage growth
- increasing complexity of need in areas such as health and community care, family support and population ageing, transport, and environmental protection.

Australia is not unique in facing difficulties such as the end of full-employment, changes in family structures and formation, and the increased complexity of need. But it is different in that it lacks the background of political support to raise the revenue it now requires to deal with the demise of the worker's welfare state, partly because this has not been a priority for either of the two main political parties. The past 20 years have seen spending increasingly financed through spending cuts in areas of low priority, tighter targeting of welfare support, greater reliance on user pays, and assets sales. The limits to an excessive use of these forms of financing may now have been reached. If we continue to rely on them, we may see a further running down of public assets and a development of a two-tier welfare state, with high quality services for those who can purchase them in the market and a poorer quality residual system operating across a range of important policy areas, including education, transport, and health (Keating 2004a). Keating (2004a) estimates that a significant increase in revenue may be needed, especially to finance the health care costs of ageing, to improve our education and training performance for economic and social reasons, to improve Australia's infrastructure and the environment, and to respond to the war on terror.

The second issue is the future of income tax. There are a number of related problems including gaps in the base, changing work-patterns, the growth of tax expenditures, high marginal tax rates facing low-income earners, the lack of indexation and the problem of bracket creep, and the move away from the individual as the unit for income tax. Overall, these problems make the income tax system more inequitable and inefficient, as well as contributing to a loss of revenue. Loopholes and concessions, such as an inadequate CGT, the abuse of negative gearing, the use of trusts, and tax expenditures such as the private health insurance rebate and superannuation tax concessions, have distorted investment decisions, driven up the price of housing and health care, and benefited higher-income earners most. Tax expenditures are a form of fiscal welfare (see Table 14.1 and Chapter 2) and their cost was estimated at almost $30 billion in 2001–02 (Warren 2004). The casualisation of work and the growth of self-employment means a move away from paying income tax through the employee-based PAYE system, with more people paying as a company to take advantage of the lower company tax rate.

The gap between the top marginal tax rate (47 per cent plus Medicare levy of 1.5 per cent) and the corporate tax rate of 30 per cent also provides an incentive to incorporate in order to minimise tax. It is generally seen as desirable to have a minimal gap between these two rates. The impact of globalisation and the greater focus on international competitiveness means that it is unlikely that this gap will be closed through an increase in the company tax rate (Eccleston 2004). This places pressure to reduce the top marginal tax rate, particularly when evidence indicates that this rate cuts in at a lower income than the top rate of other countries. However, eliminating the gap is expensive (see Warren 2004, p. 128) and it also gives most benefit to those on above average earnings. Tax cuts in the 2004–05 and 2005–06 Commonwealth Budgets have mainly focused on large increases to the income threshold at which the top rate applies. This threshold has been increased from $70 000 p.a. to $125 000 (to apply in 2006–07). The cuts give taxpayers on more than $120 000 per annum a benefit of $86.58 per week in comparison with $6.00 per week for a taxpayer on average earnings. It has, arguably, significantly reduced the need to lower the top rate, despite calls to the contrary. However, bracket creep (see Table 14.1) along with strong increases in income for many, means that more people have become subject to higher marginal tax rates, including the top tax rate, and this has become a much 'hotter' political issue over the past few years.

But, as previously indicated, the highest effective marginal tax rates (EMTRs) are faced by low-income Australians, as they move from welfare to work and as government income-tested payments are withdrawn. Unemployed people are particularly hard hit and in the past have faced EMTRs of 87 per cent or more, although these were reduced somewhat in the 2005–06 Commonwealth Budget. The main problem is the rate of withdrawal of government payments as a result of the very tightly targeted income support system in Australia, rather than the tax rates per se (see Chapter 9 on social security policy for further details). A final issue for income tax concerns the unit of tax liability. Historically this has been the individual in Australia, but this is being compromised in two ways. First, through income splitting where non-PAYE tax payers, who are able to arrange their affairs through family trusts, partnerships, and companies, can reduce their income tax liability by splitting income with family members who have a lower tax liability. Successive governments have been unwilling to take action on this loophole that is both inequitable (because it benefits higher income earners most) and inefficient, because it discourages the secondary income earner in the family unit (usually the wife) from working as that person becomes subject to the primary earner's marginal tax rate, a higher rate than would otherwise occur. The second way the individual as the unit is being compromised is through changes to family payments and other benefits, which have been increasingly paid through the tax system. Such payments are often geared towards providing greatest benefit to single income families and are withdrawn on either family income or on the income of the secondary income earner (in the case of Family Tax Benefit Part B), with the latter having similar problems of equity and efficiency to that provided by income splitting. Chapter 9 provides more discussion of the family payments system and Cass and Brennan (2003) have more detail on the move away from the single unit in the tax system and how the position of women is compromised by this move.

Another ongoing issue concerns the taxation of capital and wealth. Australia does not have a general wealth tax or taxes on death, but instead relies heavily on property taxes through local government rates and state government land taxes. This is particularly relevant in the context of the ageing of the 'baby boomers', many of whom have amassed significant amounts of wealth that will be transferred untaxed for the next generation. Economists often favour taxes on death (or inheritance) as they are less likely to distort behaviour than other taxes and can contribute to equity if well designed. However, such taxes require political courage as they, along with most wealth-related taxes, are very subject to political scare tactics. Another significant but politically loaded problem is the omission of the family home from the CGT, from a number of state land taxes, and from the assets test for social security purposes. This is said to have encouraged excessive investment in high-value houses and, alongside negative gearing, to have driven up the price of housing in Australia (Disney 2003). The impact of distortions in the tax system on the equitable distribution of housing supply and on housing affordability more generally is a significant issue requiring attention at Commonwealth and state levels.

How we tax mobile capital in a global world is a related and important issue. There has been limited action on the development of international treaties and cooperative arrangements (Smith 2004) that will reduce the scope for a race to the bottom as countries compete with each other for 'footloose' capital. However, the role of taxation needs to be kept in perspective here as other factors are also important in the decision of firms (and high-skilled individuals) to locate to particular countries: such as a skilled workforce, sound infrastructure, and services, including good schools and health care. Another issue is the absence of a broad-based environmental tax, such as a carbon tax, which could provide a price signal to limit the excessive use of environmentally damaging carbon-based fuels and also raise revenue for improvements to the environment. There is also the ongoing problem of vertical-fiscal imbalance alongside the absence of any mechanism for resolving Commonwealth/state differences in a cooperative and constructive manner. While allocating the GST revenue to the states was meant to assist in resolving this imbalance and an intergovernmental agreement was developed to help it work constructively, differences exist between the states and the Commonwealth about the terms and meaning of this agreement. The states continue to rely heavily on payroll taxes and on gambling taxes. Both taxes have been criticised—payroll taxes for discouraging employment, and gambling taxes because of the benefits that government derives from behaviour that can be extremely harmful to individuals and their families.

CONCLUSION—OPTIONS FOR REFORM AND THE TAX POLICY PROCESS

A package of reform needs to meet the objectives of adequacy, equity, and efficiency outlined earlier and hopefully also contribute to greater simplicity. It will also need to be politically acceptable and, to achieve the latter, the public needs to see a positive connection between taxation and government spending—the spending must be both worthwhile and efficient (Keating 2004a). A reform package to increase revenue in an equitable way that is also economically efficient and politically acceptable, could include:

■ action to remove or reduce loopholes and distortions in the income tax base and tightening, removing, and renovating inefficient and inequitable tax expenditures (including the private health insurance rebate, negative gearing, and superannuation tax concessions)—this could be used to fund reductions in the high EMTRs facing low-income people, improvements to areas such as housing, and the gradual introduction of some form of income tax indexation to reduce the problem of bracket creep
■ the introduction and extension of more earmarked (hypothecated) taxes—for example, a carbon tax to fund action on environmental degradation, an education and training levy to fund specially designated improvements to schools and TAFEs, or an increase in the Medicare levy to fund improvements to public hospitals or a new dental health program
■ the participation in international discussions to develop a more robust system of international taxation designed to contain destructive tax competition and to protect national revenue systems.

Other options include keeping the present system with little change and moving more to funding social policy through market-oriented arrangements and a greater use of user-pays systems, or having limited change alongside the ad hoc provision of tax cuts. With the exception of the tax reforms of 1985 and the introduction of the GST, this had been the direction of policy change for the past three decades or more in Australia. Another option would be to fund cuts to marginal tax rates through more cuts to government spending. Both of these other options would be favoured more by those with values supporting limited government involvement and a more self-reliance. However, such options will move Australia's economic and social policy arrangements closer to more unequal countries such as the USA, something that some commentators say is already occurring because of our failure to address issues such as taxation and to have a more interventionist social investment approach along the lines identified by Paul Smyth in Chapter 7.

Any substantial reform of Australia's tax system requires attention to the significant problems with our tax policy process. According to Eccleston (2004), tax reform is always difficult because the benefits of tax reform are often spread among many, occur over time, and are not readily apparent, whereas the costs can be immediate and tangible. There are also 'difficulties associated with building political support for reforms that are aimed at restructuring the tax base to further the national interest at the expense of sectional concerns' (2004, p. 7). A good tax policy process requires a combination of evidenced-based problem identification and analysis of options, and a democratic engagement of its citizens, especially of the key interest groups, in the stages of problem identification, options analysis, and decisions around implementation details. There have been a number of problems with the policy process in relation to tax reform over the past 20 years that mean that these conditions are not likely to be met. These problems include its closed nature, a lack of bi-partisan support or engagement, a lack of informed public debate, and a discontinuous approach to change. While these difficulties would be problematic for any policy area, they are especially problematic for tax reform, where most voters consider they have a strong stake in the outcomes, technical detail is very important to understanding problems and options, and strong fears and emotions can be generated.

Eccleston (2004) further comments that Australia has a poor history of tax reform because of a weak state institutional capacity to deal with matters about tax change in an open and inclusive way that generates an informed discussion and political consensus about the merits of particular proposals for change. This weak institutional capacity includes 'fragmented political institutions and pluralistic policy environment' (p. 15), which in Australia is characterised by constitutional difficulties and limitations, Executive control over the Parliament, a concentration of policy power in the Commonwealth Treasury Department that has tended to operate in a closed and dictatorial way, a two-party system that has operated in an adversarial fashion in matters of substantial tax policy change, and the lack of structures to effectively engage with the public and key interest groups in the development and analysis of policy. Similar criticisms have been made by Marsh (2003) about Australia's institutional capacity for policy change in general. Chapters 3 and 4 provide more detail.

There is arguably a need for a more open and consultative tax policy process and while the Howard government has provided for this to some extent through the introduction of a Board of Taxation to advise the government on the implementation of policy change, the membership of this Board is mainly confined to people from a business background, which limits its capacity to engage and to represent the views of a range of interests groups. It also does not report to the Parliament, but to the Treasurer. Marsh (2003) emphasises the importance of a phased approach to policy development, whereby various interest groups can be engaged, and concludes that the present policy making machinery lacks that capacity. His solution, after canvassing the alternatives of independent inquiries, summits, elections, and the floor of the House of Representatives, is to increase the use of Senate Committees. This would also allow for a more continuous and open policy process. It could mean, for example, a Senate Standing Committee of Taxation. The idea of using a Senate Committee has some merit and deserves investigation. However, possible disadvantages include the limited ability of the Senate to initiate change (rather than blocking or amending legislation) and, possibly, a restricted capacity to have the technical expertise required to undertake the problem identification and analysis needed on an ongoing basis. Further, Senate Committees are less likely to be able to operate in a robust way, questioning current policy approaches, when the government of the day also has a Senate majority, as was the case from July 2005.

The report from the United Kingdom's Fabian Society, *Paying for Progress* (The Commission on Taxation and Citizenship 2000), contains another possibility. It recommends a Standing Royal Commission on Taxation 'to enable ideas for new or reformed taxes to be assessed impartially before being subjected to party political conflict' (p. 7). This idea also deserves further consideration. It would need to be well resourced, open to community involvement, and have membership that engendered respect, both for its expertise as well as its capacity to reflect the understandings of different sections of the community. It would need to be independent of the government of the day, to retain an impartial standing, and could possibly report regularly to Parliament.

Whatever the actual mechanism to be used, whether it is an expanded Board of Taxation, an independent Commission, or a Senate Committee, the development of a better process to tax policy development in Australia would be a very important step towards our analysis and development of policies to finance social policy in Australia.

BIBLIOGRAPHY

ACOSS. See Australian Council of Social Service.

ACROD 2005, *2005 Federal Budget Submission*, January, ACROD, Canberra.

Adams, D. & Hess, M. 2002, 'Knowing and skilling in contemporary public administration', paper for *Knowledge, Networks and Joined-Up Government*, conference hosted by the Centre for Public Policy, University of Melbourne, 3–5 June, <http://www.public-policy. unimelb.edu.au/events/IPSA_Conference.html> 9 January 2005.

AIHW. See Australian Institute of Health and Welfare.

Alcock, P. 1997, *Understanding Poverty*, Macmillan, Basingstoke.

Alcock, P. 1998, 'The discipline of social policy', in P. Alcock, A. Erskine & M. May (eds), *The Students Companion to Social Policy*, Blackwell, Oxford.

Alford, R. 1975, *Health Care Politics: Ideological and Interest Group Barriers to Reform*, University of Chicago Press, Chicago.

Antonios, Z. 2000, 'The international human rights system and social change', in G. Davy, M. Mowbray & M. Raynor (eds), *Papers From The Winter School on Advocacy and Social Action, Just Policy, 19/20,* Victorian Council of Social Service, Melbourne.

Apple, M., Kenway, J. & Singh, M. 2005, *Globalizing Education: Policies, Pedagogies & Politics,* Peter Lang, New York.

Apps, P. F. 2004, 'The high taxation of working families', *Australian Review of Public Affairs*, vol. 5, no. 1, pp. 1–24.

Argy, F. 2003, *Where To From Here? Australian Egalitarianism Under Threat*, Allen & Unwin, Crows Nest, NSW.

Argy, F. 2005, 'An Analysis of Joblessness in Australia', *Economic Papers*, no. 24, pp. 75–96.

Australian Bureau of Statistics 1998, *Australian Social Trends 1998, Housing – Housing & Lifestyle: Smaller households, larger dwellings*, Australian Social Trends, Australian Bureau of Statistics, Canberra.

Australian Bureau of Statistics 2001, *Community Services*, cat. no. 869.0, Australian Bureau of Statistics, Canberra.

Australian Bureau of Statistics 2003a, *Household Income and Income Distribution, Australia*, cat. no. 6523.0, Australian Bureau of Statistics, Canberra.

Australian Bureau of Statistics 2003b, *The Health and Welfare of Australia's Aboriginal and Torres Strait Islander Peoples 2003*, cat. no. 4704.0, Australian Bureau of Statistics, Canberra.

Australian Bureau of Statistics 2003c, *Child Care Australia*, June 2002, cat. no. 4402.0, Australian Bureau of Statistics, Canberra.

Australian Bureau of Statistics 2003d, *Disability, Ageing and Carers: Summary of Findings*, cat. no. 4430.0, Australian Bureau of Statistics, Canberra.

Australian Bureau of Statistics 2004, *Australian Social Trends, Education and Training: Paying for University Education*, Australian Social Trends, Australian Bureau of Statistics, Canberra.

Australian Bureau of Statistics 2005, *Table 8. Finance Commitments For Housing (Owner Occupation and Commercial): Australia, Original, Seasonally Adjusted and Trend ($000)(d)*, 5671.0 Lending Finance, Australian Bureau of Statistics, Canberra.

Australian Bureau of Statistics Victorian Office 2004, *A Discussion of Selected Housing Issues, Victoria*, Australian Bureau of Statistics, Melbourne.

Australian Council of Social Service 2001, *Breaching the Safety Net: The Harsh Impact of Social Security Penalties*, ACOSS, Strawberry Hills, NSW.

Australian Council of Social Service 2003, *Taxation in Australia: Home Truths and International Comparisons, ACOSS Info 347*, ACOSS, , Strawberry Hills, NSW.

Australian Council of Social Service 2004a, *What Is ACOSS*, ACOSS, Strawberry Hills, NSW, <http://www.acoss.org.au/About.aspx?displayID=1?> 6 October 2005.

Australian Council of Social Service 2004b, *Australia's Social Security System: International Comparisons of Welfare Payments, ACOSS Info 360*, ACOSS, Strawberry Hills, NSW.

Australian Council of Social Service 2004c, *Blueprint for a Fairer Australia: Federal Budget Priorities Statement 2004–2005, ACOSS Paper 133*, ACOSS, Strawberry Hills, NSW.

Australian Council of Social Service 2005, *Signposts to Welfare Reform, ACOSS Info 369*, ACOSS, Strawberry Hills, NSW.

Australian Institute of Health and Welfare 1997, *Australia's Welfare*, AIHW, Canberra.

Australian Institute of Health and Welfare 2002, *Unmet Need for Disability Services: Effectiveness of Funding and Remaining Shortfalls*, AIHW, Canberra.

Australian Institute of Health and Welfare 2003, *Australia's Welfare 2003*, AIHW, Canberra.

Australian Institute of Health and Welfare 2004, *Australia's Health 2004*, Australian Government Publishing Service, Canberra.

Baldock, J. Manning, N. & Vickerstaff, S. 2003, 'Social policy, social welfare, and the welfare state', in J. Baldock, N. Manning & S. Vickerstaff (eds), *Social Policy*, 2nd edn, Oxford University Press, Oxford.

Baumann, Z. 2001, *The Individualized Society*, Polity Press, Cambridge.

Beck, U. 1992, *Risk Society: Towards a New Modernity*, Sage, London.

Beer, G. 2003, 'Work incentives under a new tax system: the distribution of effective marginal tax rates in 2002', *Economic Record*, vol. 79 (special issue), pp. S14–S25.

Beilharz, P. 1994, *Transforming Labor: Labour Tradition and the Labor Decade in Australia*, Cambridge University Press, Melbourne.

Bell, S. 1997, *Ungoverning the Economy: The Political Economy of Australian Economic Policy*, Oxford University Press, Melbourne.

Bell, S. 2000, 'Unemployment, inequality and the politics of redistribution', in S. Bell (ed.), *The Unemployment Crisis: Which Way Out?*, Cambridge University Press, Melbourne.

Bell, S. 2002, 'The contours and dynamics of unemployment', in P. Saunders & R. Taylor, *The Price of Prosperity: The Economic and Social Costs of Unemployment*, UNSW Press, Sydney.

Belli R. 2000, *Individualized Funding: One Key to Self-Determination*, paper presented at First International Conference on Self-Determination & Individualized Funding, Seattle, USA, July, <http://www.sprc.unsw.edu.au/nspc2001/NSPC%202001Papers/Laragy.pdf>.

Berry, M. 1983, 'Posing the housing question in Australia: elements of a theoretical framework for a Marxist analysis of housing', in L. Sandercock & M. Berry (eds), *Urban Political Economy: The Australian Case*, George Allen & Unwin, Sydney.

Berry, M. 2000, 'Investment in rental housing in Australia: small landlords and institutional investors', *Housing Studies*, vol. 15, no. 5, pp. 661–81.

Berry, M. 2003, 'Why it is important to boost the supply of affordable housing in Australia — and how can we do it', *Urban Policy and Research*, vol. 21, no. 4, pp. 413–35.

Berry, M. & Dalton, T. 2000, 'Home ownership into the new millennium: view from the margins', *Urban Policy and Research*, vol. 18, no. 4, pp. 435–54.

Berry, M. & Dalton, T. 2004, 'Housing prices and policy dilemmas: a peculiarly Australian problem?' *Urban Policy and Research*, vol. 22, no. 1, pp. 69–91.

Bessant, J., Dalton, T., Watts, R. & Smyth, P. 2005, *Talking Policy: Australian Social Policy*, Allen & Unwin, Sydney.

Beveridge, W.H. 1942, *Social Insurance and Allied Services*, HMSO, London

Bishop, J. 2004, *The Way Forward, A New Strategy for Community Care*, Department of Health and Ageing, Canberra, <http://www.ageing.health.gov.au>.

Black, D. 1980, *The Black Report*, HMSO, London.

Bok, D. 2003, *Universities in the Marketplace: The Commercialization of Higher Education*, Princeton University Press, Princeton.

Borland, J. 1999, 'Earnings inequality in Australia: changes, causes and consequences', *Economic Record*, vol. 75, pp. 177–202.

Botsman, P. & Latham, M. 2001, *The Enabling State: People Before Bureaucracy*, Pluto Press, Sydney.

Bradshaw, J. 1972, 'The concept of social need', *New Society*, March, no. 496, pp. 640–42.

Brennan, D. 1998a, 'Government and civil society: restructuring community services', in B. Cass & P. Smyth (eds), *Contesting the Australian Way: States, Markets and Civil Society,* Cambridge University Press, Cambridge, pp. 124–37.

Brennan, D. 1998b, *The Politics of Australian Child Care: From Philanthropy to Feminism*, 2nd edn, Cambridge University Press, Cambridge.

Bridgman, P. & Davis, G. 2004, *The Australian Policy Handbook*, 3rd edn, Allen & Unwin, Crows Nest, NSW.

Brotherhood of St Laurence 2004, *Poverty Line Update*, Brotherhood of St Laurence, Fitzroy, 16 September 2005.

Bryson, L. 1992 *Welfare and the State: Who Benefits?*, Macmillan Press, London.

Bullen, E., Kenway, J. & Robb, S. 2004, 'Can the arts and humanities survive the knowledge economy? A beginner's guide to the issues', in J. Kenway, E. Bullen & S. Robb (eds), *Innovation and Tradition: The Arts, Humanities, and the Knowledge Economy*, Peter Lang, New York.

Butlin, N.G. 1964, *Investment in Australian Economic Development, 1861–1900*, Cambridge University Press, Cambridge.

Cairns, J. 1957, *The Welfare State in Australia: A Study in the Development of Public Policy*, PhD Thesis, University of Melbourne, Melbourne.

Campbell, I. 1997, 'The challenge of increased precarious employment', *Just Policy*, no. 11, December, pp. 4–20.

Campbell, I. 2000, 'The spreading net: age and gender in the process of casualisation in Australia', *Australian Journal of Political Economy*, no. 45, pp. 68–98.

Capling, A. 2001, *Australia and the Global Trading System*, Cambridge University Press, Melbourne.

Carney, T. & Hanks, P. 1986, *Australian Social Security Law, Policy and Administration*, Oxford University Press, Melbourne.

Cass, B. 1988, *Income Support for the Unemployed in Australia: Towards a More Active System*, Australian Government Publishing Services, Canberra.

Cass, B. 1995, 'Overturning the male breadwinner model in the Australian social protection system', in P. Saunders & S. Shaver (eds), *Social Policy and the Challenges of Social Change*, Social Policy Research Centre, University of New South Wales, Sydney, pp. 47–66.

Cass, B. 1998, 'The social policy context', in P. Smyth & B. Cass (eds), *Contesting the Australian Way. States, Markets and Civil Society*, Cambridge University Press, Melbourne.

Cass, B. & Brennan, D. 2003, 'Taxing women: the politics of gender in the tax/transfer system', *eJournal of Tax Research*, vol. 1, no. 1. pp. 37–63.

Castles, F. 1985, *The Working Class and Welfare: Reflections on the Political Development of the Welfare State in Australia and New Zealand, 1890–1980*, Allen & Unwin, Wellington.

Castles, F. 1989, 'Social protection by other means', in F.G. Castles (ed.), *The Comparative History of Public Policy*, Oxford University Press, New York.

Castles, F. 2002, 'Australia's institutions and Australia's welfare', in G. Brennan & F. Castles (eds), *Australia Reshaped: 200 Years of Institutional Transformation*, Cambridge University Press, Port Melbourne.

Castles, F. 2004, *The Future of the Welfare State: Crisis Myths and Crisis Realities*, Oxford University Press, Oxford.

Castles, F. & Mitchell, D. 1992, 'Three worlds of welfare capitalism or four?' *Governance*, vol. 5, no. 1, pp. 1–26.

Castles, F. & Mitchell, D. 1994, 'Designing for the future: an institutional view of the Australian welfare state', in Economic Planning Advisory Commission (ed.), *Perspectives on Shaping Our Future: Commissioned Studies*, Vol. Conference Report 2, AGPS, Canberra.

Castles, S. & Miller, M. J. 2003, *The Age of Migration*, Macmillan, Basingstoke.

Centre for Affordable Housing 2005*, National Affordable Housing Conference*, NSW Department of Housing, Sydney, <http://www.housing.nsw.gov.au/nahc/#3>.

Centrelink 2004, *Centrelink Information: A Guide to Payments and Services 2004–05*, Centrelink, Canberra.

Centrelink 2005, *A Guide to Australian Government Payments 20 March–30 June 2005*, Centrelink, Canberra.

Chapman, B.J. 1999, 'Could increasing the skills of the jobless be the solution to Australian unemployment?', in S. Richardson (ed.), *Regulating the Labour Market: Regulation, Efficiency and Equity in Australia*, Cambridge University Press, Cambridge.

Chesterman, J. & Galligan, B. 1997, *Citizens Without Rights: Aborigines and Australian Citizenship*, Cambridge University Press, Melbourne.

Clasen, J. (ed.) 1999, *Comparative Social Policy: Concepts, Theories, and Methods*, Blackwell Publishers, Malden.

Coady, T. (ed.) 2000, *Why Universities Matter*, Allen & Unwin, Sydney.

Commission on Social Justice 1994, *Social Justice: Strategies for National Renewal*, Vintage, London.

Committee of Inquiry into the Australian Financial System (Campbell Inquiry) 1981, *Final Report,* Australian Government Publishing Service, Canberra.

Commonwealth of Australia 2001a, *Budget Measures 2001–02*, Budget Paper No. 2, Commonwealth of Australia, Canberra.

Commonwealth of Australia 2001b, *Backing Australia's Ability: An Innovation Action Plan for the Future*, Department of Education, Science and Training, Canberra, <http://www.dest.gov.au/sectors/research_sector/publications_resources/national_research_priorities/> 28 Sept 2005.

Commonwealth of Australia 2002, *Building a Simpler System to Help Jobless Families and Individuals,* Department of Family and Community Services, Canberra.

Commonwealth of Australia 2004, *Backing Australia's Ability – Building our Future through Science and Innovation*, Commonwealth of Australia, Canberra.

Considine, M. 1994, *Public Policy: A Critical Approach*, Macmillan, South Melbourne.

Considine, M. 1996, 'Market bureaucracy? Exploring the contending rationalities of contemporary administrative regimes', *Labour and Industry*, vol. 7, no. 1, pp. 1–27.

Considine, M. 2000, 'Competition, quasi-markets and the new welfare state: reflections on the challenges awaiting clients, governments and welfare professionals', in I. O'Connor, P. Smyth & J. Warburton (eds), *Contemporary Perspectives on Social Work and the Human Services: Challenges and Change*, Addison Wesley Longman, Frenchs Forest, NSW.

Considine, M. 2001, *Enterprising States: The Public Management of Welfare-to-Work*, Cambridge University Press, Cambridge.

Considine, M. 2002, 'Introduction', paper for *Knowledge, Networks and Joined-Up Government*, conference hosted by the Centre for Public Policy, University of Melbourne, 3–5 June, <http://www.public-policy.unimelb.edu.au/events/IPSA_Conference.html> 9 January 2005.

Considine, M. 2005, *Making Public Policy*, Polity Press, Cambridge.

Costello, P. 2002, *Intergenerational Report 2002–03, Budget Paper No. 5*, Commonwealth of Australia, Canberra.

Costello, P. 2005, 'Pocket brief to the Australian tax system', attachment to *Mid-Year Economic and Fiscal Outlook*, Commonwealth Department of Treasury, Canberra, <http://www.budget.gov.au/2004-05/myefo/html> 3 January 2005.

Cutright, P. 1965, 'Political structure, economic development and national social security programs', *American Journal of Sociology*, vol. 70, pp. 537–50.

Dalton, T. 2002, 'Which way housing policy? Housing markets and policy agendas', *Just Policy*, no. 25, pp. 3–12.

Dalton, T., Draper, M., Weeks, W. & Wiseman, J. (eds) 1996, *Making Social Policy in Australia: An Introduction*, Allen & Unwin, St. Leonards.

Davidson, G. 2000, *The Compassionate Eye: Research and Reform*, Oswald Barnett Oration, Ecumenical Housing Inc & Uniting Care Connections, Melbourne.

Dawkins, P. & Kelly, P. (eds) 2003, *Hard Heads: Soft Hearts: A New Reform Agenda for Australia*, Allen & Unwin, Sydney.

Dawkins, P., Beer, G., Harding, A., Johnson, D. & Scutella, R. 1998, 'Towards a negative income tax system for Australia', *The Australian Economic Review*, vol. 31, no. 3, pp. 237–57.

Deacon, A. 2002, *Perspectives on Welfare: Ideas, Ideologies and Policy Debates*, Open University Press, Buckingham.

Deacon, B., Hulse, M. & Stubb, P. 1997, *Global Social Policy: International Organizations and the Future of Welfare*, Sage, London.

Denniss, R. 2005, *Who Benefits from Private Health Insurance in Australia?*, The Australia Institute, Canberra.

Department of Education and Children's Services 2002, *Futures Connect*, Department of Education and Children's Services, Adelaide, <http://www.decs.sa.gov.au>, November 2002.

Department of Family and Community Services (FaCS) 2002, *FaCS Submission to the House of Representatives Standing Committee on Ageing*, Department of Family and Community Services, Canberra.

Department of Family and Community Services 2003, *Income Support Customers: A Statistical Overview 2001*, Department of Family and Community Services, Canberra.

Department of Family and Community Services (FaCS) 2005, *Portfolio Budget Statements 2004–05*, Part B, Department of Family and Community Services (FaCS), Canberra, p. 17, <http://www.facs.gov.au/internet/facsinternet.nsf/aboutfacs/budget/budget2004-pbs.htm#budget>.

Department of Health 1999, *Reducing Health Inequalities: An Action Report*, HMSO, London.

Department of Health 2001, *Tackling Health Inequalities: 2002 Cross Cutting Review*, HMSO, London.

Department of Health 2002, *Tackling Health Inequalities: Consultation on a Plan for Delivery*, HMSO, London.

Department of Health and Ageing 2005, *Medicare Statistics*, Department of Health and Ageing, Canberra, <http://www.health.gov.au/internet/wcms/publishing.nsf/Content/medstat-dec04-contents> 6 April 2005.

Department of Human Services 2000, *Primary Care Partnerships: Going Forward*, State of Victoria, Melbourne.

Department of Human Services 2002, *Neighbourhood Renewal: Growing Victoria Together*, State of Victoria, Melbourne.

Department of Social Security 1990, *Family Allowance Supplement: A Cash Payment for Working Families with Children*, Evaluation Report Policy Research Paper No. 57, Department of Social Security, Canberra.

De Voe, J. 2003, 'A policy transformed by politics: the case of the 1973 Australian Community Health Program', *Journal of Health Politics, Policy and Law*, vol. 28, no. 1, pp. 77–108.

Dickey, B. 1980, *No Charity There: A Short History of Social Welfare in Australia*, Nelson, Melbourne.

Disney, J. 2003, 'Strengthening social investment in Australia', in I. Marsh (ed.), *Australia's Choices: Options for a Prosperous and Fair Society*, UNSW Press, Sydney.

Ditch, J. 1999, 'Introduction: policies and current issues', in J. Ditch (ed.), *Introduction to Social Security: Policies, Benefits and Poverty*, Routledge, London.

Doyal, I. & Gough, I. 1991, *A Theory of Human Need*, Macmillan, London.

Duckett, S. & Jackson, J. 2000, 'The new private health insurance rebate: an inefficient way of assisting public hospitals', *Medical Journal of Australia*, vol. 172, pp. 430–42.

Duncan, G. 2000, 'Notes from a departed Dean', *The Australian Universities Review-Special Issue Higher Education and the Politics of Difference*, vol. 41, no 2, pp. 55–63.

Eardley, T. & Matheson, G. 2000, 'Australian attitudes to unemployment and unemployed people', *Australian Journal of Social Issues*, vol. 35, no. 3, pp. 181–202.

Eather, W. 1988, 'We only build houses: the Commission 1945–60', in R. Howe (ed.), *New Houses for Old: Fifty Years of Public Housing in Australia 1938–1988*, Ministry of Housing and Construction, Melbourne.

Eccleston, R. 2004, *The Thirty Year Problem: The Politics Of Australian Tax Reform*, Research Study 42, Australian Tax Research Foundation, Sydney.

Edwards, A. & Magarey, S. (eds) 1995, *Women in a Restructuring Australia*, Allen &Unwin, Sydney.

Edwards, J. 2004, *Policing and Practicing Subjectivities: Poor and Working Class Young Women and Girls and Australian Government Mutual Obligation Policies*. PhD Thesis, School of Education, Adelaide, University of South Australia, Adelaide.

Edwards, M. 2001, *Social Policy, Public Policy: From Problem to Practice*, Allen & Unwin, Crows Nest, NSW.

Erskine, A. 1998, 'The approach and methods of social policy', in P. Alcock, A. Erskine & M. May (eds), *The Student's Companion to Social Policy*, Blackwell, Oxford.

Esping-Andersen, G. 1990, *The Three Worlds of Welfare Capitalism*, Polity Press, Cambridge.

Etzioni, A. 2004, *A Common Good*, Polity, Maldon, Mass.

Ferrera, M, 1996, 'The "Southern model" of welfare in social Europe', *Journal of European Social Policy*, vol. 6, no. 1, pp. 17–37.

Fine, B. 2001, *Social Capital versus Social Theory : Political Economy and Social Science at the turn of the Millennium*, Routledge, London.

Fine, M. 1999, 'Ageing and the balance of responsibilities between the various providers of child care and aged care: shaping policies for the future', in Productivity Commission and Melbourne Institute of Applied Economic and Social Research, *Policy Implications of the Ageing of Australia's Population*, conference proceedings, AusInfo, Canberra.

Finer, C. J. & Smyth, P. 2004, (eds), *Social Policy and the Commonwealth: Prospects for Social Inclusion*, Palgrave Macmillan, New York.

Fitzpatrick, T. 2003, 'Cash transfers', in J. Baldock, N. Manning & S. Vickerstaff (eds), *Social Policy*, Oxford University Press, Oxford.

Fitzpatrick, T. 2005, *New Theories of Welfare*, Palgrave Macmillan, Hampshire.

Flora, P. & Heidenheimer, A.J. 1981, (eds), *The Development of Welfare States in Europe and America*, Transaction Books, New Brunswick.

Frank, A.G. 1971, *Sociology of Development and the Underdevelopment of Sociology*, Pluto Press, London.

Fraser, A. 2002, 'Is making money out of childcare as easy as ABC?', *Weekend Australian*, 12–13 October, p. 32.

Frost, L. 1991, *The New Urban Frontier: Urbanisation and City-Building in Australasia and the American West*, New South Wales University Press, Sydney.

Frost, L. 2000, 'Connections', in P. Troy (ed.), *A History of European Housing in Australia*, Cambridge University Press, Melbourne.

Galbraith, J.K. 1962, *The Affluent Society*, Penguin, Harmondsworth.

Gallagher, M. 2000, 'The emergence of entrepreneurial public universities in Australia'. Paper presented at *IMHE General Conference of the OECD*, Paris, September, OECD, Paris.

Garton, S. 1990, *Out of Luck Poor Australians and Social Welfare*, Allen & Unwin, Sydney.

Gerwitz, S. 2002, *The Managerial School: Post-Welfare and Social Justice in Education*, Routledge, London.

Giddens, A. 1999, *The Third Way: The Renewal of Social Democracy*, Polity Press, Cambridge.

Giddens, A. (ed.) 2003, *The Progressive Manifesto: New Ideas for the Centre-Left*, Polity Press, Cambridge.

Gillespie, J. 1991, *The Price of Health. Australian Governments and Medical Politics 1910–1960*, Cambridge University Press, Sydney.

Ginsburg, N. 2004, 'Structured diversity: a framework for critically comparing welfare states', in P. Kennett (ed.), *Handbook of Comparative Social Policy*, Edward Elgar, Cheltenham.

Goodin, R. & Rein, M. 2001, 'Regimes on pillars: alternative welfare state logics and dynamics', *Public Administration*, vol. 79, no. 4, pp. 769–801.

Goodman, R., White, G. & Huck-Ju Kwon (eds) 1998, *The East Asian Welfare Model: Welfare Orientalism and the State*, Routledge, London.

Gough, I. 2001, 'Globalization and regional welfare regimes: the East Asian case', *Global Social Policy*, vol. 1, no. 2, pp. 163–89.

Gray, G. 2004, *The Politics of Medicare. Who Gets What, When and How*, UNSW Press, Sydney.

Gregory, R. 2002, 'It's full time jobs that matter', *Australian Journal of Labour Economics*, vol. 5, no. 2, pp. 271–78.

Gregory, R.G. & Hunter, B. 1996, 'Increasing regional inequality and the decline in manufacturing', in P. Sheehan, B. Grewal & M. Kumnick (eds), *Dialogues on Australia's Future*, Victoria University Press, Melbourne.

Greig, A. 1992, *Structure, Organisation and Skill Formation in the Australian Housing Industry*, The National Housing Strategy, Background Paper 13, Australian Government Publishing Service, Canberra.

Hall, A. & Midgley, J. 2004, *Social Policy for Development*, Sage, London.

Hall, J. & Berry, M. 2004, *Operating Deficits and Public Housing: Policy Options for Reversing the Trend*, Australian Housing and Urban Research Institute, Melbourne, <http://www.ahuri.edu.au>.

Hall, P. & Soskice, D. (eds) 2001, *Varieties of Capitalism: The Institutional Foundations of Comparative Advantage*, Oxford University Press, Oxford.

Hamilton, C. 2003, *Growth Fetish*, Allen & Unwin, Sydney.

Hancock, K. 1999, *Economics, Industrial Relations and the Challenge of Unemployment*. Keynote address to the Association of Industrial Relations Academics of Australia and New Zealand, Adelaide, 4 February.

Harding, A. 1995, *The Impact Of Health, Education And Housing Outlays On Income Distribution in Australia in the 1990s*, NATSEM Discussion Paper No 7, <http://www.natsem.canberra.edu.au/publicationsByYear.jsp?year=1995> 5 February2005.

Harvey, K. 2005, 'The Pharmaceutical Benefits Scheme 2003–2004', *Australia and New Zealand Health Policy*, vol. 2, no. 1, p. 2.

Healy, K. 2000, *Social Work Practices: Contemporary Perspectives on Change*, Sage, London.

Healy, T. & Cote, S. 2001, *The Well-Being of Nations: the Role of Human and Social Capital*, OECD, Paris.

Held, D. &.McGrew, A (eds) 2000, *The Global Transformations Reader: An Introduction to the Globalization Debate*, Polity Press, Cambridge.

Hess, M. & Adams, D. 2002, 'Knowing and Skilling in Contemporary Public Administration', *Australian Journal Of Public Administration*, vol. 61, no. 4, pp. 68–79.

Hewett, A. & Wiseman, J. 2000, 'Memory, reflection, imagination and action: advocacy and social action strategies in a globalising world', in G. Davy, M. Mowbray & M. Raynor (eds), *Papers from the Winter School on Advocacy and Social Action, Just Policy, 19/20,* Victorian Council of Social Service, Melbourne.

Housing Industry Association (HIA) 2002, *The Housing 100: Australia's Most Active Homebuilders in 2001/2002*, Housing Industry Association, Canberra.

Higgins, B. 1968, *Economic Development: Principles, Problems and Policies*, Constable, London.

Hill, M. 1996, *Social Policy: A Comparative Analysis,* Prentice Hall, London.

Hill, M. 2003, *Understanding Social Policy*, 7th edn, Blackwell, Oxford.

Hirst, P. & Thompson, G. 1999, *Globalization in Question: The International Economy and the Possibilities of Governance*, Polity Press, Cambridge.

Holliday, I. 2000, 'Productivist welfare capitalism: social policy in East Asia', *Political Studies*, vol. 48, no. 4, pp. 706–23.

Horin, A. 2003, 'When making money is child's play', *Sydney Morning Herald*, October 4, p. 39.

Hort, S. & Kuhnle, S. 2000, 'The coming of East and South-East Asian welfare states', *Journal of European Social Policy*, vol. 10, pp. 162–84.

Howard, J. 2004, *The Fourth Howard Ministry*. Media release 22 October 2004, <http://www.pm.gov.au/news/media_releases/media_Release1134.html> 24 February 2005.

Howe, B. & Howe, R. 2005, *Transitions in Australian Labour Markets: Initial Perspectives*, CEDA Information Paper No. 82, Committee for Economic Development of Australia, Melbourne.

Howe, R. (ed.) 1988, *New Houses for Old: Fifty Years of Public Housing in Victoria 1938–1988*, Ministry of Housing and Construction, Melbourne.

Howlett, M. & Ramesh, M. 1995, *Studying Public Policy: Policy Cycles and Policy Subsystems*, Oxford University Press, Oxford.

Hughes, O. 1998, *Australian Politics*, 3rd edn, Macmillan Education, South Yarra.

Hunter, B. 2001 'Tackling poverty amongst indigenous Australians', in R. Fincher & P. Saunders (eds), *Creating Unequal Futures? Rethinking Poverty, Inequality and Disadvantage*, Allen & Unwin, Sydney.

Ignatieff, M. 1984, *The Needs of Strangers*, Chatto & Windus, London.

International Labour Office (ILO)1984, *Introduction to Social Security*, ILO, Geneva.

Jackson, A. 2003, 'ABC learning on acquisition alert', *Sydney Morning Herald*, 15 September, p. 32.

James, P. (ed.) 2000, *Burning Down the House: the Bonfire of the Universities*, Association for the Public University with Arena Publications, Melbourne.

Jarvis, P. 2001, *Universities and Corporate Universities: The Higher Learning Industry in Global Society*, Kogan Page Ltd, London.

Jayasuria, K. 2000, 'Capability, freedom and new social democracy', in A. Gamble & T. Wright (eds), *The New Social Democracy, Supplement to the Political Quarterly*, vol. 71, no. 3, pp. 282–99.

Jessop, B. 2003, *The Future of the Capitalist State*, Polity Press, Cambridge.

Jones, A. & Smyth, P. 1999, 'Social exclusion: a new framework for social policy analysis', *Just Policy*, vol. 17, pp. 11–20.

Jones, C. 1990, 'Hong Kong, Singapore, South Korea and Taiwan: oikonomic welfare states', *Government and Opposition*, vol. 25, no. 4, pp. 447–62.

Jones, M. 1972, *Housing and Poverty in Australia*, Melbourne University Press, Melbourne.

Junankar, R. 2000, 'Are cuts the answer? Theory and evidence', in S. Bell (ed.), *The Unemployment Crisis: Which Way Out?*, Cambridge University Press, Melbourne.

Kasza, G. 2002, 'The illusion of welfare regimes', *Journal of Social Policy*, vol. 31, no. 2, pp. 271–87.

Katzenstein, P. 1985, *Small States in World Markets: Industrial Policy in Europe*, Cornell University Press, Ithaca, New York.

Keating, M. 2004a, *Who Rules? How Government Retains Control of a Privatised Economy*, The Federation Press, Sydney.

Keating, M. 2004b, *The Case for Increased Taxation*, Academy of the Social Sciences, Canberra.

Keating, P. 1994, *Working Nation: Policies and Programs*, Australian Government Publishing Service, Canberra.

Kelly, P. 1992, *The End of Certainty: The Story of the 1980s,* Allen & Unwin, Sydney.

Kemshall, H. 2002, *Risk, Social Policy and Welfare*, Open University Press, Buckingham.

Kennedy, R. 1982, *Australian Welfare History Critical Essays*, Macmillan, Melbourne.

Kennedy, R. 1985, *Charity Warfare: The Charity Organisation Society in Colonial Melbourne*, Hyland House, Melbourne.

Kenway, J., Bullen, E. & Robb, S. 2004a, 'The knowledge economy, the technopreneur and the problematic future of the university', in M. Marginson & M. Peters (eds), *Policy Futures in Education, Special issue on University Futures*, vol. 2, no. 2, pp. 333–51.

Kenway, J., Bullen, E. & Robb. S. (eds) 2004b, *Innovation and Tradition: The Arts, Humanities, and the Knowledge Economy*, Peter Lang, New York.

Kewley, T. 1973, *Social Security in Australia 1900–72*, 2nd edn, Sydney University Press, Sydney.

Kingdon, J. 1995, *Agendas, Alternatives and Public Policies*, Harper & Collins, New York.

Korpi, W & Palme, J. 2004, 'Robin Hood, St Mathew, or simple egalitarianism? Strategies of equality in welfare states', in P. Kennett (ed.), *A Handbook of Comparative Social Policy*, Edward Elgar, Cheltenham, pp. 153–79.

Krimsky, S. 2004, *Science In The Private Interest: Has the Lure of Profits Corrupted Biomedical Research?*, Rowman & Littlefield Publishers Inc., Lanham.

Kwon, Huck-Ju 1997, 'Beyond European welfare regimes: comparative perspectives on East Asian welfare systems', *Journal Of Social Policy*, vol. 26, no. 4, pp. 467–84.

Lalonde, M. 1974, *A New Perspective on the Health of Canadians*, Ministry of Health and Welfare, Ottawa.

Land, H. 1998, 'Altruism, reciprocity and obligation', in P. Alcock, A. Erskine & M. May (eds), *The Students Companion to Social Policy*, Blackwell, Oxford.

Langmore, J. & Quiggin, J. 1994, *Work for All: Full Employment in the Nineties*, Melbourne University Press, Melbourne.

Laragy, C. & Frawley, P. 2004, 'Strategies in disability services for equality and inclusion: an evaluation of individualised funding/family governed initiative', VCOSS Congress 2004: *Strategies for Equality and Inclusion*, Victorian Council of Social Service, Melbourne, 4–6 August.

Latham, M. 1998, *Civilising Global Capital: New Thinking for Australian Labor*, Allen & Unwin, St Leonards.

Lauder, H. & Hughes, D. 1999, *Trading in Futures: Why Markets In Education Don't Work,* Open University Press, Buckingham.

Layard, R., Nickell S. & Jackman, R. 1991, *Unemployment: Macroeconomic Performance and the Labour Market,* Oxford University Press, Oxford.

Lee, J. 2004, 'The tyranny of home ownership: housing policy and social exclusion in colonial and post colonial Hong Kong', in C. J. Finer & P. Smyth (eds), *Social Policy and the Commonwealth: Prospects for Social Inclusion*, Palgrave Macmillan, New York, pp. 151–66.

Lee, A.T. & Miller, P.W. (2000), 'Australia's Unemployment Problem', *Economic Record*, vol. 76, pp. 74–104.

Letich, L. 1995, 'Is life outsmarting us?' *The Washington Post*, 2 April, p. 6.

Levitas, R.2005, *The Inclusive Society? Social Exclusion and New Labour*, Macmillan, Houndmills, Hampshire.

Lewis, J. 1993, *Women and Social Policies in Europe: Work, Family and the State*, Elgra, Aldershot.

Lewis, J.M. 2000, 'From "Fightback" to "Biteback": the rise and fall of a national dental program', *Australian Journal of Public Administration*, vol. 59, no. 1, pp. 84–96.

Lewis, J.M. 2002, 'Policy and profession: elite perspectives on redefining general practice in Australia and England', *Journal of Health Services Research and Policy*, vol. 7, no. S1, pp. 8–13.

Lewis, J.M. 2005, *Health Policy and Politics: Networks, Ideas and Power,* IP Communications, Melbourne.

Lewis, J.M. & Considine, M. 1999, 'Medicine, economics and agenda setting', *Social Science and Medicine*, vol. 48, no. 3, pp. 393–405.

Lindblom, C. 1959, 'The science of muddling through', *Public Administration Review*, vol. 19, pp. 79–88.

Lister, R. 2004, *Poverty*, Polity Press, Cambridge.

Lucey, H. & Reay, D. 2002, 'A market in waste: psychic and structural dimensions of school choice policy in the UK and children's narratives of "demonized" schools', *Discourse*, vol. 23, no 3. pp 253–66.

Lyons, M. 2001, *Third Sector: The Contribution of Nonprofit and Cooperative Enterprises in Australia,* Allen & Unwin, Sydney.

Lyotard, J-F. 1984, *The Postmodern Condition: A Report on Knowledge*, translation by G. Bennington & B. Massumi, Manchester University Press, Manchester.

Macfarlane, I. 1997, 'Monetary policy, growth and unemployment', *Reserve Bank of Australia Bulletin*, June, pp. 1–8.

Macintyre, S. 1985, *Winners and Losers, The Pursuit of Social Justice in Australian History*, Allen & Unwin, Sydney.

Macintyre, S. & Clark, A, 2003, *The History Wars*, Melbourne University Press, Melbourne.

Maddox, M. 2005, *God under Howard : The Rise of the Religious Right in Australian Politics*, Allen & Unwin, Sydney.

Mandel, E. 1975, *Late Capitalism*, NLB, London.

Manning, N. 1998, 'Social needs, social problems and social welfare', in P. Alcock, A. Erskine & M. May (eds), *The Students' Companion to Social Policy*, Blackwell, Oxford.

Manning, N. 2003a, 'Welfare, ideology and social theory', in J. Baldock, N. Manning & S. Vickerstaff (eds), *Social Policy,* Oxford University Press, Oxford.

Manning, N. 2003b, 'The politics of welfare', in J. Baldock, N. Manning & S. Vickerstaff (eds), *Social Policy,* Oxford University Press, Oxford.

Marginson, S. 1993, *Education and Public Policy in Australia,* Cambridge University Press, Cambridge.

Marginson, S. 1997, *Markets in Education,* Allen & Unwin, Sydney.

Marmot, M. 1999, 'Acting on the evidence to reduce inequalities in health', *Health Affairs,* vol. 18, no. 3, pp. 42–4.

Marsden, S. 2000, 'The introduction of order', in P. Troy (ed.), *A History of European Housing in Australia*, Cambridge University Press, Melbourne.

Marsh, I. 2000, 'Gaps in policy-making capacities', in M. Keating, J. Wanna & P. Weller (eds), *Institutions On The Edge? Capacity for Governance*, Allen & Unwin, Sydney.

Marsh, I. 2003, 'Introduction', in I. Marsh (ed.), *Australia's Choices: Options for a Prosperous and Fair Society,* UNSW Press, Sydney.

Marshall, T.H. 1963, *Sociology at the Crossroads*, Heinemann, London.

Martin, J. 1998, 'What works among active labour market policies: evidence from OECD countries' experiences', in G. Debelle & J. Borland (eds), *Unemployment and the Australian Labour Market*, Reserve Bank of Australia, Sydney.

May, J. 2001, 'The challenge of poverty: the case of ACOSS', in M. Sawer & G. Zappala (eds), *Speaking for the People*, Melbourne University Press, Melbourne.

McAuley, I. 2004, *Stress on Public Hospitals: Why Private Insurance Has Made It Worse*, Australian Consumers' Association and the Australian Healthcare Association, Canberra.

McClelland, A. 1999, 'Understanding the wage and social security interface', *CEDA Bulletin* October, pp. 12–13.

McClelland, A. 2001, 'Tax agendas: the position of the welfare sector', in R.F.I. Smith (ed.), *On the Way to the GST*, Centre for Public Policy, Melbourne.

McClelland, A. & Scotton, R. 1998, 'Poverty and health', in R. Fincher & J. Nieuwenhuysen (eds), *Australian Poverty: Then and Now*, Melbourne University Press, Melbourne.

McDonald, J. 2002, 'Contestability and social justice: the limits of competitive tendering of welfare services', *Australian Social Work*, vol. 55, no. 2, pp. 99–108.

Mead, L. 1997, 'The rise of paternalism', in L.M. Mead (ed.), *The New Paternalism: Supervisory Approaches to Poverty*, Brookings Institution, Washington DC.

Mead, L. 2000, 'Welfare reform and the family: lessons from America', in P. Saunders (ed.), *Reforming the Welfare State,* Australian Institute of Family Studies, Melbourne.

Meadmore, D. & Meadmore, P. 2004, 'The boundlessness of performativity in elite Australian schools', *Discourse*, vol. 25, no. 3. pp. 375–87.

Mendelsohn, R. 1954, *Social Security in the British Commonwealth: Great Britain, Canada, Australia, New Zealand*, Athlone Press, London.

Mendelsohn, R. 1979, *The Condition of the People: Social Welfare in Australia 1900–1975*, George Allen & Unwin, Sydney.

Mendes, P. 2003, *Australia's Welfare Wars: the Players; the Politics and the Ideologies*, UNSW, Sydney.

Merrett, D. 2000, 'Paying for it all', in P. Troy (ed.), *A History of European Housing in Australia*, Cambridge University Press, Melbourne.

Midgley, J. 1999, 'Growth redistribution and welfare: towards social investment', *Social Service Review*, vol. 73, no.1, pp. 3–21.

Mishra, R. 1995, 'Social policy and the challenge of globalisation', in P. Saunders & S. Shaver (eds), *Social Policy and the Challenges of Social Change*, Social Policy Research Centre, University of NSW, Sydney.

Mishra, R. 2004, 'Social protection by other means: can it survive globalization?', in P. Kennett (ed.), *A Handbook of Comparative Social Policy*, Edward Elgar, Cheltenham, pp. 68–88.

Mitchell, W.F. 2000, 'The causes of unemployment', in S. Bell (ed.), *The Unemployment Crisis: Which Way Out?*, Cambridge University Press, Melbourne.

Mitchell, W.F. 2001a, 'Hidden unemployment in Australia', in W.F. Mitchell & E. Carlson (eds), *Unemployment: The Tip of the Iceberg*, Centre for Applied Economic Research, University of New South Wales, Sydney.

Mitchell, W.F. 2001b, 'The pathology of unemployment', in W.F. Mitchell & E. Carlson (eds), *Unemployment: The Tip of the Iceberg*, Centre for Applied Economic Research, University of New South Wales, Sydney.

Mitchell, W.F. & Carlson, E. 2001, 'Labour under utilisation in Australia and the USA', in W.F. Mitchell & E. Carlson (eds), *Unemployment: The Tip of the Iceberg*, Centre for Applied Economic Research, University of New South Wales, Sydney.

Mitchell, W.F. & Watts, M. 1997, 'The path to full employment', *Australian Economic Review*, vol. 30, pp. 436–44.

Mkandawire, T. (ed.) 2004, *Social Policy in a Developmental Context*, Palgrave, London.

Moss, J. 2000, 'The ethics and politics of mutual obligation', *Australian Journal of Social Issues*, vol. 35, no. 4, pp. 1–14.

Murray, C. 1994, *Losing Ground: American Social Policy 1950–1980*, 2nd edn, Basic Books, New York.

Myrdal, G. 1972, *Asian Drama : An Inquiry into the Poverty of Nations*, Allen Lane, London.

National Aged Care Alliance (NACA) 2005, *Recommendations for Strengthening the Government Agenda for Aged Care*, NACA, Canberra, February, <http://www.naca.asn.au/publications.html>.

National Health Strategy 1992, *Enough To Make You Sick. How Income and Environment Affect Health*, Research Paper No. 1, National Health Strategy, Melbourne.

National Housing Strategy 1991, *The Affordability of Australian Housing,* Issues Paper No. 2, Australian Government Publishing Service, Canberra.

National Summit on Housing Affordability 2004, *Improving Housing Affordability: A Call for Action*, Canberra, <http://www.housingsummit.org.au>.

Neutze, M. 1997, *Funding Urban Services: Options for Physical Infrastructure,* Allen & Unwin, Sydney.

Neutze, M. & Kendig, H. 1991, 'Achievement of Home Ownership among Post-War Australian Cohorts', *Housing Studies*, vol. 6, no. 1, pp. 3–14.

Nevile, J. 2000, 'Can Keynesian policies stimulate growth in output and employment?', in S. Bell (ed.), *The Unemployment Crisis: Which Way Out?*, Cambridge University Press, Melbourne.

New Zealand Minister for Social Development and Employment 2005, 'Extending opportunities to work', New Zealand Ministry for Social Development, Wellington, <http://www.msd.govt.nz/media-information/press-releases/2005/pr-2005-22-02.html>, 8 March 2005.

Nussbaum, M, 2000, *Women and Human Development: The Capabilities Approach*, Cambridge University Press, Cambridge.

Nutbeam, D. 2003, 'Tackling health inequalities in England: developing policy, driving delivery', Paper for *VicHealth Health Inequalities Policy Forum*, 20–21 February 2003, Melbourne.

O'Connor, J. 1973, *The Fiscal Crisis of the State*, St. Martin's Press, New York.

O'Connor, I., Wilson, J. & Setterlund, D. 1998, *Social Work & Welfare Practice*, Longman, South Melbourne.

O'Connor, J, Orloff, A. & Shaver, S. 1999, *States, Markets, Families: Gender, Liberalism and Social Policy in Australia, Canada, Great Britain and the United States*, Cambridge University Press, Melbourne.

OECD. See Organisation for Economic Cooperation and Development.

Ohmae, K. 1991, *The Borderless World: Power and Strategy in the Interlocked Economy*, Harper Perennial, New York.

Olssen, M., Codd, J. & O'Neill, A. 2004, *Education Policy: Globalization, Citizenship & Democracy,* Sage Publications, London.

Organisation for Economic Cooperation and Development 1996, *The Knowledge-based Economy*, OECD, Paris.

Organisation for Economic Cooperation and Development 2001, *Innovations in Labour Market Policies: The Australian Way*, OECD, Paris.

Organisation for Economic Cooperation and Development, 2004, *OECD Health Data* 2004, 3rd edn, OECD, Paris.

Organisation for Economic Cooperation and Development 2005, *Society at a Glance*, OECD Social Indicators, Paris.

Parkin, A. & Summers J. 1994, 'The Constitutional Framework, in J. Summers, D. Woodward & A. Parkin (eds) *Government, Politics, Power and Policy in Australia*, 5th edn, Longman Cheshire, Melbourne.

Parsons, W. 2002, 'From muddling through to muddling up. Evidence based policy-making and the modernisation of British government', *Public Policy and Administration*, vol. 17, no. 3, Autumn, pp. 43–60.

Pateman, C.1989, *The Disorder of Women: Democracy, Feminism and Political Theory*, Polity Press, Cambridge.

Pearce, D., Disney, J. & Ridout, H. 2002, *Making it Work: The Report of the Independent Review of Breaches and Penalties in the Social Security System*, Independent Review of Breaches and Penalties in the Social Security System, Sydney.

Pearson, N. 2000a, *Our Right to Take Responsibility*, Noel Pearson and Associates, Cairns.

Pearson, N. 2000b, *Planting the Seeds for Change*, Workplacement's Hollingworth Trust Lecture, Workplacement, Melbourne.

Peel, M. 1995, *Good Times, Hard Times: The Past and Future in Elizabeth,* Melbourne University Press, Melbourne.

PHIAC. See Private Health Insurance Administration Council.

Pierson, C. 1994, *Dismantling the Welfare State?,* Cambridge University Press, Cambridge.

Pierson, C. 1998, *Beyond the Welfare State: The New Political Economy of Welfare*, Polity Press, Cambridge.

Pinker, R. 1998, 'The conservative tradition of social welfare', in P. Alcock, A. Erskine & M. May (eds), *The Students Companion to Social Policy*, Blackwell, Oxford.

Private Health Insurance Administration Council, *Hospital Insurance*, Commonwealth of Australia, Canberra, <http://www.phiac.gov.au/statistics/membershipcoverage/hosquar. htm> 24 March 2005.

Productivity Commission 2004, *First Home Ownership*, Report no. 28, Productivity Commission, Melbourne.

Pusey, M. 1991, *Economic Rationalism in Canberra: A Nation Building State Changes its Mind*, Cambridge University Press, Cambridge.

Pusey, M. 2003, *The Experience of Middle Australia: The Dark Side of Economic Reform*, Cambridge University Press, Cambridge.

Quiggin, J. 2000, 'The public sector as a jobs engine', in S. Bell (ed.), *The Unemployment Crisis: Which Way Out?*, Cambridge University Press, Melbourne.

Ramesh, M. & Asher, M. 2000, *Welfare Capitalism in Southeast Asia. Social Security, Health and Education Policies*, Macmillan, London.

Rawls, J. 1972, *A Theory of Justice*, Clarendon Press, Oxford.

Reference Group on Welfare Reform 2000, *Participation Support for a More Equitable Society: Final Report of the Reference Group on Welfare Reform*, Department of Family and Community Services, Canberra.

Reich, R. 1992, *The Work of Nations: Preparing Ourselves for 21st Century Capitalism*, Vintage Books, New York.

Reid, A. 2005, 'Rethinking the democratic purposes of Public Schooling' in 'Globalising World', in M. Apple, J. Kenway & M. Singh, *Globalizing Education: Policies, Pedagogies & Politics*, Peter Lang, New York.

Reiger, K. 1985, *The Disenchantment of the Home: Modernising the Australian Family*, Oxford University Press, Melbourne.

Reserve Bank of Australia 2002, 'Recent developments in housing: prices, finance and investor attitudes', *Reserve Bank of Australia Bulletin*, pp. 1–6. <http://www.rba.gov.au/ PublicationsAndResearch/Bulletin/bu_jul02/bu_0702_1.pdf> 18 September 2005.

Reserve Bank of Australia 2003, 'Housing Equity Withdrawal', *Reserve Bank of Australia Bulletin*, pp. 50–4.

Roe, J. 1976a, 'Perspectives on the present day: a postscript', in J. Roe (ed.), *Social Policy in Australia. Some Perspectives 1901–1975*, Cassell, Stanmore.

Roe, J. 1976b, 'Leading the World? 1901–1914', in J. Roe (ed.), *Social Policy in Australia: Some Perspectives, 1901–1975*, Cassell, Stanmore.

Roe, J. 1993, 'Social policy and the cultural cringe', in P. Saunders & S. Shaver (eds), *Theory and Practice in Australian Social Policy*, Social Policy Research Centre, University of NSW, Sydney.

Roe, J. 1998, 'The Australian way', in P.Smyth & B. Cass (eds), *Contesting the Australian Way. States, Markets and Civil Society*, Cambridge University Press, Melbourne.

Room, G. 2004, 'The international and comparative analysis of social exclusion: European perspectives', in P. Kennett (ed.), *A Handbook of Comparative Social Policy*, Edward Elgar, Cheltenham.

Roy Morgan Research 2000, *Community Attitudes Towards Unemployed People of Workforce Age*, DFaCS, Canberra.

Rydon, J. & Mackay, D. 1995, 'Federalism and health', in H. Gardner (ed.), *The Politics of Health: the Australian Experience*, Churchill Livingstone, Melbourne.

Sainsbury, D. 1994, *Gendering Welfare States*, Sage, London.

Sandler, T. 2001, *Economic Concepts for the Social Sciences*, Cambridge University Press, Cambridge.

Saunders, C. 2003, 'Building federal state cooperation', in I. Marsh (ed.), *Australia's Choices: Options for a Prosperous and Fair Society,* UNSW Press, Sydney.

Saunders, P. 1988, 'Guaranteed minimum income revisited: paradise lost or guiding light?', *Economic Papers*, vol. 7, no. 3, pp. 25–32.

Saunders, P. 2001, *2001 Centenary Article – Household Income and its Distribution – 1301.0*, Year Book Australia, Australian Bureau of Statistics, Canberra.

Saunders, P. 2005, *Poverty Wars: Reconnecting Research with Reality*, UNSW Press, Kensington, NSW.

Saunders, P. & Taylor, R. 2002, *The Price of Prosperity: The Economic and Social Costs of Unemployment*, UNSW Press, Sydney.

Saunders, P. & Tsumori, K. 2002, Poverty in Australia: Beyond the Rhetoric, *CIS Policy Monograph* 57, The Centre for Independent Studies, St Leonards.

Sawer, M. 2003, *The Ethical State? Social Liberalism in Australia*, Melbourne University Press, Melbourne.

Sax, S. 1984, *A Strife of Interests: Politics and Policies in Australian Health Services*, Allen & Unwin, Sydney.

Schmid, G. 1998, *Transitional Labour Markets: A New European Employment Strategy*, Discussion paper FS I 98-206, Social Science Research Centre, Berlin, <http://www.wz-berlin.de/default.en.asp> 5 September 2003.

Schmid, G. 2002, 'Transitional labour markets and the European social model: towards a new employment compact', in G. Schmid & B. Gazier (eds), *The Dynamics of Full Employment: Social Integration Through Transitional Labour Markets*, Edward Elgar, Cheltenham, UK.

Scotton, R. & Macdonald, C. 1993, *The Making of Medibank,* School of Health Services Management, University of NSW, Sydney.

Sen, A. 2001, *Development as Freedom*, Oxford University Press, Oxford.

Senate Community Affairs References Committee 2004, *A Hand Up not a Hand Out: Renewing the Fight Against Poverty*, Commonwealth of Australia, Canberra.

Senate Select Committee on Superannuation 1994, *Super for Housing,* Twelfth Report of the Senate Select Committee on Superannuation, Senate Printing Unit, Parliament House, Canberra.

Sheehan, P. 1998, 'Rebirth of Australian industry revisited', in R. Genoff & R. Green (eds), *Manufacturing Prosperity*, Federation Press, Sydney.

Sherraden, M. 2003, 'From the social welfare state to the social investment state', *Shelterforce Online* Issue 128, March/April, <http://www.nhi.org/online/issues/128/socialinvest.html>4 June 2004.

Simon, H. 1972, 'Theories of bounded rationality', in C. McGuire & R. Radner (eds), *Decision and Organization*, North-Holland, Amsterdam-London.

Smart, D. 1978, *Federal Aid to Australian Schools,* University of Queensland Press, Brisbane.

Smith, J. 2004, *Taxing Popularity: The Story of Taxation in Australia*, Research Study 43, Australian Tax Research Foundation, Sydney.

Smyth, P. 1994, *Australian Social Policy: The Keynesian Chapter*, UNSW Press, Kensington.

Smyth, P. 1998, 'Remaking the Australian way', in P. Smyth & B. Cass (eds), *Contesting the Australian Way,* Cambridge University Press, Melbourne.

Smyth, P. 2004, 'The British social policy legacy and the Australian way', in C.J. Finer & P. Smyth (eds), *Social Policy and the Commonwealth Prospects for Social Inclusion*, Palgrave, Basingstoke.

Smyth, P. 2005, '"Australian way", Australian settlement and the Australian legend', in T. Battin (ed.) *Passion for Politics Essays in Honour of Graham Maddox*, Pearson Education, Sydney.

Smyth, P & Cass B. (eds) 1998, *Contesting the Australian Way: States, Markets and Civil Society*, Cambridge University Press, Melbourne.

Smyth, P. & Wearing, M. 2002, 'After the welfare state: welfare governance and the communitarian revival', in S. Bell (ed.), *Economic Governance and Institutional Dynamics,* Oxford University Press, Melbourne.

Social Inclusion Unit, *Social Inclusion Initiative*, Government of South Australia, Adelaide, <http://www.socialinclusion.sa.gov.au/site/page.cfm> 23 May 2005.

Stafford, A. 2005, 'Razor gang targets health safety net', *Australian Financial Review*, 8 April 2005.

Standing, G. 1997, 'Globalisation, Labour Flexibility and Insecurity: The Era of Market Regulation', *European Journal of Industrial Relations*, vol. 3, pp. 7–37.

Steering Committee for the Review of Government Service Provision (SCRGSP) 2005, *Report on Government Services 2005*, Productivity Commission, Canberra.

Stiglitz, J. 2002, *Globalization and its Discontents*, Allen Lane, London.

Stilwell, F. 2000, *Changing Track*, Pluto Press, Sydney.

Stokes, G. 2002, 'Australian democracy and Indigenous self-determination', in G. Brennan & F. G. Castles (eds) *Australia Reshaped: 200 Years of Institutional Transformation*, Cambridge University Press, Melbourne.

Stretton, H. 1999, *Economics: An Introduction*, University of New South Wales, Sydney.

Swerrisen, H. 2004, 'Australian primary health policy in 2004: two tiers or one for Medicare?', *Australia and New Zealand Health Policy*, vol. 1, no. 1, p. 2.

Tawney, R. 1964, *Equality,* Unwin Books, London.

Taylor, S., Rizvi, F., Lingard, B. & Henry, M. 1997, *Educational Policy and the Politics of Change*, Routledge, London.

Taylor-Gooby, P. 1998, 'Equality, rights and social justice', in P. Alcock, A. Erskine & M. May (eds), *The Students Companion to Social Policy*, Blackwell, Oxford.

Teghtsoonian, K. 1993, 'Neo-conservative ideology and opposition to federal regulation of child care services in the United States and Canada', *Canadian Journal of Political Science*, vol. 26, pp. 97–121.

The Commission on Taxation and Citizenship 2000, *Paying for Progress: A New Politics of Tax for Public Spending*, Fabian Society, London.

The Myer Foundation 2003, *2020 A Vision for Aged Care in Australia*, <http://www.myerfoundation.org.au/main.asp> 10 January 2005.

Thomson, P. 2002, *Schooling the Rustbelt Kids: Making the Difference in Changing Times*, Allen & Unwin, Sydney.

Tilly, J. 1999, 'Consumer-directed long-term care: participants' experiences in five countries', Public Policy Institute, AARP, Washington DC, <http://www.aarp.org/research/housing-mobility/homecare/aresearch-import-196-IB36.html> 25 April, 2005.

Titmuss, R.1970, *The Gift Relationship: From Human Blood to Social Policy*, Allen & Unwin, London.

Titmuss, R. 1974, *Social Policy: An Introduction*, Allen & Unwin, London.

Titmuss, R. 1976, *Essays on the Welfare State*, Allen & Unwin, London.

Tomlinson, S. 2001, *Education in a Post-Welfare Society*, Open University Press, Buckingham.

Townsend, T. (ed.) 1998, *Issues for the Primary School in the Age of Restructuring*, Routledge, London.

Uhr, J. & Wanna, J. 2000, 'The future roles of parliament', in M. Keating, J. Wanna & P. Weller (eds), *Institutions on the Edge? Capacity for Governance*, Allen & Unwin, Sydney.

Valuer General – Victoria 2002, *A Guide to Property Valuers: Data Analysis from the Records of the Valuer General Victoria*, Landata, Department of Natural Resources and Environment, Melbourne.

van Kersbergen, K. 1995, *Social Capitalism. A Study of Christian Democracy and the Welfare State*, Routledge, London.

Vanstone, A. & Abbott, T. 2001, *Australians Working Together: Helping People to Move Forward. Joint Ministerial Statement*, Commonwealth of Australia, Canberra.

Walzer, M. 1997, 'Complex equality', in L. Pojman & R. Westmoreland (eds), *Equality: Selected Readings*, Oxford University Press, Oxford.

Wanna, J. & Keating, M. 2000, 'Conclusion: institutional adaptability and coherence', M. Keating, J. Wanna & P. Weller (eds), *Institutions on the Edge? Capacity for Governance*, Allen & Unwin, Sydney.

Warren, N. 2004, *Tax: Facts, Fiction and Reform*, Research Study 41, Australian Research Foundation, Sydney.

Watson, D. 2002, *Recollections of a Bleeding Heart: A Portrait of Paul Keating PM*, Random House, Milsons Point, NSW.

Watson, D. 2003, *Death Sentence: The Decay of Public Language*, Knopf, Sydney.

Watson, D. 2004, *Watson's Dictionary of Weasel Words: Contemporary Clichés, Cant and Management Jargon*, Knopf, Sydney.

Watts, M. 2000, 'The dimensions and costs of unemployment in Australia', in S. Bell (ed.), *The Unemployment Crisis: Which Way Out?*, Cambridge University Press, Melbourne.

Watts, R. 1987, *The Foundations of the National Welfare State*, Allen & Unwin, Sydney.

Webster, E. 2000, 'What Role for Labour Market Programs', in S.Bell (ed.), *The Unemployment Crisis in Australia: Which Way Out?*, Cambridge University Press, Melbourne.

Weller, P. 2000, 'Introduction: the institutions of governance', in M. Keating, J. Wanna & P. Weller (eds), *Institutions on the Edge? Capacity for Governance*, Allen & Unwin, Sydney.

Wells, A. 1989, *Constructing Capitalism: An Economic History of Eastern Australia 1788–1901*, Allen & Unwin, Sydney.

Western, R., Millward, C. & Lazzarini V. 1995, *Facets of Living Standards*, Department of Social Security (DSS) Research Paper No. 70, AGPS, Canberra.

Weiss, L. 2003, *States in the Global Economy: Bringing Domestic Institutions Back In*, Cambridge University Press, Cambridge.

Whiteford, P. & Angenent, G. 2002, *The Australian System of Social Protection: An Overview*, 2nd edn, Department of Family and Community Services, Canberra.

WHO. See World Health Organization.

Wilensky, H.L. 1975, *The Welfare State and Equality: Structural and Ideological Roots of Public Expenditures*, University of California Press, Berkeley.

Wilensky, H.L. & Lebeaux, C. 1965, *Industrial Society and Social Welfare*, Free Press, New York.

Wilkins, R. 2003, *Labour Market Outcomes and Welfare Dependence of People with Disabilities in Australia*, Melbourne Institute Working Papers No. 02/2003, Melbourne Institute of Applied Social and Economic Research, Melbourne, <http://www.melbourneinstitute.com>.

Wilson, J., McMahon & Thompson 1996, *Australian Welfare State: Key Documents and Themes*, Macmillan, Sydney.

Winter, I. & Stone, W. 1999, 'Social polarisation and housing careers: exploring the interrelationship of labour and housing markets in Australia', in K. O'Connor (ed.), *Houses and Jobs in Cities and Regions: Research in Honour of Chris Maher*, University of Queensland Press, Brisbane.

Wiseman, J. 1998, *Global Nation? Australia and the Politics of Globalisation*, Cambridge University Press, Melbourne.

Wood, G., Berry, M., Dalton, T., Pettit, C., Allan, I., Leong, K. & Stokes, A. 2005, *Affordable Housing for Low Income Victorians: A Summary of a Report on Research on Recent Trends and Issues in Affordable Housing Carried out for the Victorian Department of Premier and Cabinet*, AHURI, RMIT University, Melbourne.

Wood, G.A. 1990, 'Housing finance and subsidy systems in Australia', *Urban Studies*, vol. 27, no. 6, pp. 847–76.

Wooden, M. (1996), *Hidden Unemployment and Underemployment: Their Nature and Possible Impact on Future Labour Force Participation and Unemployment*, National Institute of Labour Studies, Working Paper no. 40, National Institute of Labour Studies, Flinders University, Adelaide.

World Health Organization 1978, *Declaration of Alma-Ata*, WHO, Geneva.

World Health Organization 2005, *Action on the Social Determinants of Health: Learning from Previous Experiences*, WHO, Geneva.

Wulff, M. & Maher, C. 1998, 'Long-term renters in the Australian housing market', *Housing Studies*, vol. 13, no. 1, pp. 83–98.

Yates, J. 1981, 'The demand for owner-occupied housing', *Australian Economic Papers*, vol. 20, no. 37, pp. 309–24.

Yates, J. 1996, 'Towards a reassessment of the private rental market', *Housing Studies*, vol. 11, no. 1, pp. 35–50.

Yates, J. 1999, 'Decomposing Australia's home ownership trends', in M. Wulff & J. Yates (eds), *Australia's Housing Choices,* University of Queensland Press, Brisbane.

Yates, J. 2000, 'Is Australia's home ownership rate really stable? An examination of change between 1975 and 1994' *Urban Studies*, vol. 37, no. 2, pp. 319–42.

Yates, J. 2003, 'Has home ownership in Australia declined?', *AHURI Research and Policy Bulletin*, issue 21, May.

Yates, J. & Wulff, M. 2000, 'W(h)ither low cost private rental housing?' *Urban Policy and Research,* vol. 18, no. 1. pp. 45–64.

Yates, J. Wulff, M. & Reynolds, M. 2004, *Changes in the Supply of and Need for Low Rent Dwellings in the Private Rental Marke*t, Australian Housing and Urban Research Institute, Melbourne.

Yeatman, A. 1998, 'Introduction', in A. Yeatman (ed.), *Activism and the Policy Process*, Allen & Unwin, North Sydney.

Ziguras, C. 2005, 'International trade in educational services: governing the liberalisation and regulation of private enterprize', in M. Apple, J. Kenway, & M. Singh, *Globalizing Education: Policies, Pedagogies & Politics,* Peter Lang, New York.

Ziguras, S., Dufty, M. & Considine, M. 2003, *Much Obliged: Disadvantaged Jobseekers Experiences of the Mutual Obligation Regime*, Brotherhood of St Laurence, Fitzroy.

Ziguras, S., Considine, M., Hancock, L. & Howe, B. 2004, *From Risk to Opportunity: Labour Markets in Transition*, Centre for Public Policy, University of Melbourne, Melbourne.

INDEX

ABC Learning Centres   230–1
Aboriginal Health Services   198
Aboriginal people *see* Indigenous people
Accord   109–10
Administrative Appeals Tribunal (AAT)   88, 163
advisory committees   59, 60
Age Pension   103, 104, 106, 121, 150, 161–2, 165, 168, 170, 173, 232
aged care   8, 10, 48, 52, 85, 86, 196–7, 224–5, 227, 228, 232–4, 236
aged community care   49–50, 51, 52, 53, 54
ageing   232–4
agency freedom   29
Alford, Robert   201
altruism   32–3
Australian Assistance Plan   101, 107
Australian Association of Social Workers (AASW)   79
Australian Confederation of Commerce and Industry   71
Australian Council of Social Service (ACOSS)   42, 55, 56, 76–8, 165, 172
Australian Council of Trade Unions (ACTU)   45, 73
Australian Housing and Urban Research Institute (AHURI)   180
Australian Industries Group (AIG)   71
Australian Institute of Health and Welfare (AIHW)   227
Australian Labour Party (ALP)   102, 107, 109–10
Australian Technical Colleges (ATCs)   212
Australian Way of social and economic policy   97, 102, 104, 109, 121, 129, 131, 173, 182, 239
Australian Youth Policy Action Coalition (AYPAC)   77
Australians Working Together (AWT)   10, 163

Barnett, Oswald   12, 134, 163, 165

Bell, Stephen   144
Bentham, Jeremy   22
Beveridge, William   106
biomedicine   202–3
Blainey, Geoffrey   95
Blair, Tony   138
    Blair government   41
bounded rationality   42
Brennan, Deborah   145
Bretton Woods agencies   126, 129, 131
Brotherhood of St Laurence   42, 74, 76, 100, 165, 172
Burke, Edmund   23
business and social policy   70–2
Business Council of Australia (BCA)   71
Business Round Table for Tax Reform   71

Cabinet   86–8, 90
Canada   114, 117, 120, 181, 203, 204, 234, 242
Capital Gains Tax (CGT)   180, 247, 248, 250
capitalist economy   147–8
Cass, Bettina   19, 48, 164, 172
Centre for Independent Studies (CIS)   71, 172
Centrelink   37, 65, 163, 169, 171
change, social, economic and political aspects   187–92
charities   74, 99–101
child care   6, 18, 37, 73, 84, 86, 109, 224, 225, 228–32, 236
Child Endowment   6, 106, 162
China   125
churches and social policy   79–81
Clark, Manning   96
Committee of Inquiry into the Australian Financial System   189
Commonwealth Employment Service   163
Commonwealth State Housing Agreement (CSHA)   182
Communism   105
communitarianism and society   23, 26

community groups   59, 60, 89
community health centres   40, 75, 85
community health programs   199, 200, 202, 208
community-managed service organisations   74
community networks   174
community organisations   17, 19, 20, 40, 51, 53, 62, 65, 70, 71, 78, 224, 226, 230, 236
community services   16, 76, 86, 144, 145, 224–8, 236, 237
  historical context   225–7
  size and scope of sector   227–8
community welfare organisations (CWOs)   72, 74–9
comprehensive analysis   41
conservative ideology   24
conservative tradition and society   23
Considine, M.   15, 40, 44, 47–8, 63, 225
Constitution   83–4, 86–8
consultation process   53, 55, 56, 58–61, 62, 63, 205
consumer groups   172
Consumer Price Index (CPI)   170
corporatisation   217, 218
Corporatist model of power   44–5
Council for the Ageing   172
Council for the Single Mother and her Child   172
Council of Australian Governments (COAG)   86, 226
Curtin government   163

Dalton, Tony   144
Dawkins, John   71
Dawkins, Peter   172
Deakin, Alfred   102
decision-making   2, 17, 61, 216, 225–6, 237
  elitist model   44
  government   71, 78, 91
  organisational   75
  policy   41–3, 45, 47, 55, 62–3, 82
decommodification   24, 104, 116–17, 118–19, 124, 126, 127
Denmark   114, 118, 119, 242
dental services   197–8
Disability Reform Package   164
disability services   234–6
Disability Support Pension (DSP)   163, 167, 168, 170, 173, 235
discourse and power   45–6
Downer, Alexander   96

earnings inequality   153, 188, 248
East Asian model   123–5
economic depression   102
economic development   127
  Australia   102–4, 130
economic globalisation   71, 90, 128
Economic Planning Advisory Council (EPAC)   45
economic policy   109, 110, 134–6, 163, 252
  Australian Way of   97, 102, 104, 109, 121, 129, 131, 173, 182, 239
economic rationalism   34, 94, 101, 109, 128–9, 134, 213
Edwards, Meredith   48, 55, 59
education   132, 144

future directions   220–3
and private schools   211
public funding   211
education policy   209–23
  assessment of market approaches   219–20
  in Australia   210–14
  policy issue   214–18
effective marginal tax rates (EMTRs)   56, 161, 169, 249, 251
efficiency   33–5, 38, 52, 62, 68, 206, 243, 250, 251
egalitarianism and society   22–3
Elitist model of power   44
employment   104–7, 132, 152, 163
equality   30–3
equity   30–3
Erskine, A.   12–13
Esping-Andersen, G.   19, 24, 116, 117, 118–19, 120–1, 122–3, 124, 125
evaluation of policy framework   64–7

families   6, 32–3, 119
Family Allowance   6, 106, 109, 162, 163
family reunion scheme   167
Family Tax benefit   37, 163, 169, 170, 173, 250
Fascism   105
federalism   84–6
Federation   83, 94, 97, 98, 101, 102–4, 106, 107, 109, 129, 134, 184, 194, 196, 243–4
feminist analysis   25, 33, 118–19
financial system deregulation   130
Finland   114, 118, 119, 242
fiscal welfare   27, 36–8, 54, 248
Foucault, Michel   45, 46, 217
framework for action   54–67
framework for understanding   48–54
France   114, 118, 119, 120, 137
Fraser government   7, 163, 199, 200, 232, 244
free market liberalism   213, 221
Friedman, Milton   214

Galbraith, John K.   107
gender   120
General Agreement on Tariffs and Trade (GATT)   129
General Agreement and Trade and Services (GATS)   216
Germany   24, 103, 115, 117, 118, 119, 120, 242
Giddens, Anthony   29, 135, 140, 221
Gillespie, James   199, 200
globalisation   18, 44, 94, 95, 97, 109, 113, 121, 129, 130–3, 134, 141, 249
  economic   71, 90, 128
Goods and Services Tax (GST)   40, 56, 243, 245, 251, 252
government
  and child care   228–9
  and community services   226
  departments   88–9
  funding   217
  and health services   196
  institutional arrangements   82–9
  and policy framework   53–4, 71
Great Depression   102, 105
Green, T.H.   102
guaranteed minimum income (GMI)   163, 175

Harvester judgment 104, 107
Hawke government 7, 44, 57, 71, 73, 77, 78, 86,
   137, 199, 200, 247
Hayek, Fredrick 22, 126, 214
HECS 109, 188
health 144
   social determinants 202–3
health care 6
   expenditure 203–4
Health Inequalities Research
   Collaborations 206
health insurance
   national 196, 198–201, 206
   private 198, 199, 200–1, 205, 207, 248, 251
health policy in Australia 195–208
   actors and interests 201–2
   elements and structures 196–8
   future directions 206–8
   pressures on 203–4
Henderson Poverty Inquiry 12, 136, 163, 165
Henderson, Ronald 12, 136
Higgins, Justice 104
Home and Community Care Program
   (HACC) 50, 53, 54, 75, 78, 233
household
   movements 190–2
   types 187–8
housing 144, 178–80
   affordability 187, 193
   prices 187, 188, 189, 190, 191–2, 193, 194
   public 6, 12, 85, 86, 178, 179–80, 182, 185–6,
      192, 193
   rental 178, 182, 183, 185, 189–90, 192
housing affordability 187
housing development 190
housing finance 189–90
housing policy 178–94
   elements 184–6
   historical context 181–4
   market-replacement 185
   market-supplementing 184–5
   market-supporting 184
   non-government organisations 179
   state government responsibility 179
housing stress 186–92
Howard government 7, 10, 23, 35, 56, 59, 64,
   67, 71, 77, 78, 83, 86, 87, 94, 95, 110, 121, 132,
   133, 155, 164, 171, 174, 175, 193, 199, 201, 205,
   226, 233, 247, 253
Howe, Brian 48
human capital theory 213, 221, 222
human rights 81, 83, 88, 91, 234

immigration 104–7
implementation of policy framework 53–4,
   64–7
income inequality 155, 157, 188, 193
income support 144, 173
India 125
Indigenous people 98–9, 108, 111, 138, 174, 198,
   206, 208
individual and society 22–4
industrial achievement performance model 24
industrial relations 104
Innovative Community Action Networks
   Program 222
Institute of Public Affairs (IPA) 71

institutional arrangements of government 82–9
institutions and policy decision-making 47
International Monetary Fund (IMF) 113, 126,
   129, 130
issue identification 55–8, 63, 66

Japan 26, 107, 114, 118, 120, 124, 125, 130, 204,
   242, 245
Job Network 171
Jobs, Education and Training (JET) 164

Keating government 9–10, 11, 44, 59, 67, 71, 73,
   77, 78, 82, 86, 87, 198, 245
Kelly, P. 97
Kenway, Jane 145
Keynesian economic ideas 106, 126, 134–5, 136,
   153–4, 213
knowledge-based economy 140, 158

labour market 147–53, 157–8, 159, 176, 188
labour supply 154
laissez-faire capitalism 100, 102
Lasswell, Harold 44
Letich, Larry 158
Lewis, Jenny 145
liberal ideology 24
liberal welfare regime 24
libertarianism and society 22
Lindblom, Charles 42

McClelland, Alison 145
McClure report 175
Macfarlane, Ian 154–5
marketisation 218
Marshal, T.H. 116, 119
Marxism 97
Marxist model of power 44
media 81–2
Medicare 5, 6–7, 15, 40, 73, 109, 195, 197, 200–1,
   206–7
Medicare Levy 6, 35, 198, 199, 205, 246, 249, 251
Medicare Plus 205
medicine 201–2
Melbourne Institute 172
Mill, John Stuart 22, 102
mixed scanning 42
mortgages 178, 180, 185, 188, 189
mutual obligation regime 46, 103, 144, 159, 163,
   164, 174, 175, 221

National Aged Care Alliance (NACA) 233–4
National Competition Policy 86, 226
national health insurance 196, 198–201, 206
National Housing Strategy 186, 188
National Industry Association for Disability
   Services 235
National Tertiary Education Industry Union
   (NTEU) 212
Neighbourhood Renewal 208
neo-liberal (pro-market) economic policies 22,
   25, 34, 44, 71–2, 80, 90, 108, 109, 110, 126–7,
   133, 134, 136, 140, 141, 142, 153–4, 156, 173–4,
   189, 210, 221, 222, 226, 239, 246

Netherlands 119, 242
New Zealand 117, 121, 137, 155, 170, 175, 181, 213, 242
Newstart Allowance 173, 175
non-government organisations 17, 46, 58, 72, 74–81, 101, 107, 126, 179, 185, 225
North American Free Trade Agreement (NAFTA) 131

occupational welfare 27, 36–8, 54
Organisation for Economic Cooperation and Development (OECD) 113, 114, 130, 131, 133, 166, 204, 213, 217, 218, 245
O'Sullivan, E.W. 103

paid work 8, 11, 46, 51, 107, 108, 115, 119, 132, 140, 141, 144
Parenting Payment (PP) 37, 163, 168, 173, 175
parliament 86–8
Pearson, Noel 174
pensions 37, 103, 161, 163, 167, 168–70, 173, 237
    see also Age Pension, Disability Support Pension (DSP)
Pharmaceutical Benefits Scheme (PBS) 5, 198, 199, 203
pluralist model of power 45
policy activist 40
policy actors 40
policy analysis 2, 42, 49, 55, 61–2, 63, 66, 67, 68, 77, 89, 112
policy as a rational exercise 41–3
policy assessment of market approaches 219–20
policy context 50–2
policy definition 49–50
policy development 47–9
policy framework
    consultation 58–61
    decision stage 62–4
    evaluation 64–7
    impacts and options 52–3
    implementation 53–5, 64–7
    issue identification 55–8
    policy analysis 61–2
    policy context 50–2
policy issue 214–18
policy practice 39, 40, 67
policy process 13–14, 40–8
policy statements 10–11
policy systems 47–9
politics and power 43–6
Poor Law 100, 165
poverty 9, 12, 30, 44, 46, 48, 51, 57, 71–2, 74, 76, 79, 81, 99–100, 107, 109, 113–15, 122, 132–3, 136–9, 140, 144, 163, 165–6, 169, 170, 175, 176–7, 179, 207
power
    Corporatist model 44–5
    definition 43
    and discourse 45–6
    Elitist model 44
    Marxist model 44
    Pluralist model 45
    and politics 43–6
Primary Care Partnerships 208

private health insurance 198, 199, 200–1, 205, 207, 248, 251
Private Health Insurance Rebate 7, 37, 53, 67, 199, 205, 207, 248, 251
private schools 211
Productivity Commission 89, 187, 189, 190, 191–2, 227
Program Planning Budgeting Systems (PPBS) 41
public interest organisations 80
Putman, Robert 138

Quiggin, John 144

race 120
Rawls, J. 30–1
reciprocity 32–3
redistribution of welfare 30–3
Reference Group on Welfare Reform 164
residual welfare model 24
risk society 139–41
Roe, Jill 121

Saunders, Peter 71, 132
Scandinavia 24, 44, 109, 119, 121, 122, 123, 133, 239
Schon, Donald 43
Schumpeterian Workfare Post-national Regime (SWPR) 134, 135
Second World War 104–7, 163
self-help organisations 74
Sen, Amartya 29, 31, 137, 139
Simon, Herbert 42
Smith, Adam 102
social citizenship 28–9
social coalitions 71
social equality 30–3
social inclusion 136–9, 221–2
social insurance, compulsory 117
social justice 30–3
social liberalism 22
social movement organisations 74
social needs 26–8, 38
social policy
    area of study 12–13
    assessment 173–4
    Australian 12–13, 22, 97, 101–2, 104, 109, 112–13, 120–2, 128–9, 131–3, 141, 173, 182, 239, 252
    and business 70–2
    changing perspectives 96–7
    and churches 79–81
    concepts 26–33
    decision stage 62–4
    definition 5, 14–16
    designing 36
    and development 103, 104, 125–7
    and distribution of welfare 30–2
    East Asian model 123–5
    and economic policy 134–6
    evaluation 64–7
    features 14–16
    as formal statements 9–10
    forms and meanings 8–14
    framework for action 54–67

framework for understanding 48–54
future options 175–7
global context 128–31
goals 164–6
historical overview 161–4
impacts and options 52–3
implementation 53–5, 64–7
importance of 5–8
indigenous people 98–9, 108
as informal agreements 11
and media 81–2
national histories 139–41
nineteenth century 97–102
as output 8–11
as a process 13–14, 40–8
research 113–16, 119–20
scope 16–18
and unions 72–3
and the welfare state 18–20
social reform organisations 74, 107
social security 103, 105, 109
administration 171–2
changes 162–3
future options 175–7
institutions 171–2
key elements of the current system 166–70
payments 166–70
policy, Australian 161–77
policy assessment 173–4
policy development 171–2
policy goals 164–6
Social Security Appeals Tribunal (SSAT) 171–2
Social Security Review 163, 172, 173
social solidarity 32
social welfare expenditures 128
social welfare system 132
society and the individual 22–4
state welfare 27, 36–8, 54
superannuation 166
Superannuation Guarantee Charge (SGC) 166, 246
Supporting Parents Payment 163
Sweden 114, 117, 118, 119–20, 123, 203, 240, 242
Switzerland 118

targeting 33, 35–6, 38, 109–10, 122, 142, 175, 192
Tasmanian Institute 71
tax, consumption 243
taxation 238–54
of capital 250
changing context 247–51
and Commonwealth government 245
effective marginal tax rates (EMTRs) 56, 161, 169, 249, 251
expenditures 248
income 56, 84, 103, 105, 169, 175, 185, 240, 241, 243–7, 248–9, 251
inquiries 247
reform 252
structure, Australian 244
of wealth 250
see also Capital Gains Tax (CGT), Goods and Services Tax (GST), Wholesale Sales Tax (WST)

Thatcher, Margaret 22, 108, 124, 129, 133
Third Way 29, 109, 134, 135, 136, 140, 210, 221, 222
Titmuss, Richard 12, 15, 24, 25, 32, 36, 54, 107, 116
transitional labour markets (TLMs) 141, 176

underemployment 144, 147, 149, 150, 152, 153, 155, 156, 159, 185, 188
unemployment 108, 132, 144, 149–54
benefits 166, 170, 174
long-term 9–10, 59, 60, 132, 149, 151, 152, 164, 173, 174
unions and social policy 72–3
United Kingdom 25, 26, 41, 100, 101, 102, 117, 119, 120, 121, 123, 129, 133, 135, 137, 138, 204, 207–8, 242, 253
United States (USA) 18, 25, 26, 81, 83, 102, 107, 114, 117, 120, 121, 129, 132–3, 135, 155, 169, 181, 198, 203–4, 214, 229, 234, 240, 242, 245, 246, 252
universalism 33, 35–6, 109, 145, 205

Victorian Council of Social Service (VCOSS) 172

wages 103–4, 144, 183
Weber, Max 43, 99
welfare 6
distribution 30–3
means and design 33–8
values, ideologies and frameworks 21–6
welfare dependence 173, 174
welfare regimes 116–18
welfare rights 172
welfare society 107
welfare state
analysis, critiques of 118–20
arrangements, national diversity 120–3
Australian 97, 107, 246
decommodified 24, 104, 116–17, 118–19, 124, 126, 127
definition 19
development 115
expenditure 128
and social policy 18–20
White Australia Policy 106
Whitlam government 6, 107, 163, 199, 200
Wholesale Sales Tax (WST) 56, 153, 245, 247
Women's Electoral Lobby 172
women's refuges 75
Work for the Dole scheme 164
Working Nation 9, 10, 59, 60, 67, 162
World Bank 113, 125, 126, 127, 129, 130, 138–9
World Trade Organization (WTO) 129, 130, 216

Youth Allowance 212

Ziguras, Stephen 89, 140, 144